# ACCLAIM FOR BRE

# BREAKING KOLA

An Inside View of African Customs

CATHERINE ONYEMELUKWE

A PEACE CORPS WRITERS BOOK

Breaking Kola: An Inside View of African Customs
A Peace Corps Writers Book
An imprint of Peace Corps Worldwide

Printed in the United States of America
by Peace Corps Writers of Oakland, California.

Peace Corps Writers and the Peace Corps Writers colophon
are trademarks of PeaceCorpsWorldwide.org.
Cover design by Miggs Burroughs
Book design by Opal Roengchai

ISBN-13: 978-1-935925-96-5

Library of Congress Control Number: 2014953038
First Peace Corps Writers Edition, December 2018

A PEACE CORPS WRITERS BOOK

To my husband Clement, my most important source of knowledge about Igbo customs, our children Chinaku, Beth, and Sam, and our grandchildren, Kenechi, Nkiru, Teya, Bruche, and Ikem to whom I pass the responsibility to remember and honor the traditions of their Igbo heritage.

*Onye wetelu oji wetelu ndu.* He who brings kola brings life.

# Table of Contents

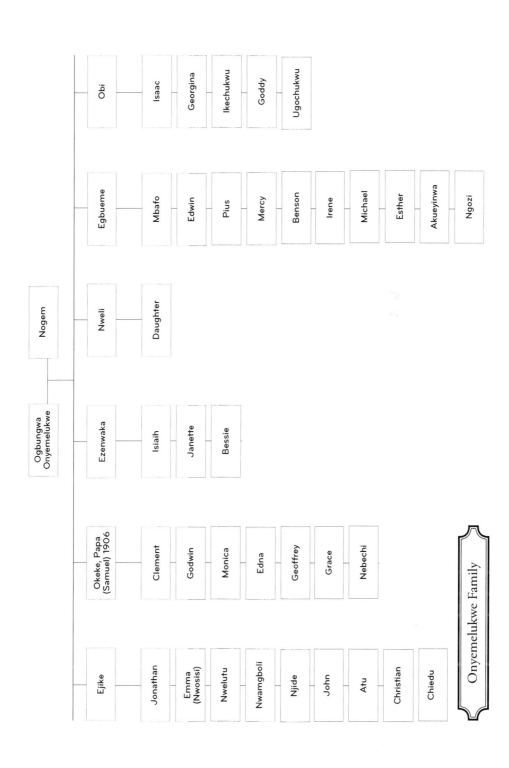

Onyemelukwe Family

# ACKNOWLEDGEMENTS

I could not have written this book without the constant support of my husband Clement. Though I had a taste of Igbo and wider Nigerian customs from my Peace Corps training and months in the country before I met him, it was through him that I became fully immersed in Igbo and wider African traditions. His appreciation for his own culture is reflected daily in his attention to family, both near and extended. He also shows his debt to African tradition, specifically his Igbo customs, in his desire for respect for himself as the father of our three children and in the respect he shows to those senior to him. He wishes that I would show more respect to him as my husband, as a dutiful Igbo wife would do, but he has learned to accommodate my American ways and only tries occasionally, knowing he will not succeed, to convince me to be more compliant.

I am grateful to his parents, long deceased, the Mama and Papa of my story as I came to know them, for teaching me Igbo ways and telling me enough about their backgrounds that I could tell their stories. Emmanuel, also called Nwosisi, is my husband's oldest cousin, and the only one remaining senior to him. He has been a source of entertainment, traditional practice, and family knowledge. Isaiah, the first cousin I met and the one who introduced me to other family members, has shared his knowledge and stories. His wife Rebecca enjoys explaining Igbo customs to me, and I have learned from her.

Several other younger cousins have also been sources of information. Christian, Atu and Chiedu have answered my frequent questions. Their mother, whose 90th birthday we celebrated a few years ago, remains a source of strength in the family, though she can barely see and has finally given up her tobacco grinding business. The younger generation cousins, Ejike and Osita, have taken us on visits to the Nanka Erosion site and joined us at parties and family events.

I am grateful to Yvonne Mbanefo has been an organizer of the annual Igbo Conference at SOAS in London and has provided a platform for me to speak about family and traditions. Gloria Chuku organized a conference in 2018 on Biafra and again gave me a chance to present my views.

I want to thank the audiences at my book talks and the students in my classes for their comments, criticism and encouragement. I always come away from a presentation with renewed appreciation for the opportunity I've had to understand African customs and share my knowledge with others. My publicist Aline Weiller has helped me with many arrangements and been a frequent source of positive feedback.

My Sister Grannies and my two book groups, Baker's Dozen and the Mount Holyoke Alumnae of Bridgeport, have provided support and encouragement. Members of both book groups and the Sister Grannies read my memoir and gave me useful ideas for this book.

I am grateful to our children, Chinaku, Beth and Sam, for helping me see the customs through their eyes as they were growing up and today, as they act on their own interpretations. Our two older grandchildren, Kenechi and Nkiru, have demonstrated curiosity about their Igbo heritage; I've been encouraged to explain the traditions for them through the stories of their relatives. And for our younger grandchildren Teya, Bruche, and Ikem, the stories I've told here about their kin will be waiting for them.

# Introduction

## African Customs
## Create Community

AT EVERY CELEBRATION AMONG THE Igbo people of Nigeria, the kola nut is held up as a venerated symbol of community. No event can begin without the ceremonial breaking and sharing of kola nut. It signifies hospitality and welcome.

Two popular sayings among the Igbo people are "He who brings kola brings life," and "When the kola reaches home, it will say where it came from." The first is like a statement of affirmation, declaring the important role of the kola. What can be more important than bringing life? There is a risk that without kola, there will be no life.

When someone attends a ceremony or pays a visit, he is frequently given a kola nut to take home. The second proverb tells us that when a guest reaches his home, he will speak well of the people he has visited. Not only that, he and his own people will feel a connection with those he visited. The kola he is given demonstrates how well he was treated and builds trust between his people and those where he was a guest. Sharing the kola nut is just one example of the practices that build community among African people.

We long for community, for a place to feel at home, to belong, and to know we are needed. African customs build this community. In our Western society today, we often lack this strong sense of belonging and connection. Although holidays, weddings, funerals, christenings, or bar and bat mitzvahs provide occasions to unite with extended family, we are usually not connected at other times. Social media now may help us stay in touch, but the connection is not deep. Nor are we tied to a specific place that grounds us.

Figure 1 Kola nuts from Dr. Y at www.afrolegends.com

This is significantly different from being part of an African family. African traditions of belonging encompass generations past and generations to come. The extended family includes many nuclear families who are members of the same clan. The clan is part of a village, and the village part of a town. The largest grouping is the tribe, or ethnic group.

An Igbo person, like Africans elsewhere, is part of the clan, village, and tribe forever. Even though he or she may never visit the village, he or she still belongs to it. An American or European may say they come from a place—"I came from Illinois," or "I'm German." But they may change to become another nationality or to come from another state. Our "homes" are not fixed. An African's home is fixed.

I grew up in a modern Western society in a nuclear family with no definitive sense of belonging anywhere. We moved every two years until I was eleven, in 1951. In the northern Kentucky town where I lived from then until I joined the Peace Corps, I established few lasting bonds.

In June 1962, newly graduated from Mount Holyoke College in Massachusetts, I traveled to the University of California, Los Angeles (UCLA) for ten weeks of intense training for Peace Corps volunteers headed for Nigeria. My assignment was to teach German at a sixth-form, or postsecondary, school for students who had excelled in sciences and mathematics. They were destined to go overseas for their university training. At the time, German was regarded as a requirement for people pursuing science and math subjects.

My sense of community changed during my two years as a Peace Corps volunteer in Nigeria. As I made friends and observed the closeness Nigerians felt with their people, I saw that the isolation we can experience in the West didn't exist. During my second year as a Peace Corps volunteer teacher, I met a Nigerian man who had just returned to his country two years earlier after nine years away. We began dating.

After I started seeing Clem, but before I knew we would marry, I visited his part of the country. He asked his cousin who lived in the area to take me to meet his family and to visit their village. Without knowing this would become my family and my village, I was drawn to both, sensing the warmth inherent in an Igbo family and town. When I found myself falling in love, I knew that I could make Nigeria my home. After my Peace Corps service concluded, I returned to Nigeria as a private citizen. Clement and I married in December 1964.

We continued living in Lagos, the capital, and had our first child in 1965. But in three years, Nigeria was torn by a civil strife. Differences in religion and tribal identity were factors. But so were differences of opinion about the nature of the central government as opposed to the power of the regions. How to share the proceeds of oil was also a critical factor.

The Igbo people were determined to make their way independently. Just before our second child was born, we fled Lagos for the Eastern Region, the home of the Igbo people and the secessionist movement. Biafra declared itself an independent country in May 1967, and in July the Nigerian army invaded, determined not to let the breakaway nation succeed.

Two months later we escaped Biafra's capital, Enugu, for my husband's village of Nanka. I had visited and found it friendly, but would I still really feel at home, surrounded by his family, clan, and fellow villagers, with no other expatriates nearby, in this unexpected situation?

I lived there, without electricity, running water, or supermarkets, and with two small children, for a year. Though I couldn't ignore the obvious fact that I was different, I was not only accepted but cherished. I came to care for others in the family, the clan, and the town. I suffered with them through the hardships of wartime inflation and increasing lack of medicine and foreign goods. I went to market with the other women, ate the local food, and watched my children thrive as they played outside all day.

I experienced the strong sense of community and belonging that pervaded the village. The common threat of war emphasized the feeling. What I had sensed before and knew on the surface became deeply personal for me. I understood, as Igbo people do, what it means to belong and to care for one another.

I left Biafra halfway through the war, in September 1968, spent several months with my parents, who had retired to the Portuguese island of Madeira, and then lived in the US until the war finished. In 1970 I returned to the reunited Nigeria and resumed teaching. Our third child was born the following year. I continued teaching for several years, including an academic year in the US to earn a master's degree in education. In 1980 I started my own business of garment manufacturing.

In 1986 I returned to the US for a master's degree in business administration, or MBA, at Yale University. A few years after that, my husband joined me in the US, where we live today. I published my memoir, *Nigeria Revisited: My Life and Loves Abroad,* in 2014. It recounts my experiences as a Peace Corps volunteer, teacher, wife and mother, resident of my husband's village, businesswoman, and community participant and leader. Throughout the memoir, I describe my interactions with, and fondness for, members of the family and community I had joined.

When I speak about my memoir and about Nigeria, my audience always comments on my visible love for the country and its people. And they ask, "Is there anything you miss?" I don't hesitate. I tell people that I miss the powerful sense of community that I came to know so well in Nigeria. I feel it most strongly when I think of my husband's village of Nanka. When I respond to an audience member's question and speak of the sense of belonging, of being part of an all-embracing community, people nod. "We do not have that here in the same way," they say. "That sense of community sounds wonderful."

*Breaking Kola* is my attempt to explain African, especially Igbo, customs that build this deep sense of community. To bring the experience of an African community and culture to you, I share stories of my husband's parents, Grace and Samuel. I begin by telling you about my father-in-law, who changed the course of his life when he ran away from a traditional ceremony he feared, a story I have heard from my husband many times.

Both my husband's parents became Christian early in life and I've created stories about those circumstances. I relied on my knowledge of the customs, my imagination, and historical research about Nigeria's early colonial period to tell their stories. I portray the story of their marriage, again drawing on research of marriage customs of the period and my own experiences.

My husband was their first son. From his memory he has given me details of customs practiced by his family. He even told me about the challenge to the sense of belonging he experienced when his parents sent him away from home at age six to give him a better chance at later success.

You will find the story of a female cousin who was given the task of preserving land ownership by not marrying and yet producing heirs. I introduce you to her and others in my husband's extended family. You will come to know the relationships that form the layers of belonging and give an Igbo person an enduring and unbreakable sense of being rooted forever.

I show how a woman joins her husband's family when she marries but maintains ties to her own place of birth. The practices of widowhood are shown at the time of my husband's grandfather's death from leprosy in 1944 and my father-in-law's death in 1979. The first is from my imagination and research, the second from my experience.

I also bring you the organization Nigerwives, which I helped create in the 1970s. It has become a "tribe" for foreign wives of Nigerian men. I relate the importance of Nigerwives for its members today.

Throughout, I explain my relationship with the people, places, and events I describe, and what they mean to me. As you read about the customs of Nigeria that I love, I hope you will experience the sense of connection and community that I—and maybe you too—miss in our Western lives in the twenty-first century.

# 1

## COMING OF AGE:
## THE MISSING SON

THE DAY HAD COME FOR the final ritual of becoming Igbo men. The two oldest sons of Ogbungwa had completed the other requirements for their coming-of-age ceremony. This morning they were to have the marks carved on their faces, called ibu ichi, to show their identity as men from the town of Nanka. After completing this final step, they would be recognized as men.

But one son was missing.

*"Ebea k'Okeke no?* Where is Okeke?" Ogbungwa glared at his oldest son, who came to stand before him.

Ejike could not meet his father's gaze. He knew he would be blamed for failing to ensure his brother's presence at this all-important event. His eyes on the ground, he said, "I thought he was sleeping. When I woke up this morning, he was not there."

The three younger brothers, the younger sons of Ogbungwa, were watching from a distance, torn between relief that they were not yet old enough to be among the initiates and envy of the attention their brothers had been receiving. Ejike was the same height as his father's five feet, nine inches, and the eldest at nineteen; his missing brother, Okeke, an inch shorter, was seventeen.

All the boys had smooth black skin that shone in the morning sunlight. They had the oval face and evenly spaced black eyes of their father.

Twelve initiates, Ogbungwa's two sons among them, had spent the previous eight days in the forest deepening their knowledge of the gods and the ancestors, and demonstrating their ability to withstand hardships. They had undergone tests of their manhood, showing they could go without food for a day, sleep on the ground, and face insults hurled at them from their elders. They'd learned about the responsibilities of being a man and the secrets of the *mmuo*, the masked figures who represent spirits.

In 1924, Nigeria was firmly in the grip of the British colonial masters, but during the preceding centuries men from Igbo towns had fought one another regularly. The defeated people were often taken captive. Sometimes they were kept by the victors; sometimes they were sold to traders who took them to the coast to sell to the foreign merchants. But the British had outlawed warfare between villages, so the young men practiced wrestling, the only way they could physically demonstrate their bravery and strength. The time in the forest had seen several matches, with the winners carried around the circle of young men on the shoulders of those they defeated. Okeke had often been the victor.

The initiates had returned to their own homes in the village the night before the rite of scarification to get ready for the final step. Ejike and Okeke had been preparing for this ceremony with a mix of eagerness and dread, but now Okeke was nowhere to be seen.

The youngest sibling, Obi, approached his father from his spot beside the wall. "I saw him after he returned from the forest. He was gathering his things. I asked what he was doing. He said he wasn't going to have anyone cut his face."

His father reached out and slapped Obi. "Why did you not tell me?"

"He said the *masquerades* would take me," Obi said, looking everywhere except at his father.

It was clear that Okeke had bolted. He must have jumped over the wall. The boys' father was furious, his anger intensified by the shame he felt that a son of his would be so lacking in courage. But the number of cowries to be paid for this service had already been agreed upon. The father gestured to the cutter, who approached, laid a mat on the ground, and told Ejike to lie down. "Close your eyes and do not move," the man said.

Ejike called on every ounce of his strength to stay still and not show any sign of pain. He knew he had to make up for his brother's disgraceful behavior. Using first the tip and then the blade of a knife shaped like a palm leaf, the expert made several deep cuts on each side of Ejike's face. He worked slowly and deliberately, spending a few minutes on each incision. When he had finished, he directed his assistant to bring thick red palm oil, which he spread over the cuts. Then he covered them with strips of banana leaves. "Remain on the mat," the man said. "I will tell you when to get up."

After an hour, Ejike was told to rise. "Stay away from fire," the man said. "Do not put any water on your face. Tomorrow you can remove the leaves."

Okeke was already several miles from Nanka and widening the distance when his brother was lying on the mat. He knew his father would be enraged when his absence was discovered.

Figure 2 Nanka man, 1972

But he had been overcome with fear of the pain. One of his younger brothers had seen him late the previous evening as he was collecting his few items of clothing. He had threatened his sibling. "The masquerades will take you if you tell!" he'd said.

When he and Ejike had returned to their compound after the days in the forest, Okeke had not yet made up his mind. They had eaten the dinner of garri and okra soup prepared by their mother, with the chicken their father had killed to honor their coming adulthood. As he finished eating, Okeke had noticed the stack of firewood piled against the wall near the yam barn. The mud wall, six feet high, enclosed the compound. It was built of palm stems covered with the reddish-brown mud of the area and made smooth by the women of the compound who rubbed the surface as it dried.

Suddenly he knew that he would run. He would wait for the moon to set and make his move. He could use the firewood to help him over the wall. The carved wooden gate, where he knew there would be a watchman, was twenty yards away. If he was careful and quiet, he would not be spotted.

When everyone was asleep and the moon had gone to bed, he crept from his sleeping mat to the open door of the one-room hut, grabbed his small bundle, and stepped out into the dark. He did not need light to know the way to the wall. Every inch was familiar; he had lived here since he was born. He dropped his belongings over the wall. Then he backed up for a running start. His bare feet hardly made a sound. Using the pile of wood and scrambling to get a handhold, he was over the wall in seconds.

He did not hesitate. He grabbed his bundle as he ran along the path beside the ridges where the yams were planted, reached the path leading to the road, and then burst out on the dirt road itself. He did not stop running until he was at the market, nearly two miles from his home. Sweat was pouring from his face and he was panting like he had in the wrestling matches. The sun was just peeping over the horizon when he turned right, heading west toward Onitsha.

He knew he dared not return for a long time, maybe not for many years. But he had a plan. He knew men from Nanka who had gone to the Nigerian Midwest and returned with stories of cutting down and hauling timber for pay. When he leapt over the wall, he already had in mind that he could follow them. He was proud of his strength. When he reached Onitsha, the big city on the Niger River, he would find other Nanka people. They would tell him how to travel on to find his townspeople at the logging camp.

He walked for the first ten of the twenty-seven miles. The sun was high overhead when he reached Aguata, a town larger than Nanka, where there was a motor park. He spoke to the driver of a lorry, a truck with an open back where passengers sat on benches. The driver agreed to take him to Onitsha for one shilling, half the money he had. On the way into the city of many thousands with its famous market, he passed the new secondary school established by the missionaries. He could not read the name, Dennis Memorial Grammar School, but he recognized the buildings as an educational institution. He had no idea that his son would one day excel at that school.

It was late afternoon when he reached the home of his clansman from Nanka. Okeke did not explain why he had left Nanka. The clansman and his wife gave him a meal and a mat to sleep on. The next morning, they directed him to a canoe for passage across the mile-wide Niger River, and explained how to continue the journey to Sapoba. "You will find your way to the logging company from there. If you carry bundles for other passengers, they may let you ride for free," his relative told him.

Okeke felt the pull of home as he left Nanka farther and farther behind. He thought of his mother, Nogem, and knew she would be crying for him. His father would be furious; he would find it difficult to forgive this transgression of custom. But Okeke had not been ready for the pain. Perhaps he could return one day. His shameful behavior wouldn't prevent that. Now he had to earn a living.

Okeke reached Sapoba. He found an Igbo speaker who directed him to the logging camp, another hour away. There he found a Nanka man who directed him to an office where he spoke to another Igbo, a supervisor, who hired him immediately. The United Africa Company, or UAC, had the headquarters of its logging operations in the heart of the tropical rain forest. Men like Okeke cut down the ebony and mahogany trees and shaped them into logs for UAC to ship to England.

UAC controlled much more than the timber industry. The company and its predecessors had been active in Nigeria since the 1600s. Their first business had been slave trading. British merchants and ship captains had formed alliances with Africans who saw the opportunities for profit. By the time the British outlawed the slave trade in 1806, traders were already shipping timber and other raw materials out of West Africa and bringing in manufactured products to sell. Palm oil from the eastern part of the country, cotton and groundnuts from the North, and timber from the Midwest were valuable exports.

Missionaries accompanied the British as their trade expanded. The Church Missionary Society, or CMS, had started in London at the end of the eighteenth century, developed out of the evangelical spirit of the time. Its goals were to abolish slavery and "endeavor to propagate the knowledge of the Gospel among the Heathen."[1] Eventually it became part of the Anglican Church. As British traders grew more interested in access to African goods other than slaves, they encouraged CMS expansion. When the British Colonial Office took over all of Nigeria in 1914, CMS was the most active religious organization. They and other religious bodies established schools with the dual goal of conversion and education, training people who could be employed in industry and the colonial structure.

Okeke was poised to take advantage of the religious and commercial zeal of the colonizers. CMS staff in Sapoba provided religious services for the few British workers managing the facility. Occasionally a British priest or missionary was present, but there were also Nigerians, including Igbo men, who had converted and become catechists or pastors who could lead services. The workers were given Sundays off and encouraged to attend. From the quarters where they lived four to a room, they could hear the voices singing the strange-sounding hymns. Okeke had been brought up to believe in authority. Running away, disobeying what he knew his father wanted, was almost unheard of.

When the supervisors suggested their workers go to the service, it seemed like an instruction. He had run for fear of the knife, but he still saw the importance of listening to those in power. He was also aware that joining the foreigners' religion would help his chances of advancing in the new world of British domination. Eventually, Okeke joined other loggers and ventured to the hall where the services were held.

Toward the end of his first year with UAC, he approached the Igbo pastor. "I would like to join your group of church people," he said. "How would I do that?"

"I have seen you during the services. I am very happy that you would like to devote your life to Jesus," the pastor said. "Next month I will start classes for you and the others who want to become Christian and give up your old pagan ways. I will tell you which evening, and you will come to the church once a week until you are ready."

After a few months, Okeke spoke to the pastor after class. "Am I not ready yet?" he said.

"You are ready. The priest will be coming soon. He is the one who will baptize you. Have you considered what Christian name you will take?"

Choosing a name when preparing for baptism was common practice at the time. How he made his choice I do not know. He had surely learned passages of the Bible, probably Old and New Testaments. He may have heard about Samuel, the Old Testament judge who anointed the first kings of Israel. Perhaps that name conveyed power. Maybe the pastor suggested it. Or it might have been the name of someone he respected in the management. He became a Christian with the name Samuel in 1926.

His story is hardly unique; he was part of a wave of conversions. Many men working in Sapoba or in other British-run operations were encouraged to join the Anglican Church. At the same time, missionaries from CMS were becoming active in his home region and had established a primary school in Agulu, the town to the northwest of Nanka. The Roman Catholics were also promoting their own religion and were equally active among the Igbo people.

Like others in Nigeria who became Christian, he was not abandoning his traditional religious beliefs. No matter what was said during the baptism, he was adding on, not replacing. He did not forget what he had been taught about the importance of honoring the ancestors during his training for initiation, nor did he cease to believe in the power of the *mmuo,* or spirits. Chukwu, the supreme Igbo god, did not seem different from the Christian God. The angels were like ancestors, living on after their earthly death. The power ascribed to the first son, Jesus, was like power that always went to the first son.

Samuel's adoption of the religion, his hard work, and his ability to influence others brought him to the notice of his superiors. In 1928, after four years and still only twenty-one years old, he was made a supervisor. He liked overseeing other men. His confidence in his own ability grew. A year after his promotion, he decided it was time to marry. During the Christmas holidays at the end of 1929, he returned home to Nanka to find a wife.

The connection that drew him homeward is the first and strongest pillar of Igbo communal life, so powerful that even the shame that lingered could not keep him away. This sense of belonging to a place that provides one's identity is immutable. Every Igbo person belongs to and identifies with a town and usually a village within the town. This identity is part of him and gives him a foundation; it makes him rooted. His whole being is connected to that place.

Added to this strong base because of the location is the sense of belonging to a family and clan. Every Igbo man is part of the chain of his family, including the generations that have gone before and are yet to come. He cannot break away and belong somewhere else. There was no doubt he had to return home to his village and his family for marriage.

As Okeke, now Samuel, made the journey home, he looked forward to seeing his mother. He did not know how his father would react to his return but hoped enough time had elapsed for his father's anger to diminish. His was aware that his declaration of his new religion and his desire to seek a wife who was also a Christian, or would convert, would be a shock to his parents. Would they support him or turn him away?

No young women in Nanka had yet joined the Christians. A girl growing up in Agulu, near Nanka, had been drawn to the Christian church by her teachers. She had been baptized and was now called Grace. She was of marriageable age but not yet promised.

# 2

## GOING TO SCHOOL:
## THE DAUGHTER PREPARES

CLEM'S MOTHER WAS BORN IN 1913, the year before the Colony and Protectorate of Nigeria came into being. Most Igbo men at the time were farmers, dependent on their crops for their livelihood and to feed their families. But trade with the British was growing steadily. The palm oil that the Igbo people produced was valuable, needed to lubricate the machines of the British factories and to make soap and margarine. Women and a few men gathered palm kernels and extracted the oil. They would take it themselves or sell it to others who would take it to the British traders. The British in turn sold or traded the manufactured products from their home factories to the Nigerians.

Her father, Ezeonodu, was a prosperous farmer in Agulu, about ten miles northwest of Nanka. His yam barn was the largest in the area. His many children helped him. He and his family grew most of what they ate. The wives sold a few items—extra cassava tubers, yams, and vegetables such as okra and spinach—in the Agulu market. They raised chickens and goats, which were slaughtered for special occasions. He even had two cows.

Eye (pronounced ā-yāh) was the most senior of Ezeonodu's wives. Her hut was the first to be built near her husband's in their compound. The other two wives had their own in the back. Her children, one son named Okeke and one daughter named Mgbeke, lived there with her. She and her co-wives would have dressed like the women in Figure 2. They may have worn the ivory leg ornaments.

Figure 3 Pagan trading women; probably Igbo, early 1900s. NigeriaCollection (MS 1553). Manuscripts and Archives, Yale University Library

At around the age of seven, Mgbeke began asking her father to let her attend the new CMS school. A boy from the next compound left every morning in his school uniform, and she wanted to follow. A few times she met him as he returned and asked him to tell her what he had learned that day. Her older brother, Okeke, was not interested in learning letters or numbers. By the age of nine he was helping his mother in the fields and caring for his father's goats. But Mgbeke was curious and eager. She began begging Ezeonodu to enroll her.

"Why do you want to go to school?" her father said. "What is there for you to learn?"

She hardly knew how to answer, but she said, "I want to count and say words in the new language, like Obi, the son of our neighbor."

"I don't have money to send you to school," he said. "Besides, you have to help your mother." She did help. She was accustomed to carrying her half siblings on her back as she fetched water from the nearby stream or went on errands for her mother or one of the other wives. But she did not give up.

One day he was complaining to a kinsman about his daughter's persistent request. "I heard the new term at the CMS school will start soon," the man said, then drained the last of his palm wine from his drinking gourd. "Maybe you should let her go. A few years of school could make her an attractive marriage partner."

Her father knew about the CMS school in his town. It was founded and administered by missionaries from the Church Missionary Society, a branch of the Anglican Church and an important part of the colonial administration. He had no use for the missionaries or other colonial administrators, white or African, whom he had seen. The white men looked ill, with their pasty skin. He regarded the Igbo people who had joined them as traitors or fools. Why would he let his daughter join them?

Ezeonodu was not one to fear what others thought. He just did not understand the point. But gradually his daughter's pleading wore him down. The rainy season was ending. One morning her father called her. "We will go to this school today," he said.

Like other children, she normally wore nothing. She raced to grab her "wrapper," a piece of fabric a yard long, which she wrapped around her waist, so it covered her lower body. She had no shoes or sandals. She preceded her father out of their compound, dancing with joy. Neither the ninety-degree heat from the sun climbing overhead nor the humid air dimmed her enthusiasm.

They reached the school nearly an hour later. Her father paused in front of the raffia-covered structure. They were approached by an Igbo man. "Bring your child to me," he said as he led them into the two-room school.

They saw fifteen or sixteen boys and two girls, some seated at desks and holding slates, and others on two benches at the back. A teacher stood in front. Mgbeke longed to be among them.

The man brought them into the second room. He took a seat behind a large wooden desk and motioned for her father to sit in the chair facing him. The two men exchanged Igbo greetings.

"I am the head teacher of the school," he said. "You are coming at a good time. The term has just started. What is your child's name?"

Her father told him. Then the man turned to her. "You are sure you want to come to school?" he said.

She nodded, suddenly too frightened to speak. "You know you will have to work hard. You must tell me why you want to come," he said to her.

"I want to wear a uniform. I want to learn," she said.

"How old are you?"

She did not answer, but her father said, "She was born in the year when the rains were very heavy."

The head addressed her. "Stand up straight. Now reach your right hand over your head. Can you touch your left ear?" He demonstrated.

She mimicked him and reached her ear easily. She had passed the "entrance exam" used in Nigeria and other British colonies where birth certificates did not exist. "You can start now, in this term," the teacher said.

Mgbeke was happy but worried. She did not have a uniform. How could she come without that?

As if reading her thoughts, the teacher said, "She will need a uniform." He gave her father the name of the tailor who kept the fabric and sewed the uniforms for the pupils at the school. "You must wear your uniform every day and it must be clean," he said, addressing her. "Come back as soon as you have your uniform."

Her father grumbled as he led her away. "You see that this will cost me a lot," he said. "I have to pay the tailor. You will not be able to help your mother as you should." But he could see how important this was for his daughter, whom he loved. With his limited experience of the colonial masters, he also suspected that an education could be useful later. Perhaps it would be helpful for his child to understand the ways of the white men. Better to try it out on a daughter, who would marry and leave, than on his son, who would inherit his land and his position.

They went straight to the tailor, who lived along their way home. He measured her and said, "I will sew your uniform big so you can wear it for two years."

"No, make it fit her now," her father said. He did not want his daughter to look too poor to have a well-fitting uniform. He had a reputation to uphold. "We will pick up the uniform tomorrow."

She followed her father home, skipping and humming. The next day she accompanied her father to the tailor's. The tailor had her try on the white blouse and dark skirt and showed her how to fasten the buttons. She carried her new clothes home and put them on to show her mother and siblings. Then she placed them by her sleeping mat to be ready for the next morning.

She barely slept that night. She was up before dawn and sweeping the compound, her daily task. Then she took a metal bucket half-full of cold water and went to the back of the compound, where the women bathed. After drying off, she put on her new outfit and joined her neighbor for the four-mile walk. prophets and disciples. She loved the stories about Jesus speaking to crowds of people.

A few children were already lining up outside the building when she and her friend arrived. The head teacher led the assembly in prayers in Igbo. When the pupils filed into the mud-walled classroom, a child near her size led her to one of the benches. The head teacher called out names, adding hers to the list, then left the room for the younger teacher to take over.

He led the children in number sequences for them to practice while he turned his attention to the children seated at desks. He wrote sentences on the blackboard for them to copy on their slates.

Mgbeke learned to say the alphabet and to count, first up to ten, then twenty. They were drilled on spelling a few simple Igbo words. The learning was all by rote. There were no books for the youngest children nor were they expected to write.

By the second term, she needed her own slate. She was trembling as she asked her father to buy it for her; he might refuse, and she would not be able to keep up with the other children. She was relieved when he brought her a slate two days later. She began to write the alphabet and the numbers up to one hundred. She learned to read and write a few Igbo words and do simple addition and subtraction. Gradually, English words were added to the children's vocabulary.

Religious education was as important as the reading, writing, and counting. Mgbeke and the other children memorized Bible verses and the names of prophets and disciples. She loved the stories about Jesus speaking to crowds of people.

During her third year Mgbeke was introduced to the story of Samuel Ajayi Crowther, who had translated the Bible into Igbo. Crowther was the most famous of the early Nigerian converts. He was Yoruba, from west of the Niger River, later Western Nigeria. He had been captured with other family members in 1821, when he was twelve, and sold to Portuguese slave traders. The British—who were dedicated to ending the slave trade, in which they had been eager participants a few years earlier—seized the ship and released the captives in Sierra Leone. Crowther was cared for by CMS, learned English, and converted to Christianity.

He developed an early interest in languages, studied in England, and returned to Nigeria. He took part in an expedition along the Niger River to promote the end of slave trading, encourage commerce, and convert the local people. The British noticed his deep dedication and he was sent to England to become a priest. He translated the Bible not only into Igbo but first into his own native Yoruba. Later he did translations and wrote dictionaries in several other Nigerian languages. He became the first African bishop in the Anglican Church in the 1860s.

Mgbeke loved all her classes. There were daily prayers, Bible stories, and singing in addition to classes in more advanced reading, writing, and arithmetic. The girls were also given lessons in food preparation, though they had already learned to cook from their mothers. She never missed a day.

In her fourth year, her teacher announced that baptisms would take place the following month. Addressing each child in turn, he said, "Do you wish to become a Christian and be baptized?"

She answered without hesitation. "Yes, I want to be baptized."

"You must ask your parents tonight. If you will be baptized, you will need to choose a Christian name as your baptismal name," the teacher told her.

That evening she took her father's meal to him in his hut, the *obi* at the center of the compound. "My teacher asked me if I want to be baptized and become a Christian," she said. "I have to choose a baptismal name."

"I said you could go to school. I did not say you could join their religion. Do you think that our gods are not good enough?" he said, his voice shaking with anger.

"The teachers say that our gods are not real, but their God is. They say that we should pray to their God and his son, Jesus." She was shaking as she spoke. Her voice trailed off.

He raised his hand to strike her. But he stopped himself. He had agreed to send her. Now he wondered if he had done the right thing. "They are not our people and they do not understand our customs. They do not know how important it is to honor the ancestors."

"I will still honor our ancestors," she said.

"Talk to your mother. If you still want to join them after that, I will not stop you."

She spoke to her mother that night. Her mother must have recognized how much her daughter wished to join the new religion. Perhaps she had a sense that times were changing. Maybe she even admired her daughter for her willingness to break with tradition.

The next day, Mgbeke told the teacher, "I will be baptized."

"What name do you choose?" he asked her.

"I like the name Grace." *Grace* was an important word in the passages of the Bible that she knew best, such as "Mary, full of grace," and other references to Jesus's mother. "Can I take that name?"

He liked her choice. A month later the teacher took his group of ten- and eleven-year-old boys and girls to the Anglican Church in Aguata, where the priest who was part of the Mission on the Niger came to baptize them. Other groups of children from different schools were also present. After the rite of baptism, where he anointed the head of each child with water, he conducted the full service of Holy Communion. Grace fell in love with the flowery language, the elaborate robes of the priest and other clergy, and the ritual of the Anglican Church.

Her parents did not accompany her, nor did her father change his opinion. He believed that the traditional gods were more influential than any invisible Christian God. He was sure that she would forget about her new faith. When she married in a few years, her husband could set her back on the right path. Ezeonodu stopped sending her to school but allowed her to attend church services on many Sunday mornings.

At home, she was occupied with improving her knowledge of what was required of an Igbo wife and mother. She could already pound the cassava or yam, the starchy component that accompanied the soup for evening meals.

She had learned how long to soak the cassava to remove the poison. Making *akamu,* custard from corn flour, was a special skill. After ruining it once and getting beaten by her father, she became adept at pouring just the right amount of boiling water at the right slow speed to cause the custard to set.

She was popular in Agulu as she reached her teens. Attractive, with her round face, smooth dark skin, wide lips, and shy smile, young men noticed her. She had completed four years of school, more than most other children, especially girls. She was a tempting target. For the occasions when the young unmarried women danced in the moonlight, she wore glass beads around her waist and around her neck. If she went off with one of the young men after dancing, her father did not know about it.

Ezeonodu did know the time was coming for her to marry. He expected to be approached by the family of one of the young men of the town. When that happened, he would consider the prospects of the man and, even more importantly, the character of the man's family. Ezeonodu and his brothers and other men of the clan would send someone to investigate the family before agreeing to pursue the marriage. And he would make the final decision on the man she would marry. But instead of being approached by his towns-men, he was surprised to learn about inquires by a visitor from the nearby town of Nanka.

My husband recalls seeing Eze-onodu dressed in a fashion similar to the man in figure 4. Men of his status and wealth could have carried the ivo-ry tusk and the staff. A hat somewhat like the one in the photo is worn by Delta men today.

Figure 4 Niger Delta Chief; probably Igbo, early 1900s, Nigeria Collection (MS 1553). Manuscripts and Archives, Yale University Library.

# 3

# TO FIND A WIFE,
## SAMUEL GOES HOME

GRACE WAS ALREADY SIXTEEN IN 1929. Some of her age-mates had married. Her father was beginning to wonder if her acceptance of the new Christian faith was causing suitors to stay away. At the same time, Samuel came home from the logging camp with marriage on his mind. "You will marry and have a family," his father and other men had always told him. "It is your responsibility to continue the family line."

He had reached the proper age and with his promotion, he was ready. He never thought of taking a wife in Sapoba. He had to return home, where his family would help in the choice of his bride. Belonging to the community meant that your clansmen were involved in helping you find the right person to marry. The marriage was, after all, a union between two families, not just two people.

Samuel had sent two letters, written for him in English by a scribe in the market. His parents took the letters to the market, where they also paid a scribe to read the strange English language and translate for them. He informed them that he was well, working hard, and living among other Igbo people, though the native population spoke a different language called Edo. In his second letter he told them that he was attending the white man's church. The best news had been that he would be coming home soon.

It was *Afor,* the town's major market day, when he reached Nanka. The women had piled their unsold produce and their purchases into wide raffia baskets to carry home on their heads. Ogbungwa's sister recognized him immediately. "Our son has returned," she said as she embraced him. A neighbor heard the greeting and hastened from the market to be the first to tell his parents.

He was welcomed by others and paused to speak with them. By the time he reached home, his parents had already been alerted. Nogem had killed a chicken and was preparing his favorite soup. "Our son is home," she shouted when she saw him approaching. She dropped her cooking spoon and threw her arms around him. His upper body was full of muscles, and he was very dark from spending his days in the sun. He smiled at her welcome. His brothers, whose facial scars reminded him of how he had departed so suddenly, gathered to welcome him. His older brother, Ejike, had married in his absence and introduced his pregnant wife.

Ogbungwa approached Samuel and grabbed his arm, squeezing to make sure he was real. *"Ikwere inata n'uno!* You decided to return home," he said. He led his son to the *obi,* the central hut of the compound. "We must call our *umunna,* the men of the clan, to welcome him," he said to his older brother, the head of the family, who occupied the obi.

Later that evening, after Samuel had eaten garri and the *ofe onugbu,* bitterleaf soup, with chicken that his mother had prepared, he sat with his father, Uncle Nwafor, and other male relatives in the obi. The sweet smell of fresh palm wine filled the hut as the men drank from their gourds and animal horns.

Samuel told stories about life in the white man's world of the logging camp. "The trees are as tall as two of our palm trees," he said. "The white men have saws longer than a big snake, with teeth. Two men must pull the saw, back and forth, to cut down the trees. We cut the trees into logs, which are shipped to the white man's country."

His audience responded with surprise and appreciation. "Eh, eh," they said, or *"O di egwu.* It is amazing."

After a couple of hours, the others departed to their own huts and compounds. Samuel turned to his father. "It is time for me to marry. I have come home to find a wife," he said. "I have been working for the white man for several years. I get paid six shillings every week. I've been given a title of native supervisor."

"So, you did well after you left us. I was angry. But I am proud of you. You are right to come home to marry."

Samuel hesitated before telling his father about his new religion. Finally, he said, "I have joined the white man's church. I have taken the name Samuel. I want a wife who will come to church with me."

"Eh, why would you do that?" his father said, his voice several notches louder. "What medicine did they give you?"

"They didn't give me any medicine. I decided on my own that I would accept their message and join their faith."

"Is this what you ran away for? Aren't our gods good enough for you? The ancestors will be offended. Do you even still honor our ancestors?"

"Yes, I honor our ancestors, and I believe our gods are good. But their God has great power," he said. "They pray to their God every Sunday. I go to their church and sing their songs. I want to take a wife who will come back with me to Sapoba and join me in their church."

Ogbungwa protested. But he saw that he could not change his son's mind. "I will speak to the umunna tomorrow. We will find someone for you to marry."

After all, this was his duty. Even though his son had abandoned their traditional religion, the father's role was to bring other family and clan members into the decision process. It was unheard of for a son to search for a bride on his own.

"Thank you, father," Samuel said, standing up to go to his older brother's hut for a place to sleep. His mind was almost at rest. He was home, his parents were well, one brother was married, and other relatives had welcomed him without reservation. But he was not sure what they would say the next morning when his father took his request for a Christian wife to the umunna.

The Harmattan, the wind carrying sand south from the Sahara in December and January, had coated the compound with dust. The sky was gray when Ogbungwa gathered his brothers, his oldest son, and others of the umunna the next morning. He brought out a jug of fresh palm wine and announced, "My son Okeke has told me that he wants to marry. I have asked you here today to help me find a wife for him."

Obiora, a clansman near the age of Ogbungwa, said, "It is good that he wants to marry. We will look at the girls of our town the next time they are dancing together."

His father shook his head. "No, we need to find a wife for him right away. He wants to go back to Sapoba and his work. He does not need a village girl. He wants to marry a Christian! He even says he has a name from the new religion. He told me his name is now Samuel."

One of the older men said, "Why would he do that? Does he want to disgrace you further?"

Ogbungwa was prepared. He had not been surprised by his son's intention to marry. But he had not slept well after his son's other announcement. Though Samuel had mentioned his attendance at the white man's church in one of his letters, his father had not expected that his son would have adopted the new religion. During the night he had thought about his son's decision. He was disappointed but he knew what he would say.

He also realized that his son was right to adapt to the new times. There was a priest who visited the village occasionally, and Ogbungwa knew that a few people who joined his religion were gaining advantages. One had been given a job with the district officer in Onitsha. Despite the warnings from some of the elders who opposed the missionaries, he knew of nothing bad that had happened to those who joined or to their families.

Now it was time to show support and accede to his son's wishes. "He has made his decision. We have to find a wife for him or he will marry someone from the place where he is living."

Obiora had recovered from his shock and spoke again. "There is a young woman in Agulu who has become a Christian in a family I know of. She has even been to school."

Another clansman said, "Do you mean Ezeonodu's daughter? I know the father a little. He is a successful farmer. I have seen him in the market. He is doing well."

Two other men who traveled to other markets in the four-day market rotation nodded their agreement. "People speak well of him," one said.

Ogbungwa's brother Nwafor spoke. "Other men in our town have married women from Agulu. The women behave well."

"It's true," said another man. "Not one has been sent away by her husband and returned to her parents with nothing except a request for repayment of the bride price."

"They have all produced children, and they all have at least one son," said a third.

The jug of palm wine was half-empty. Ogbungwa took another drink from his horn before speaking. "We need to send someone."

Several men spoke at once, each suggesting a name for the role of *abaeke*. Others opposed or supported the different choices. After a few minutes, Ogbungwa said, "Enough! Obiora should go. He will ask about the woman and her family. He can call on the family that lives near Ezeonodu."

He turned to Obiora. "Do you understand what you must do?"

"I do. I am not a small boy," Obiora said. "I have carried out these inquiries before. I will ask about the family. Are there any mad people, or sickly? Are they hardworking?"

"Don't forget to be sure they are not osu," Nwafor reminded him.

"Of course. I know we would never allow our son to marry a slave," Obiora said.

The osu were either people dedicated to serving the gods, or people who had been captured in warfare or taken in payment of a debt. No respectable Igbo person would marry an osu.

Obiora set out early the next morning. The Harmattan was even heavier; the air was cool and dusty with the sand blowing south from the Sahara Desert. He knew the compound of the girl in question. He entered a compound near it and approached the obi in the center. "Pam, pam," he said, in imitation of knocking on a door. He was copying the custom he had learned from a townsman who now worked in Onitsha. He had also seen the English-trained priest who visited use this expression.

"*Nno,* welcome," said a woman who appeared from the side of the hut. After Obiora gave a brief introduction of himself and his mission, she called her husband from inside the obi, set chairs for them outside, and disappeared to return a moment later with a small plate holding two kola nuts, with a shape between ovoid and spherical, with a length of roughly an inch and a half.

The two men exchanged greetings. The host held one kola up as he said, "He who brings kola brings life." He broke the pink nut into two pieces, took one himself, and offered the plate to his visitor. Obiora took the other piece and dropped the whole nut into his leather bag to take back with him. He recited a familiar proverb, "When the kola nut reaches home, it can say where it came from," before chewing and swallowing the smaller piece.

After the required pleasantries about family, Obiora introduced the purpose of his visit. "I have come from Nanka, from the Onyemelukwe family," he said. "They asked me to come to Agulu. I have come to you for your advice and help."

He quoted a familiar proverb: "The bush where a child got a snail, there is where his eyes are drawn." He continued, "Several Nanka men have taken wives from your town and our eyes are drawn here again. We know there is a daughter in one of your families who has become a Christian. One of our sons has also joined that faith. He is seeking a bride."

Then he listened carefully. "The family is well regarded here in Agulu," his host said. "Their daughter Grace has indeed become a Christian, though her father is not happy about that. She is attractive and well behaved, despite abandoning our traditional religion."

After a few more comments about the merits of the young woman, Obiora took a sip of the palm wine he had been given. Then he said, "Has she been overly free with any of your men?" His host told Obiora that to his knowledge, though she danced with the other young women at celebrations, she did not follow anyone into the bush after the dance was over.

Obiora then broached the critical topic. "Can you assure me her family does not come from slave origins?"

"No," his host assured his visitor. "They are not osu. Her father comes from a long line of Agulu men. He is a successful farmer and a leader in our town."

Satisfied, Obiora returned to Nanka and his relatives with news of Ezeonodu and his daughter. The family was not osu. The father was well known and respected. His daughter had attended the CMS school. She was a Christian and had taken the name Grace. She was beautiful and of acceptable marrying age, though older than some who had already wed. She was available. She was said to be well behaved, a virgin, and knowledgeable about women's work.

Obiora was then deputized as an emissary. He now had a specific role: to make the first approach to the girl's family with a statement of interest. He took two other family members with him. Going alone would not be respectful to her family. Nor would it show sufficient commitment.

Ezeonodu had heard whispers of their interest. He was ready.

After Ezeonodu had given them kola and palm wine, Obiora stood. He explained the purpose of their visit, repeating the proverb he had used on his first visit.

"You say the man is a Christian?" Ezeonodu said, his voice booming. "Why should I let my daughter marry someone in that strange religion? Nothing good can come from it!"

The visitors persisted. "Samuel has been working for the white man. He cuts huge logs, which are shipped to the white man's country. They have made him a supervisor." Though they spoke in Igbo, the word *supervisor* was said in English as "supa visa," no Igbo translation coming readily to mind. "He is strong, and he will be able to provide well for his family."

With his tone a few notches lower, Ezeonodu questioned them about the man they were calling Samuel. Was his family respectable? Would they welcome Grace as their son's wife? Would she be treated well? Did Samuel intend to take other wives?

One by one the visitors replied. Obiora spoke first. "Samuel's father, Ogbungwa, has a large compound. His yam barn is always full at the end of the harvest, and he gives thanks to the ancestors."

The next man followed. "Even though Samuel has adopted the new religion, he also continues to show deference to his elders and to the ancestors." He added, "This new religion does not like men to have more than one wife."

The third visitor spoke. "The Onyemelukwe family plays a leading role in the village and in the town of Nanka. Samuel has four brothers. The oldest is already married and provides well for his wife."

"I will consider your request," Ezeonodu said, now calmed down. "I will consult my umunna. You may return in a few weeks for my answer."

"We have to move quickly," his visitors said. "Samuel must return to Sapoba soon."

The visitors and Ezeonodu finally agreed to return in one market week, four days, for his answer. As soon as the Nanka emissaries had departed, Ezeonodu sent a message to his umunna that he had been approached about his daughter Grace. He needed to meet with them the next day.

Later, when his daughter brought him the evening meal, he said, "I had a visitor today. A man from Nanka is interested in marrying you."

She was full of questions, but he would answer only that the man was a Christian. "You will meet him if I decide to proceed."

Now that the interest had been declared, her family delegated members of their umunna to undertake their own background check of the Onyemeluk-we family in Nanka. The Agulu women married to Nanka men were their first source of information. They also spoke to people they had met in markets or in travel. Her family asked about the son's prospects as a good provider, if he had a propensity for chasing women, and whether he had respect for his elders and other family members.

If the prospective bride or groom was clearly not osu, there were still other concerns. Mental soundness was one. Had other family members, past or present, shown any signs of instability? Had anyone become a madman or madwoman, wandering the village and ostracized by the family? Good character was another. Was there any history of criminal activity in the family?

Further discreet inquiries from Samuel's side included questions about whether Grace was a virgin. Would she be a loyal wife? Were there women in her family who had not been able to produce children? On the plus side, did women directly related to the prospective bride—her mother, sisters, or aunts by blood—give birth to sons?

Because Samuel was eager to return to Sapoba as soon as possible, the inquiries were made rapidly, and the results reported promptly to each family's umunna. When the emissaries returned to Ezeonodu after four days, he agreed to proceed. They set the next step for the following week.

The ceremonial visit, *iku aka na uzo,* or "knocking on the door," by the intended groom's family to Grace's was next. This essential step in the process of arranging the marriage was the first time the prospective bride and groom would see each other. *See* was all they would do. They would not be given time to converse, share a meal, or be alone.

The day before the visitors were due, Grace's father killed a goat and placed it on the fire to burn off the hair, filling the compound with the acrid smell. He cut it into quarters and then even smaller pieces. Tradition required that certain parts of the goat be given to relatives, so her brother was sent with the right front leg to give to their father's oldest brother. Grace took the left back leg to the widow of an uncle. One of her sisters was dispatched with part of the back to another relative. When the necessary portions had been distributed, Grace stood before her father.

"Take the head and the remainder of the meat to your mother," he said. "You must watch her closely and listen carefully, so you know how to prepare *ngwo ngwo* and the other dishes for our visitors tomorrow."

"I know how to cook ngwo ngwo, and I can cook *ofe egusi,* pumpkin seed soup, and other soups," she said as she placed the meat on the banana leaves laid out on the ground.

"Then go and help your mother and the others. Make sure the food is very tasty," he said, cleaning his machete on another banana leaf lying beside the carcass.

Grace was proud of her cooking skills. She took the head and the rest of the meat to her mother's kitchen, a shed behind the hut. "Let me cook the ngwo ngwo," she said to her mother, Eye, as she lifted the goat's head, the main ingredient for the delicacy.

"Cook it the way I showed you. Don't spoil it!" As usual, there was a fire going under one of the iron tripods by the small kitchen. Grace placed the three stones she would use as her makeshift tripod, fetched firewood from the heap a few yards away, added kindling from the stack nearby, and carried a burning piece of wood from the other fire to light her own. She went to the large stone water jug at the entrance to the kitchen. Using the calabash kept there, she filled the large pot she had pulled out from its storage spot in the corner and set it on the stones. With more scoops of water, she filled an enamel pan, where she washed the head thoroughly while the water heated.

In a few minutes the water was boiling, and the head was clean, ready for the pot. She cut off the ears but left the protruding buckteeth. Then she plunged it into the pot.

"Grind the onions," she directed her youngest sister, Mbafor, who had come to watch. "I'll cut the tomatoes and the peppers," she said, picking up the knife that her mother had set down. In less than an hour the meat was coming off the bones. She removed that pot, placed another on the fire, and poured in a large spoonful of palm oil. As the thick red oil became clear, the pungent smell filled her nostrils. She added the onion and other ingredients. When they were browned, she added the meat from the goat's head, a little water, salt, and leaves from the uziza plant, like spinach, and let it all cook for another hour. The spicy aroma filled the surrounding space.

"Try it," she said to her mother. The second wife, Mama John, also tasted the dish.

"You have learned well," they said, smacking their lips. Grace took her pot off the fire and set it on a shelf her father had built along the side wall of the kitchen hut. She would reheat the dish tomorrow to give to the visitors.

She woke early the next day, brimming with curiosity about the man. She had learned from her spies in the household, servants who had been able to listen in on conversations among the men, that his name was Samuel and he worked in the logging industry. But no one had seen him. Was he good-looking? Most important, would she like him?

Eye and Mama John were already busy in the kitchen. There were several fires going. Grace joined them to lend a hand in preparing pounded yam, egusi soup with the goat meat, rice, and tomato stew. Mama John caught and killed two chickens. Grace was given the task of plucking, washing, and cutting them into pieces, ready for the pot.

Still the time seemed to pass so slowly. The wait was nearly unbearable. She was grinding tomatoes around one in the afternoon when a couple of the young children burst into the kitchen area. "They're coming," they shouted.

Grace and her sister dashed out and hid at the side of the obi. They could hardly see the young man walking behind his elders. Fearing they would be spotted, they retreated to the kitchen, finished their tasks, and headed for their own hut to prepare.

Samuel—still called Okeke by his older relatives—had asked Obiora about the woman he was to marry. He did not get much satisfaction. Obiora would only say, "She is lovely. You will not be disappointed."

Samuel had dressed in his favorite dashiki, a loose cotton top of bright green and blue that he had brought from Sapoba. He wore trousers and sandals. "Ah-ah. You are looking like a white man," his uncle said. Others among the eight men congregated for the visit laughed, but the younger ones looked at Samuel's outfit with envy.

Ogbungwa and the other older men each wore two yards of multi-colored cotton fabric wrapped around the waist, with one end thrown over the left shoulder to anchor it. Each man carried a decrepit leather briefcase. The women, including Samuel's mother, wore similar cotton wrappers that nearly reached the ground and tied at the waist, with a second, shorter piece of the same fabric over the first. They each had another piece of fabric over their breasts like a midriff. Their head covers were of a similar fabric that was wrapped twice around and then had the ends tucked in to hold them in place. Two of the men wore sandals; the others were barefoot. The youngest men carried the obligatory gifts, two jugs of palm wine and one bottle of Dutch gin. This precious drink had been imported into Nigeria since the late 1800s. They would show the girl's family that they were both traditional and modern.

Ezeonodu had assembled his own family members, a group similar in composition to those coming. They were seated on wooden benches in front of the obi. His father, the oldest man present and the head of the umunna, was at the center. They remained dignified and unsmiling as the visitors came forward. They had to show that they were a substantial family. Their daughter would not be cheap!

The guests halted in front of the seated men. The two carrying the gifts came forward and placed the jugs of palm wine and the bottle of gin on the table in front of the hosts. "We have come from the town of Nanka, not far from here, to honor you," the most senior man among Ogbungwa's umunna said. "We are pleased to give you these small gifts of palm wine and gin. Please accept them with our compliments."

The elder responded in a gravelly voice. "We are grateful for your gifts and pleased to make your acquaintance." He motioned to the women hovering nearby. "Show the visitors their seats," he said. The women came forward to indicate the benches to the right of the hosts. Ezeonodu called his senior wife, Eye, Grace's mother, to bring kola nuts to welcome the visitors. She came with a tray holding ten of the purplish-pink nuts and handed it to her husband. He, in turn, called his youngest son to take the tray to Samuel's father, who touched the tray with his right hand, then directed the boy to take it around to show everyone in the group.

After the visitors had admired and touched the kola nuts, Ogbungwa took one of the nuts and held it up in his right hand. He repeated the proverb used a few days earlier by Obiora. *"Oji luo uno okwua ebe osi abia.* When the kola nut reaches home, it will tell where it came from." He put the kola in the ancient leather briefcase he had by his side. Everyone present understood the meaning: the kola that he would take home with him was a sign of the welcome he received. Once back in his village, he would relate the story of the visit to his people, helping to cement the tie between the two families and two clans.

When the tray was back in Ezeonodu's hands, it was time to bless the kola. But Ezeonodu could not do this himself. The act of breaking kola is reserved for the oldest man present among the hosts, so he told the son to pass the tray on to his father, who lifted one of the nuts high as he spoke. *"Ife dï mma onye n'acho, o ga afu ya.* Whatever good a person is looking for, he will see it." Most of the hosts took the proverb as a direct reference to the mission that brought the Onyemelukwe family to their home. They knew the man coming on the mission to find a good wife would be successful here, and they affirmed the wisdom of the proverb with mumbled sounds of approval.

A few of the guests interpreted the proverb to say that the woman should look for the best aspects of the man she would marry. They likewise made low sounds of agreement. It was a fine proverb, an essential element of any Igbo conversation, and everyone present could make his or her own interpretation!

Next the elder broke the kola along its seam, using his hands. When it split into four pieces, he said, "We are fortunate. Our kola has given us the same number of pieces as the days of our market week. This tells us that harmony is coming." He handed the tray to Ezeonodu, who again called his son to break the remaining nuts and pass them to the guests, and then to the host family.

After the kola nuts were shared, the most senior man among the visitors stood. "We thank you for the kola you have shared with us. It is time to say why we are here."

Everyone knew why they were there, but custom required that they state their purpose formally. He introduced the men with him by name and lineage, omitting the intended groom. Then he said, "We have among us a young man who wishes to marry. He is the son of Ogbungwa, a respected member of our umunna.

"He has been living among the white people in Sapoba and will return to them, where he cuts wood and ships it to the white man's land. He is hardworking and has been made a supervisor." Again, though the speech was in

Igbo, the word *supervisor* was in English. He pointed to Samuel. "You can see that he is a strong man."

Other men among the visitors spoke about the strength of the Onyemelukwe family, the virtues of the man they were introducing, and the reputation of their town. Ogbungwa introduced his wife, Samuel's mother. Another man named a family from Nanka where one of the Agulu women was living happily with her husband to illustrate that they would protect the daughter of their hosts.

Ezeonodu's father responded. "We welcome you. Thank you for your introductions. We in Agulu are also proud of our town and our people." Like the visitors had done, he introduced the people around him. He praised their town, their lineage and family, and the young woman who had not yet appeared.

During the speeches, the young men served palm wine. Every man present had his own drinking horn or calabash with him and took it out as the men passed among them. The hosts handed cups to the servers for their drinks. The formal talk wound down after two hours. The wives brought out the food and placed it on the table. Ezeonodu's father thanked the ancestors for the gift of the food and directed the women to serve the visitors and then their own family members. More palm wine was served.

When everyone had eaten their fill, Ezeonodu called for his daughter Grace to come out and join the party. She was dressed in a red-and-green cotton wrapper around her waist. A piece of the same fabric was tied on her head, and she wore glass beads around her neck.

"Come, daughter," her father said. "Take this cup of palm wine. If you see any man here whom you want to marry, you are to take it to him." He handed her a calabash fashioned into a cup. She looked around. At first, she did not see the man she thought she had glimpsed when he was arriving with his family. Her heart stopped. Was one of the older men her intended husband? Samuel, as custom demanded, had half hidden himself behind one of his relatives. Then she spotted his slight movement, breathed a sigh of relief, and went toward him. She approached, knelt in front of him, sipped the wine, and gave him the cup to finish. She had indicated her agreement to the marriage.

The day's events concluded with negotiations over bride price. Two uncles, along with both fathers, were the principal participants in this discussion. The usual amount in Agulu was known to Samuel's family. Grace's uncle opened with a speech. "You have seen our daughter Grace. You have spoken with others about her. She has been to school and can read, write, and do numbers. She is a Christian, following the new ways of the white men. It will be difficult for us to let her go."

Samuel's uncle countered with his own comments. "We understand that Grace is a remarkable young woman. That is what has brought us to you. Our son is also an outstanding young man. He has been working for the white men for several years and, as we told you, is now a supervisor. His prospects are excellent. Grace will be fortunate to marry him. Your family will not regret this joining of our children."

Soon the men began to speak of actual numbers. After an hour of back and forth discussion, the bride price was settled at one goat, six chickens, twelve yams, and twenty shillings. They did not need to include in the list the standard gifts the man's family would bring: several jugs of palm wine and tobacco. The price was steep, but with Grace's education and Christian faith, it seemed fair.

The date for the next step in the marriage rites was again set for one native week, or four days, later. Again, Samuel's family would come to Grace's home, bringing the bride price, the gifts, and more relatives. At the end of that day's events, Grace would leave with her new husband.

The couple had barely met. Grace had brought the palm wine to Samuel, but they had not been given a chance to speak. Surely, they wondered whether they would like, much less love, each other. But they expected nothing different nor were other options available. At that time, 1929, in Igboland, there was almost no opportunity for young men and women to meet one another in a casual setting where they could become acquainted.

Their parents had married in the same way, as had generations before them. No one recalled any time in either family when a woman had to be returned to her family for misbehaving. No wife they knew of had been badly mistreated by her husband.

# 4

# PALM WINE CONFIRMS THE MARRIAGE

FOUR DAYS AFTER SAMUEL AND his family had "knocked on the door," and been accepted, came the culminating ceremony of the marriage, *igba nkwu,* carrying palm wine. On this day Samuel was accompanied by the same senior men and their wives, including his parents, who had come four days earlier. He was also joined by several members of his own age grade, the group of people born within three or four years of one another who form a community of equals. His older brother, Ejike, led this contingent. Again, the men had exchanged their loincloths, their usual wear, for wrappers. The green and blue lines on a white background were a stark contrast with their dark skin.

The Onyemelukwe family brought along three musicians. The drummer came first, his instrument held over his left shoulder by a leather strap, his right hand holding the striker. He was followed by a man playing an Igbo flute, a hand-carved wooden instrument about eight inches long, with a wide opening to fit the lower lip, and holes to cover to make the melodies. The third musician struck an *ogene,* an iron hand bell, with a short piece of wood.

The women held the six chickens and the yams, while the young men carried the calabashes of palm wine. Ejike led the goat. Samuel's junior uncle had the twenty shillings tied in a tattered cloth and the tobacco in a round tin container.

The musicians began playing well before they reached the compound. People living along the way came out to watch the procession. Some even followed them into the compound as they danced their way to the benches outside the obi where their hosts were seated.

Ezeonodu had assembled more relatives for the *igba nkwu*. The family members wore wrappers of a purple-and-green cotton fabric to identify themselves. Grace's father, grandfather, uncles, and mother were in the center. Other male relatives were next to them. The *umuada,* the women born into the family, had seats near the men. The *ndi anutara di,* women married into the family, had their place on the opposite side of the clearing, though many of them were busy preparing the food.

After the procession of the visitors, Grace appeared at the entrance to the compound, leading five of her age-mates, all in red-and-green cotton wrappers. She carried a jug of palm wine on her head, stretching one hand up to steady it. When she reached her father, her mate helped her lift the palm wine from her head to place it before him. She moved to a chair that had been placed for her at the front of the assembly.

"We have brought the gifts that you require," Samuel's uncle said, standing before Ezeonodu and motioning to the bearers of the gifts to bring them forward. Ejike dragged the goat while the women and boys brought the yams, chickens, and kegs of palm wine, placing them all on the ground in front of the hosts. Obi, Samuel's youngest brother, unwrapped the shillings and placed them with the container of tobacco on the table.

Ezeonodu's senior brother spoke. "Count the money," he directed one of the younger men. Turning to another, he said, "See if the number of yams meets our request."

Accompanied by the bleating goat and squawking chickens, the first youth stacked the coins into piles of five each. "It is correct. Twenty shillings," he said.

His colleague moved the yams from the pile the visitors had placed into another heap as he counted. "The yams are complete," he said.

The senior uncle spoke. "We are grateful for your visit, and for the gifts you have brought. We accept them as the bride price for our daughter Grace." He directed the young men to take the chickens and goat away, leaving the yams and other gifts in place.

Then, as always for an Igbo event—a marriage, a funeral, or any social gathering, even a visit to someone's home—the hosts presented kola nuts.

They performed the same ceremonies as they had four days earlier, showing the kola nuts around, praising the ancestors, and welcoming the visitors. Then the kola nuts were broken and shared. The young men came out to serve palm wine, each man holding his own horn or calabash and the women again accepting cups from their hosts.

Ogbungwa stood up. *"Ndi be anyi, kwenu!* Our people, shout!" he said.

"Yah," the assembly responded. Three more times he repeated his call, and each time the answer was louder—"Yah!"—until the nearby palm trees seemed to reverberate. Then he turned to the hosts. "We are here to celebrate our son's marriage to your daughter. We thank you for welcoming us."

He took a lengthy drink of palm wine and continued. "Our towns have a long relationship," he said. "The men of Nanka are known as great wrestlers. One time our best wrestlers were competing in the town of Igbo Ukwu. They had defeated everyone that the people of Igbo Ukwu could present against them. Then wrestlers came from Agulu to compete. Our youngest wrestler fought with an older, experienced man from Agulu. Our man held the leg of the older man until he fell and was being pinned to the ground. But then he remembered that he had to respect his elders, and he let the man overturn him and hold him down. This was in the days before we were born."

The crowd shouted their approval. "He was right. He had to show respect!"

Samuel's father took his seat again and Grace's father rose. He called out, "Ndi be anyi, kwenu!" Just as the guests had, he and his people repeated the call before he began his own comments. "Thank you for telling us this story about our ancestors," he said. "We do well to learn from the experiences of those who came before us."

He turned to his father. *"Bia, nna anyi.* Come, our father. Tell us about the time you wrestled with the men of Nanka."

The older man, walking with a stick to support his stooped body, came forward. "Ndi be anyi, kwenu!"

He was answered with an enthusiastic "Yah!"

He began. "Before the time of the white men, we Igbo men wrestled for many reasons. Sometimes it was part of a battle with another village. But sometimes it was against other men in our town. We wrestled at that time to see who could marry the most attractive woman. When I was a young man, I was the strongest wrestler, and I was sure I could win the beautiful daughter of our chief. But she had seen another man she liked. He also liked her. He visited the *Dibia* to get him to put a curse on me."

He paused in his story while the crowd voiced sympathy and reproach. "Shame on him," one man said.

"What a cowardly thing to do!" another cried out.

The elder picked up his story again. "On the day we were to wrestle, I had fever and chills. I still fought like a champion, but I was weak. He defeated me." More sympathetic noises came from his audience. "He married the beautiful woman. She had several children for him but no sons. Even his second wife had more daughters than sons. When I later married my first wife, she gave me two sons before she ever had a daughter." He laughed at the misfortune of his competitor and his own good luck. The crowd shouted their appreciation.

Grace knew the stories, and she knew that the men were building the essential relationship between her family and her new husband's family. Finally, her father turned to her. "This man from Nanka has brought the bride price and wants you to go with him as his wife. Do you accept him as your husband?" he said.

She nodded her assent. He asked her to rise, took her arm, and walked with her to stand in front of Samuel. "You are going from our family to his. You will obey him, serve him well, and have his children. We will welcome you back as a visitor, but your home is now with him."

With the two principal celebrants seated together, the *ndi anutara di* brought out the food. They piled mounds of pounded yam and placed bowls of steaming rich soup on the tables in front of the visitors. The visiting women took charge of the food for their group, spooning large quantities onto the enamel plates their hosts had supplied. Equal quantities of food were placed before Ezeonodu and his relatives, and the women shared it out, giving each person their own plate. The *umuada,* seated in their own section, were given their own containers of yam and soup. Young people brought out bowls of water and carried them to each person for the obligatory hand washing before eating. The food disappeared quickly, accompanied by hums of satisfaction.

When everyone had eaten, the women cleared the tables and the boys brought out more palm wine. It was time for the dancers. The umuada of Grace's family were the first. Her father's sisters, his father's sisters, and female cousins born to the family had been practicing for weeks. They all wore cotton wrappers and *bubas,* tops, of the same purple-and-green geometric print, just as the men of their group did.

One of the women dragged out the *ekwe,* a two-foot-long hollowed-out log, with two rectangular cavities on the top. She began beating rhythmically with a stick. She varied the tone by covering one hole or the other, partially or fully, with her free hand. Another woman played the *ogene.* And a third led her relatives in their dance. They began slowly in a circle, moving their feet in the same pattern. After two minutes, the *ekwe* and gong picked up the pace; the women turned around and danced more rapidly. Soon they were stamping their feet and the crowd was applauding. With sweat pouring down their faces, they withdrew to their seats. The instrumentalists remained to accompany the next dancers.

Grace and her age-mates came forward. The unmarried girls had bare breasts, while the two already married wore *bubas* to cover their tops. Their dance was more vigorous, as befitted their younger age. Obiora, the original emissary, turned to the man seated next to him, pointing as he did so. "Look at the girl behind Grace," he said. "I've been considering taking a second wife."

"Isn't she too young for you? Do you think she would have you?"

"Why not? She looks ready. See how her breasts stand up. I could teach her how to be a good wife!" He lifted his drinking horn to take more of the palm wine. He knew that his role as emissary for Samuel should preclude him from seeking a bride among Grace's age-mates now. If he waited a year or two, and she had not married, he might send an emissary for himself, he thought. The girls went back to their bench.

The *ndi anutara di* had completed their work of cooking, serving, and cleaning up, and they were joyous as they danced last.

By late afternoon everyone was full of food and palm wine. Ogbungwa stood. "We thank you for entertaining us so well," he said, addressing Grace's father and the other men of her family. "It is time for us to take our new bride and return to Nanka." A few of the guests had drunk a little too much and had to be dragged to their feet.

Grace's mother embraced her daughter. She spoke softly, "You must show your husband proper respect. Obey him but let him know you also deserve respect."

"Yes, Mama," Grace said. "I will behave well. You will not be ashamed of me."

"He will show you what to do as a married woman. Do not let him beat you but follow his direction." Grace nodded before turning to the other members of her family to bid them a tearful farewell.

From now on, she and her husband were bound together. Samuel could return her to her family only if she publicly humiliated him so deeply that the elders of his family agreed she was beyond redemption. Her family would then have to accept her fault, take her back, and return the bride price. If he mistreated her severely so that the elders in her family agreed he could no longer be trusted, she could return to her family and they would keep the bride price. Otherwise, they would be together for life. Grace would be part of the Onyemelukwe family and the town of Nanka, though she would always retain her close ties to her family in Agulu, including her role as one of the umuada, the children of the family.

She departed with her husband and his family, taking the gifts the couple had been given to support them in their home. She herself carried a mortar and pestle on her head. Her new mother-in-law, Nogem, balanced two cooking pots, and other family members carried a water pot and the battered suitcase holding Grace's clothes. They returned to Nanka, where Samuel and Grace spent their first two nights together on a mat in his mother's hut. Two days later they set out for Sapoba.

Figure 5 Male relatives in Agulu, 2009, Clem 2nd from left, granddaughter Nkiru on right

The ceremonies "knocking on the door" and "palm wine carrying" bind the couple's families forever. The individuals who are marrying are the central figures in the drama, but their roles are minor compared to the efforts of their families who have made all the major decisions: whom they will marry, what the bride price will be, and when the two events will occur. The young people are on the stage, but not speaking. At the first, *iku aka na uzo,* the woman barely appears. And at the second, *igba nkwu,* the wife leaves her family and joins her husband's, with full support of the two families. Her family has agreed that she will stay with her husband and behave like an Igbo wife should. His family has committed to his good conduct in the relationship.

The ties between the families continue for the next generations too. Grace's sister Mbafor, who stayed with her to help with her first two children, Clement and Godwin, married a few years later. In 1965, twenty-two years after Mbafor had gone to Sapoba to help care for her sister's children, her daughter Rosa came to live with us and serve as our nanny when our first child was born. My husband agreed to take one of Grace's younger brothers to Lagos and helped him get a job in the Electricity Corporation. He assisted with school fees for another.

The families are still closely connected. Members of Ezeonodu's family attend any major Onyemelukwe event in Nanka. Two or three relatives came

Figure 6 Female relatives in Agulu, 2009

to the funeral for Jonathan, Clem's cousin. They were present for our fiftieth wedding anniversary. Whenever we are in Nanka, we visit Agulu to see the relatives.

The formal acknowledgment of family ties, established through the ceremonies with their set routines, is an aspect of Igbo culture that I love. It has become second nature to me to feel connected to my mother-in-law's family and other in-laws. The Igbo word *ogum*, "my in-law," extends to members of the clan, the umunna, who are all joined because of the marriage of their sons and daughters.

Is it different from what I experience in my own culture? I think of my brother and his wife. Two of their three sons live nearby and visit their parents often, more than just on major occasions. My sister-in-law has family members in the area. Her brother has employed my nephew in his construction business. When my husband and I are in town to visit, we may have dinner with her brother and his family.

My sister, who is divorced from her husband, still sees his sister, even attending Thanksgiving at the sister's home. My husband and I know members of our son-in-law's family and have observed holidays with them. We invited his mother to have dinner with us when we were in Nashville for a Peace Corps reunion.

Yet there is a major difference. For Nigerian families connected by marriage, the tie is indissoluble, intergenerational, and forever. The bond creates a sense of responsibility. My husband insists that he has a role to play in any family difficulties or disputes within a marriage. He is reflecting the belief that the family members are responsible for ensuring that disagreements are resolved. He corresponded with the father of our daughter-in-law to try to resolve conflict in our children's marital life.

I cannot do this. For me, my role is to listen with sympathy, and to offer advice only if specifically asked. This difference has led to arguments. Clem says, "You don't care about what happens." I say, "I do care, but it is not my place to tell them what to do!" While I embrace this custom of closeness when among the Igbo people, it does not translate for me into directing people's actions.

# 5

## SAMUEL AND GRACE JOURNEY FROM NEWLYWEDS TO PARENTS

SAMUEL AND GRACE BEGAN THEIR married life after the two nights in Nanka by traveling on foot and in a lorry to Onitsha. They crossed the Niger River in a canoe, then boarded another lorry to reach Sapoba. From there it was another nearly hour-long journey on foot to reach the logging camp. For her, it was an introduction to a new world. For him, it was an opportunity to show others that he had moved up. He had already achieved the status of supervisor. Now, instead of living in a hut with other workers, his rank and his position as a married man entitled him to his own accommodations.

Grace was brave. She had, after all, gone to school for a few years when not many girls did. She had made the decision on her own to become a Christian. Still, at the age of sixteen, the change from living with her family to living with a husband she barely knew, at a logging camp of mostly men, in an area where many people spoke another language was jarring.

But Igbo women look out for one another. There were other women married to men from Nanka, and they took her under their wing. She went with them to the market in the town of Sapoba, and they introduced her to other Igbo women selling there. When it was time for planting, they gave her okra and *ugu* seeds. Several were also Christian and sat with her in church while the husbands sat on their own benches across the aisle in the open-sided building.

A new Igbo wife was expected to get pregnant in her first few months of marriage. But Grace did not. One morning after she had been in the camp for nearly a year, she sat with the wife of another Igbo supervisor. "My father said I would not be able to conceive because of our religion," she said. "He put a curse on me. Can it be true that I won't have children because I joined the Christians?"

"I am a Christian too," the woman said, "and you can see my two children. I'm pregnant again and expect to have more offspring. No, it's not true."

As she began her second year in the camp, she decided to seek help. On the next market day, she approached one of the healers selling traditional medicines. It was embarrassing to explain her need, but she did. She came home with the dried bark of an evergreen tree. "Soak the bark in hot water for some time. Then drink a cup of the water every day for the next week," the healer had told her. It did nothing but make her feel slightly ill.

A few market weeks later, she sought out another healer, who sold her the leaves of a plant called *ogilisi* and told her to use it in a soup to eat with pounded yam. Again, there was no result.

They sent letters home, reassuring their families they were well. But they knew everyone was waiting to hear about a child. Finally, one Sunday morning as they were beginning their third year of marriage, Samuel said, "We are not going to church today. We are going to the *Dibia*. Maybe he can help."

"What will the mission priest say? Does he allow us to consult a native doctor?"

"We do not need to tell him. The mission priest does not understand our need to consult the ancestors. I think in their land they don't even know their ancestors. This Dibia may help us find the reason you are not conceiving. Even if your father's curse is at work, he may be able to remove its effect."

She had her bath and dressed quickly, warmed the *ora* soup left from the night before, boiled water and made garri, took her husband's food to him, and returned to her cooking shed to eat her own. As soon as they finished eating, he stood and called to her. "We will go now before the church people are arriving," he said. Their path would take them near the church. She understood that even though he did not think the priest needed to know, he did not want to be questioned.

In less than an hour they were near the market in Sapoba, the same market where she had bought her useless remedies. Samuel paused to ask the way to the Dibia. A few minutes later they had reached his hut.

"Pam, pam," Samuel said, hitching up his wrapper.

"Enter," he heard. He stooped to go through the low doorway under the thatch roof, Grace following behind. In the dimness she made out the shrine in one corner of the hut, and the native doctor seated opposite. He greeted them as they sat on the floor in front of him. After breaking kola, he said, "What brings you here today, my children?"

"I have been at the UAC camp for six years. Three years ago, I went home to marry. I brought my wife here. My wife is not conceiving. It is past time for her to bear a child. We have come to ask for your help."

On their way they had decided not to offer information about the curse. If the Dibia asked whether they knew any reason for her not becoming pregnant, then they would tell him. He did not ask.

He did ask if they had tried any traditional medicines. Grace explained the cures she had bought and used to no effect. "I will ask the ancestors for help," he said. He reached into his raffia bag and pulled out a handful of seeds, which he threw on the ground. He passed his hand over them, picked them up, and threw them again. Twice more he collected and threw the seeds. Then he turned to Samuel. "You must lay with your wife when the moon is full. She must be underneath you. Afterward, she should lie still until the cock crows."

Samuel thanked him and gave him a small bag of cowrie shells he had brought. For three months they tried his plan, but she did not get pregnant. She prayed every Sunday in church and every morning and night at home. One morning she went to the church and spoke to the priest about her problem. He prayed with her. "When God says it is time for you to have a child, you will conceive," he said in a steady voice. She did not share his sense of confidence, but the next month, she did not have her monthly bleeding. After another month she was sure.

"I think I am with child," she said to Samuel when she lay down beside him on their mat. "I haven't had my flow for two months. I have asked the other women. They say it is the right sign."

"It is a good thing. I was beginning to think I would have to take another wife, even though the Christians say I should not."

Her breasts got tender. Then, in her fifth month, she felt the baby move.

She remembered women at home who were pregnant and had let her, when she was younger, feel their bellies when their babies moved. She talked with the other Igbo women, who assured her the baby's movement was an ordinary part of her pregnancy. They offered advice: "You must not take kola nut. You should not use too much pepper in your soup."

One early morning in 1933, at the beginning of the rainy season, Grace felt the pain her women friends had told her to expect. She prepared Samuel's breakfast of yam and oil, as she did every day. "Today may be the time for the baby to come," she said as he left for the work site.

A couple of hours later, when her pain had increased, she went to the house nearby where her friend lived. "I think it is time," she said. Her friend summoned the local traditional midwife. Together the women led Grace to the goat shed behind the house. They helped her lie down, urged her to push when it was time, and wiped away the sweat that poured off her. Three hours later the baby emerged, and the midwife cut the cord.

"Praise God. You have a baby boy," she said to Grace as she placed the baby in her arms. An hour later Grace was back at home to greet her husband when he returned from work. He was ecstatic when she showed him their baby. He wondered aloud how they would send a message to tell their families at home.

Grace's friends had come home with her and prepared the evening meal. "You know that our cousin is going home to Nanka tomorrow," one of them said to Samuel. "He was visiting us for a few days. He could take a message for you."

Samuel thanked her and promised to visit the man early in the morning before his departure. He did not need to tell the man how to find his parents. The community of people from Nanka knew who the families of their colleagues were and how to find them in the village. But he did want to thank the man personally for taking the message home.

The messenger reached Nanka a few days later. With shouts of joy and praise to the ancestors, Ogbungwa gave the news to his wife, Nogem, and to all the other relatives. Samuel's mother was as happy as her son and her husband at this addition to their family. Members of the umunna, mostly accompanied by their wives, came to offer congratulations. The next day one brother and one cousin accompanied Ogbungwa when he went to Agulu to share the news with Grace's family. They had visited back and forth every few months since the newlyweds had left. They were, after all, united by their children's marriage.

Now that Grace and Samuel have become parents, I will call them by the names I always knew them by. They were introduced to me in 1963 as Mama and Papa by Clem's cousin. I did not even learn their names until the time of our wedding, a year later, when I wanted to introduce them to my own parents!

Two days after hearing the news about the baby, Mama's mother, Eye, set out, taking Mama's younger sister Mbafor with her, to stay with her daughter for the next few weeks to give her support in her new role. Her father sent a message with his wife. He had chosen a name for his first grandson. "He has said you must call the baby Chukwukadibia," Eye told Mama and Papa. "He now recognizes that your God is greater than the Dibia."

Usually the father of a new baby will ask his own father to provide the name, to ensure the connection between the generations and declare the child's place in the lineage. The baby's paternal grandfather may consult a Dibia or other senior members of his umunna. They may consult the ancestors before deciding what name to give the baby.

But this was a special case, and Papa accepted the choice of Mama's father as the middle name, the Igbo name, for their son. He selected the name Clement because it was the name of a good friend, a man he admired.

Clem and I relied on Papa decades later to give us the names for our three children. Two have their Igbo names as middle names; the oldest uses his Igbo name, though shortened for convenience.

Mama was glad to have her mother to help. The custom called *Omugwo* is standard practice among the Igbo people. The baby's matrilineal grandmother comes as soon as possible after the baby's birth. She always brings the ingredients for her daughter's favorite foods. She cooks for her daughter and son-in-law and for any other children if this isn't the first baby. She does all she can to make her daughter comfortable.

On the first morning Eye was there, after preparing and clearing up breakfast, she sat with Mama. "Rub his gums with your finger, and then bring his mouth to your breast," Eye said. "If he doesn't latch on right away, press him toward you. He will smell your milk."

"Ow. He's hurting me," Mama said, pulling the baby away from her breast.

"Put him back. That is nothing," her mother told her. Eye gave Mama other lessons about caring for her baby. Most of Eye's directions only reinforced what Mama had learned growing up, as older children habitually take care of younger ones. She had often carried other babies on her back, so she needed no instruction on how to make the baby secure, but not tie the wrapper too tightly. She knew the correct temperature for the baby's bath water, though that did not stop her mother from telling her!

After eight market weeks, Eye said to her daughter, now fully recovered from childbirth, "It is time for me to go home. But I will leave your sister Mbafor here to help you."

Mama's mother departed taking with her the obligatory presents of cloth and money from her daughter and son-in-law. After a day on a lorry to Asaba, she crossed the Niger River in a canoe and reached Agulu that evening on another lorry. She reported on the new mother and baby to her own family and the next day went with her husband to Nanka to fill Papa's family in on news about the long-awaited child.

A few months later, during the 1933 Christmas holidays, Mama and Papa took their new baby home to Nanka and visited Agulu too. Everyone was thrilled with the infant. Ezeonodu, after providing the name, was no longer angry or upset about his daughter's conversion to the new religion. Like grandparents everywhere, he was charmed by this addition to the family.

The next son, Godwin, was born in 1935. Again, Eye came to help. Mama was now respected in the Igbo community as the mother of two boys, for her bargaining skill in the market, and for her husband's role as a supervisor in the white man's company.

But their sojourn in the Midwest ended abruptly two years later. Papa was known for being strict with the workers he supervised. He could also be violent when displeased. One day he struck a worker across the face. When the man became blind in one eye his townspeople from the neighboring village wanted revenge.

"He has told his people what you did. They are angry," another Nanka man told Papa two days later. "They are coming to attack you and your family."

"But we have to cut a certain number of logs each day. This man was not doing his share." Papa threw his hands up in disgust. "If someone does not work, I have to discipline him."

He turned to his townsman. "Won't the white men stop them from coming to attack me?"

"They will do nothing. They do not care about our quarrels. This is your problem. If I were you, I would leave before they come for you."

Papa went straight home and told Mama to pack their belongings. She called her neighbor and gave her the mortar and pestle, the largest cooking pot, and a water jug, the items she knew they could not carry. She divided their other property into baskets and bags. She helped four-year-old Clement place a small basket with three yams on his head. Two-year-old Godwin lifted a bag of cocoyams to his head, copying his older brother's posture. Mbafor balanced a tin of palm oil, with a cloth wrapped into a circle under it to give support. Mama bent down and lifted to her own head a raffia tray holding two cooking pots loaded with crayfish, peppers, and the fresh okra she had picked that day. Papa led the procession, carrying on his head a suitcase with their few items of clothing, and holding the saw he owned.

It was late, and there was barely any moonlight when they left the logging camp, heading for Sapoba on their way back to Nanka.

# 6

## MAMA AND PAPA
## RETURN HOME

"CAN'T YOU WALK FASTER?" PAPA said. "We should be passing the Sapoba market by now."

He remembered that he and Mama had completed the journey on foot in less than an hour a few years earlier. But now their pace was much slower with two small children and all their loads, and it was night. Godwin was crying and refused to carry the cocoyams any farther.

"Give me the yams," Mama said, adding them to the raffia tray on her head. She untied her top wrapper, placed her younger son on her back, and tied him in securely. "Take Clement's hand," she said, pushing her four-year-old toward her sister and nanny, Mbafor. "I need both hands to balance my load." They reached the Sapoba market and the main road after nearly two hours of walking.

"We can rest here," Papa said, leaning against a tree. Mama took Godwin from her back, laid her outer wrapper on the ground, and put the sleeping child down. Clement needed no encouragement to lie down beside his brother. He was asleep in seconds. Mbafor placed her own wrapper on the ground, lay down beside them, and closed her eyes, while Mama slept on the opposite side.

The sound of a lorry's motor woke them after too few hours of sleep. It was early morning. "Wait here while I find passage for us to Asaba," Papa said. He returned a few minutes later. "Pick up your loads. We must go now," he said. Mama tied Godwin on her back again, helped Mbafor place her load on her head, and lifted her tray to her own head. They climbed into the back of the waiting lorry and took seats on the wooden bench nearest the front. Then they waited while the lorry driver and his conductor negotiated with more passengers.

"Buy *akara!*" shouted a seller walking past the lorry and showing his wares. "Fresh akara!" Papa leaned over the side and bought five of the fried bean cakes, handing one to Mbafor, one to each child, and one to his wife.

"Put your loads under the bench," the conductor said. "You have to hold the boy unless you want to pay full fare for him." Godwin was already asleep in his mother's arms, and Mbafor lifted Clement onto her lap. As more passengers climbed in and joined them on the bench, they squeezed closer together. One passenger's chicken tried to escape but was caught and secured under the bench. It took two hours for the lorry to be full enough to satisfy the driver. Then they departed for Asaba. Mama nearly toppled off the backless bench when she fell asleep.

After two stops, they reached Asaba and saw the Niger River. They disembarked and waited another two hours for the new ferry that carried them across the river to Onitsha. Papa led them to the house of the townsperson who had helped him on his first trip years earlier. But he had moved, and the neighbors did not know where he lived. So, they slept in a crude hotel near the Onitsha lorry park. The next day they got another lorry to Nanka.

An Igbo man always belongs to his home, and he can return whenever he needs or wants to. His family must take him in. Even Papa's unceremonious disappearance years earlier did not stop his return when he wanted to marry. This time Papa and his family were crammed in with his brothers until he could build his own house. His married brother, Ejike, had his own thatched mud-walled house in the compound and another smaller hut for his wife. Ogbungwa gave his second son, Papa, a spot, and Papa's brothers helped him begin. He built a house like his brother's, packing the mud securely to a height of about four feet. Within a few days they had nearly completed the sides. Papa and his youngest brother, Obi, went off to cut palm leaves for the roof while the others smoothed the mud and placed the beams that would hold the thatch. When the two men returned, they found a clansman waiting for them.

After they exchanged greetings, the man said, "I live in Onitsha. I trade palm oil with UAC. I am going back to Onitsha tomorrow. I have a stall in the market and I could use your help."

I knew Papa much later, when he was no longer selling palm oil. I do not think he would have been content to stay in the village when he could find work outside. Like all Igbo men and women, he was part of a strong network of mutual support. It was natural for someone from his extended family to invite him to assist. And it was normal to expect that he could bring his family to stay with this relative. Two days later Papa and Mama took their two children with them to Onitsha, and Papa began learning the palm oil trade.

UAC, the same British company that owned the logging operation in Sapoba, also owned a large part of the Onitsha market. Spread over many acres near the bank of the Niger River, in 1937 the market was already a hub for traders from all over the southeastern part of Nigeria. It was also a center for the British merchants who bought the raw materials from the colony to be processed in England.

Papa had become a cog in the machinery of the British colonial structure in the logging camp near Sapoba. He continued to serve the colonial masters. First the lumber and now the palm oil were shipped to Britain and used to make products that were sold in the UK and exported back to the colonies. It was the right time, the late 1930s, when the British demand for palm oil, with its slightly sweet, musky smell, was increasing rapidly. But now Papa was selling to UAC, no longer employed by them.

Papa's relative shared a six-by-six-foot shack in the section of the market that was devoted to trade in palm products. "Take this drum of oil to the UAC office," the more experienced man instructed him. "Wait for them to tell you if they accept it. If they refuse, do not argue."

"They didn't take it," Papa said when he returned with the barrel of the thick red palm oil in the wheelbarrow the men used. "They said it had too much water."

The next morning the women who had brought the oil came for their payment. "Your oil was not satisfactory. You will not be paid. You can take it."

Papa poured it into their buckets. It would still do for cooking. Papa too had to go home that day without any money. But more often he and his friend were successful. He became strict with the women who brought their product to him. Soon he knew what UAC would accept.

He found a couple of rooms to rent from another Nanka man. By the end of the first year he had his own market stall. He still cooperated with other men from his town but could keep more of the profit. "I visited him in the market when I was little," my husband, Clem, told me. "The ground was slippery with oil everywhere. The odor of palm oil filled the whole area. Papa even came home smelling of palm oil!"

Over the next months and years, the bond between Papa's family and Mama's was strengthened. After Mama gave birth to her first daughter, Monica, they took the three children to Nanka occasionally, and always stopped in Agulu on the way. Their families visited back and forth, even when Papa and Mama were not with them.

Papa's disgraceful flight from the scarification ceremony was forgotten as he earned the respect of his townspeople. He had traveled, worked for the white men, and now had his own business. He had completed his two-room house in the village. Although Papa had flouted tradition when he fled years earlier, he had reintegrated himself into his community despite following the nontraditional path of working for wages and then trading with the colonialists. He did not need to live in Nanka to show his commitment. The small house he had built and his occasional visits were adequate.

This lifelong tie to one's home is powerful, even extending back to one's forebears and forward to next generations. It is another example of a cultural practice that appealed to me and drew me in. The opposite was true for my own parents. Once they left their homes, they barely returned. They did not belong to the place where they were born and brought up. My father left his home in Rostock, Germany, when he was in his twenties, around 1930. He saw the city only once after that, when he took my brother there for a few hours' visit in 1964. My mother left her home in St. Louis, Missouri, for college. She graduated in 1929 and began teaching in New York, where she met my father. By the time I knew her parents, they had retired to the small town of Danforth, Illinois.

When my own parents retired, they moved to Germany for a year. It was, I believe, an attempt at re-establishing connections. They did not try to go to Rostock, in prohibited East Germany. Instead they found an apartment in Hamburg. Father contacted people he had known earlier, but they were not able to make meaningful bonds. My mother did not speak German, and

Father, I imagine, was not helpful in her effort to learn. At the end of the year my parents moved to the Portuguese island of Madeira.

In the capital city, Funchal, they made friends among Portuguese and foreigners alike. They built a community for themselves. It helped that many other non-Portuguese people, Germans, Brits, and Americans, had retired to the lovely island. They spent happy afternoons and evenings in bridge games. When my mother died there in 1989, we buried her in the cemetery of the English church where she had played the organ for several years. My father eventually returned to the US after he became confined to a wheelchair and needed assistance. For a couple of days, I considered bringing him into our home in Connecticut. My years in Africa said that was my duty as the older daughter. But I could not envision how his care would work, or even how he would be able to get into the house! Finally, my sister-in-law suggested we move him to Chicago to be near her and my brother. They found a nursing home where we hoped he would be comfortable. But I often reflected on the difference. If we were an African family, there would have been no hesitation, and we would have accommodated him in our home, no matter the difficulties.

My father was like so many immigrants to the US, people who leave their homes never to return. There is no tie holding them to their father's and ancestors' place, as part of a lineage. Nothing tells them they have a home where they belong. They may take some customs with them, but they are not bound by them. In our home we had the Advent calendars, which my father knew from his childhood. But by then they were popular in the US, so he did not have to search to find them for us. Apart from a couple of stories that my father told about his childhood, we did not get introduced to the wider family or to his ancestors. earlier relatives.

My mother too told us little about her forebears. We knew her parents but only through visits for a week or two in the summer. In those brief summer stays, we sometimes saw her siblings and their children. Once, her brother brought his family to our home for Thanksgiving. Another time, but only once that I recall, we visited her sister for a few days.

The common mobility of much of our Western society has its benefits. People are free to move away from the place where they grew up. Indeed, they may have grown up in many places, as I did, since my father was transferred by his company roughly every two years until I was in seventh grade. Even then, I did not put down strong roots in the town where I attended junior and senior high school. Especially in the US, there is little pressure to live near relatives. This freedom to settle far away from one's home made it easy for me to go to Nigeria in the first place, and then decide to stay for twenty-four years.

For my parents-in-law, and other Nigerian parents, training their children to respect older family members, the ancestors, and the in-laws was natural and important. The tie to place was paramount, and the children were expected to grow up with the knowledge of their heritage and their sense of belonging. They should feel the same devotion to their village that their parents do or did.

But Papa recognized that life was changing. Education in the white man's ways would be important in years to come. Already he could see that the colonial masters controlled the economy. He had to ensure that his sons could be part of this new life.

# 7

## SCHOOL DAYS: PAPA PREPARES FOR THE NEW NIGERIA

AT THE SAME TIME AS Papa was starting his palm oil trade, he was beginning to focus on education for his children. He had seen with his own eyes how the white men respected the Nigerians who spoke their language and adopted their customs. He wanted all his children to go to school, but he had to start with his first son, Clement. He would give him the best educational opportunity possible, even if it meant sending him away from home.

The colonial government had not yet instituted the practice of birth certificates. Papa had been observing Clement's growth and checked often to see if he met the test for school readiness. Just like Mama's "examination" that demonstrated she was old enough for school when her father took her, Clement was deemed of the right age when he could reach his left ear by stretching his right arm over his head.

When Papa returned from market one evening, he said, "He is ready. I will take him to the catechist in Nanka. The catechist and his wife do not have children. They may welcome a young boy as a substitute. He can help out while they train him."

"Can't he go to school here in Onitsha?" Mama said. "I know other children who are attending."

Papa was adamant. "Yes, I know there is a school here. But I know that CMS has trained the catechist to run the school and church in Nanka. I believe CMS puts their best people in the villages away from the city."

"He's too young," Mama said, gripping her oldest son by his hand. "He can wait another year."

She could not persuade Papa. When the family went to Nanka a few weeks later, Papa took his son to *Afor Udo,* the market area. The catechist lived in a two-story building across the major road, and the church was opposite the shrine, along the local road that led down to the family's home.

After exchanging pleasantries and accepting the obligatory kola, Papa introduced his purpose. "I believe my son is ready for school. I want him to attend your school," he said.

"Let me see if he is old enough for school," the catechist said. He demonstrated the maneuver, right hand over the head to touch the left ear, which Papa had made Clement practice many times. "Yes, he is ready."

Papa smiled and nodded. "I thought so," he said. "But I do not live in Nanka. My family and my business are in Onitsha. That is why I am coming to you. Could he live with you and attend the school? He is obedient and will not be any trouble for you. He can be a houseboy for you."

The catechist asked his wife to join them. She looked the small boy over carefully.

"I would like to have him living with us," she told her husband. "We are unlikely to have a child of our own now."

Then the couple conferred quickly. "Yes, we can keep your son," the catechist said. "We will take good care of him and see that he attends school."

Clement knew he was expected to be grateful. But he wondered what it would be like living with this man who had so much authority. No one asked his opinion.

"Bring him when the term is starting in one month," the catechist said. "He will have to bring his uniform." He explained what was required and Papa agreed.

A month later, in September 1939, Papa told Clement to pack his new uniform and his one other pair of shorts and a shirt. "Say goodbye to your mother and your brother and sister. You will come home for the Christmas vacation," he said.

Suddenly, Clement realized that he was really being taken away and would not see his mother for many weeks. He sobbed and begged to stay at home, but his father ignored his pleas. "You have to get a good education. You should be grateful that the catechist and his wife agreed to take you. I expect you to do well in your classes and behave well for the catechist's wife."

At the age of six, Clem became a boarder and a servant. Lying on his mat in an upstairs room, he cried softly for the first few nights, covering his head with his arms so the catechist would not hear him. Each morning he woke at the cock's crow, went downstairs, grabbed a small pot, and joined the other children who lived nearby to fetch water from the stream a mile away. He poured most of the water into the large pot in the kitchen and put the rest into a bucket for his bath in the enclosed area outside. He was given a small breakfast from the remainder of the last night's dinner. Then he swept the yard and the parlor. By eight o'clock, he was ready for school.

He longed for his mother but gradually stopped crying at night. He sobbed only a few times, when the desire for her overcame him. The catechist and his wife coddled Clem as if he were their own child, just as his father had hoped. The wife gave him special food, told him stories at night, and let him sleep with her. His homesickness diminished. He had been with the catechist for more than a month when Papa and Mama visited one evening. "We came to ask how our son is doing," Papa said. "Is he behaving well?"

"He is not a problem. He is not keen on his studies, but I hope he will improve soon," the catechist said. Clement knew that his parents would stay in Nanka at least for the night, and maybe longer. The school was across the road from the market, and the next day was *Afor*, the town's major market day. In the morning he watched from his classroom with its low mud wall. Just before two in the afternoon, the end of the school day, he spotted his mother leaving the market and heading to their home a couple of miles downhill. Keeping his head low, he crept out of the school and raced to their home to get there before her.

Mama embraced him, but Papa was angry. "How do you expect to improve if you run away?" He allowed him to stay for a couple of hours but then sent him back to the catechist. Twice more when his parents were in Nanka, he ran home to them. Seeing Clement's yearning to be with his family did not shake Papa's stubbornness when it came to his commitment to his son's education, and he always sent Clem back to the catechist. His mother missed him dreadfully, but she could not change her husband's mind. Instead she anticipated each school holiday, when her oldest son returned to Onitsha or the family went to Nanka together.

By the end of Clement's first year in the catechist's home, the relationship changed, and he was no longer pampered. He had done nothing that could account for the difference, but he became just a houseboy for them. The food he was given was barely adequate. When he was sent to market, he sometimes even stole bits of meat from the food sellers and now and then kept small change, instead of returning it to the catechist's wife, to use on his next market visit.

At the same time as Papa was ensuring his own son's education, he looked after his nephew's training. Papa took his responsibility to his siblings and other family members seriously, as custom demanded. Usually the oldest brother would be responsible for his younger siblings and their children. But Papa's older brother, Ejike, had never lived outside the village and had no sense of the changes coming. Ejike's son Okoli was at least four years older than Clement. But when Clement started school, Papa insisted that Okoli also enroll.

"He does not need to attend school," Ejike protested.

"I want to go," Okoli said to his father. "I will do my tasks and help on the farm." While Clement was living close to the school, Okoli had to walk from their home in the village every day to the school by the market. The next year, the catechist was transferred, taking Clement with him to his new post, a few miles away. Papa, ever vigilant about educational opportunities, moved Okoli from the Nanka school to a better school a few miles in the other direction. The following year, Clement moved again with the catechist, and Papa took Okoli to live with the family in Onitsha.

As the son of Ejike, Papa's older brother, Okoli had a slight position of seniority. And with his age advantage he also gained status. The result was that Papa treated his nephew as the oldest son in the household. But Mama was not happy; her own dear son Clement was away most of the time, and her nephew was usurping Clem's rightful place.

When Clement did come home, she fussed over him, remarking on his skin rashes and small, skinny body. His father refused to change his mind, regarding the harsh treatment his son received as training to be tough. Staying with the catechist, being connected to the church, also gave status to his son and would prepare him better for the modern life, in Papa's mind.

When Clem turned ten in 1943, he absolutely refused to go back to the catechist. "You may stay home, but you will go to school," his father said. Papa enrolled him in standard 4, the fourth year of primary school, at Central School Onitsha, with his cousin to complete the last two years.

Figure 7 Clem at his final primary school, still standing today, when he was with catechist

"I was good at school. I usually came first in class," Clem loves to say. "Papa was a big believer in rewards and punishment. He never missed a chance to give me a prize for having the highest marks."

"What was the prize?" I said.

"Papa would take me to the Bata shoe shop and buy me a pair of shoes. Or he would kill a chicken for me. I was given the cooked head, a coveted delicacy." That didn't sound like a reward to me. But Clem said, "The others wanted me to share it with them. They thought the brain of the chicken was making me smart and could do the same for them!"

In his first week at Central School Onitsha, Clement saw boys wearing a uniform—a green shirt, khaki shorts, beret, and neck scarf. He asked one of the boys what the uniform was for and learned it signified membership in the Cub Scouts.

"You can come to the Cubs with me on Saturday," the boy said. "You'll meet our leader, Akela. He'll tell you what you need to do to become a member."

A week later he asked his mother for the six pence to join and get the uniform. "If I join the Cubs, I will learn to march like a soldier. I can get badges and learn how to salute the flag properly," he told his mother.

Clem still speaks fondly of Akela. His happiest memories of his young school days are of the Cubs and the times they spent at Akela's house or at the school, playing, marching, and enjoying the time together with their leader.

Just as his father had joined the economy of the colonial power by cutting logs and now by selling palm oil, Clem was participating in the social order of the colonialists. Without knowing, he was helping to reinforce the changes underway in Nigeria. Even though his father warned him against forgetting traditions, the pressure from the colonial power bringing in an attractive movement like scouting was hard to resist. Scouting gave the boys who were already receiving an education another opportunity to connect to the British Empire. Clement's father was acutely aware of the need to take advantage of these opportunities. His son was following suit.

Figure 8 "Sam, an Igbo Boy Scout" from Nigerian Magazine, Vol.34 (1950) Courtesy of the National Archives Ibadan

In a book about Nigerian childhood, edited by Saheed Aderinto, I found useful background to the appeal of scouting. He quoted Adam Paddock who helped me understand. "Many key features of scouting resonated with African concepts of what children should do, how they should interact with society, and the ways in which children were organized."[2] The children were reaffirming their values but using them in a new context.

The introduction of the Boy Scout movement was not just for the sake of the boys, helping them adopt Western ways. Bringing the movement to the colony "had close connections to ideas of empire, the civilizing mission, and British nationalism," Paddock said.

He continues, "Gradual replacement of indigenous institutions created incentives among Yoruba and Igbo boys to support new social organizations. In addition to British interference in local institutions, African elites quickly realized that close associations with the British administration opened new opportunities, and thus scouting functioned to access benefits from the British colonial government that were otherwise unavailable."[3]

Clement's father could not have stated this more clearly! Yet the juxtaposition of Western concepts with Igbo traditional practices is sometimes jarring. The British colonial masters were clearly convinced that their ways were superior to the natives' traditions. In some areas of life, I would have to agree. No doubt the elimination of killing twins was admirable. The gradual decline in disease through better health practices and broader knowledge is worthwhile. Women can have fewer children when fewer die in childbirth or infancy. The Igbo practice of taking slaves when victorious in a war between towns is gone and not missed.

But I cannot forget that the British were major slave traders before they had a change of heart and condemned the practice just a little over two hundred years ago. Nor that a hundred years before that, witches were hunted and condemned in some "civilized" societies. Today the US, often seen as a leader of liberal human rights beliefs, is rightly found guilty of structural racism toward people of color, including the original settlers of our land.

Considering these historical and current contradictions in beliefs and behaviors, I would not say one set of practices is preferable to another. I find strength in the Western customs with which I grew up. I love the stress on individualism, thinking for oneself, and challenging authority, all opposite to Igbo, and many African, customs. At the same time, I have learned practices from Igbo and other African traditions that can inform our lives. Especially in the sense of building community, I find many strengths in the Igbo customs, those of Africa that I know best, and I—along with Clem's father—hope these traditions will not be lost.

The other childhood memories Clem cherishes are of his aspirations as an artist and of the stories with Nogem. "We visited Nanka often, staying longer during the school breaks. I was still young enough to love Nogem's stories," he said. "When the evening meal was over, we gathered near her hut. She sat on a log just a few feet from the fire that had died down after she'd finished cooking. I got as near as I could, so I wouldn't miss a word."

"What stories did she tell you?" I asked.

"The key figures in the stories were animals. My favorite was about the tortoise," Clem said. "He was often in a race or a contest."

"I know that story about the race between the tortoise and the hare. The tortoise is slow and plodding, but because he is persistent, he wins the race."

"That's not the story Nogem told us. In her stories, the tortoise was constantly tricking the other animals. Then he would get punished for his trickery."

I was intrigued. I assumed the tortoise always served the moral purpose of showing that "slow and steady wins the race!" But Clem's lesson was different. "The lesson we understood, or that I understood later, was that being dishonest and trying to deceive others to gain an advantage will only bring you trouble," he said.

Storytelling has a rich history in African cultures. The practice of gathering to hear stories from elders has gone on for ages. The older women usually tell folktales about animals, like the tortoise or the spider, while older men will often relate the history of the family going back generations. They speak of battles won, great feats of strength, and mythic celebrations. Storytelling helps bind the community together. All the children learn the same tales and share joy over the triumphs that are related, whether of the animals or the ancestors. They listen together and carry the stories with them. The tradition was a powerful element of the culture that enslaved Africans brought to the Western world, helping to hold people together even when families were cruelly separated.

"I never wanted Nogem's stories to end," Clem said. "She could have continued all night and I would have been happy."

"You must have loved her dearly," I said.

Clem surprised me with his answer. "I didn't love her the same way I loved my other grandmother, in Agulu," he said. "I admired and respected her, but she wasn't warm and embracing the way Eye was."

He explained his feelings for Eye, his maternal grandmother. A special treat during the school holidays was a visit to Mama's hometown. "Go to sleep early. We're going to Agulu tomorrow," Mama told her children at least once every time they were in the village. Clement and the others were so excited they could barely sleep the night before. They had no problem rising early. They knew the day's journey to her home, five miles away, was full of adventure.

After a quick breakfast of garri with whatever soup was left from the night before, they made their way downhill to the ravine that separated the two towns. At the bottom there was a river, where Mama let the children swim. She gave them the food she had prepared for lunch: steamed ground beans, called mai-mai, or packets of cassava. Then they climbed the opposite side of the ravine to reach Agulu. Eye and Ezeonodu embraced their grandchildren, making them feel welcome and valued.

"How you have grown!" they said, just as grandparents everywhere do when they see their grandchildren only intermittently.

My husband's smile as he reflects on these visits shows how fond he was of the Agulu relatives, especially Eye. He says, "Our grandmother would cook special foods for us. She'd roast corn and *ube,* an Igbo pear, and buy us *akara,* bean cakes."

He continues, "Sometimes we visited the neighbors in Agulu. Everyone knew who we were, so we could wander freely. We were always indulged. We went to the stream where they fetched water. We could swim and play for half the day there."

Though Clem does not say it, I suspect that being with their mother but away from their authoritarian father for a day or so was at least a small piece of the pleasure in these visits to Agulu.

Papa maintained his own mud-and-stone house at the spot he had been given by his father when he'd returned from Sapoba in 1938. "Our house was about sixty feet away from Ejike's obi," Clem said. "It was on the side opposite the goat shed." It had a sitting room and two more rooms, as far as he can recall. "Our parents slept in one room and we children slept on the floor in another.

"I also imagined myself as an artist in those days." He does not recall how he got the drawing materials, but he decorated one entire wall of the sitting room with a picture of a man's head and shoulders, perhaps Jesus, and another of St. Francis of Assisi surrounded by birds. He was pleased with his work.

His father too admired the effort and kept the mural in place, even pointing it out to visitors as his son's work. When Clem told me this story in recent years, he was still expressing surprise that he had not been punished! I too was surprised. But why should we be? For Papa, unless his oldest son was behaving badly and needed correction, anything and everything he did was a source of pride. Depicting heroes of the Christian canon was to be admired. Papa, after all, was proud of his new religion and his family's acceptance of Western ways.

While his son was getting the desired education and becoming a Cub, building for his future, Papa was actively building for the family. By 1941, when Clem was in his second year with the catechist, Papa had accumulated enough money to buy a plot of land in Onitsha.

"You need to come to my new land and help me build," he said to several of his townspeople. "You will help me construct our house." Several times over the next few months, during the dry season, three or four men came to assist. At the end of hours of work, they followed Papa back to his rented rooms for the meal Mama provided. As soon as there was the beginning of a structure, the family moved from the two rooms to their own place. For the first two months they slept in the courtyard or on a floor with no roof. But soon they had a comfortable one-story dwelling with a sitting room, a pantry and kitchen, and three other rooms. They also had a concrete veranda in the front, where Mama could sit on a mat with her children by her side. When Clement, exiled to life away, came home for holidays, she made sure to have him near her whenever she could.

The address, 5 St. John's Cross, has always intrigued me. Only in the last few years did I realize that St. John's Church, at one end of the short street, was probably the destination of people coming from the other end. They must have "crossed" to get to the church.

Soon more houses were built around them. They became an anchor on the street for newer neighbors. As soon as he had saved again for more construction, Papa built rooms at the back on one side of the courtyard. He rented these out to townspeople and others. He had additional income to add to the profit from the palm oil sales.

All the families cooked outside in the courtyard when there was no rain. Papa built a small covered area where women could cook during the rainy season. There were common latrines emptied by the "night soil" men, people employed by the town to visit outhouses and remove the waste, on a regular basis.

"I need to build a house in Nanka," Papa said to one of his townsmen. "But I do not have any land of my own."

"Can you buy land from someone else?" his townsman said.

"I do not want to move away from my father's place. My elder brother should share what our father left. There is enough land for my brothers and me. What can I do to make him give me my portion?"

"That is a difficult position and I don't have an answer. Use your money for something else instead," his friend advised.

He liked the suggestion. He invested the money he could spare in a lorry and hired a driver to ferry passengers back and forth to their towns or villages. Lorries like his were becoming popular, as the colonial masters were building a growing network of roads to serve their needs for local labor and products. Papa's lorry was a truck with an open flatbed behind the cabin, like the one he had traveled in to reach Sapoba years earlier. Forty or more passengers sat on benches in the back, lined up in rows, with their produce, chickens, and goats beside them or under the benches. For his last two years with the catechist, Clem was taken to and from home in the lorry, giving him a little comfort and prestige to relieve the suffering he endured.

The family visited Nanka, maintaining and strengthening the valuable ties that Papa had risked so many years earlier. Like every Igbo town, Nanka by this time had a town-wide organization, called the Nanka Patriotic Union, sometimes referred to as the Nanka Progressive Union.

"Put on your uniform," Papa said to his son one day when they were in Nanka during the Christmas break. "I will take you with me to the meeting of the Nanka Patriotic Union."

Clem recalls being bored on the two occasions he was taken along, but he was aware that his father became the deputy chair. "I think he wanted to show me that he was a leader, hoping that I would learn by his example," Clem said.

Whenever they went to Nanka, they stopped in Agulu as well to greet Mama's family. Papa was called on once to sit with his in-laws to receive prospective grooms for Mama's younger sister. When there was a death among the members of the clan, Papa and Mama were there for the burial ceremony.

Papa also participated in the regular meetings of his townsmen, Ndi Nanka, who lived in Onitsha. Once a month they gathered in the home of one of their members. Each time, the host's wife brought out kola nuts on a tray, with alligator pepper and sometimes groundnut dip as an accompaniment. "With this kola I welcome you to our home," the host said. Then he would direct one of the younger men to carry the tray to the oldest, who offered his own prayers to the ancestors, ending with "*N'afa*—in the name of—Jesus Christ." Years later I heard the same traditional prayers ending with the call to Jesus.

Papa's palm oil trade was going well. Mama had begun sewing and selling children's clothes in the Onitsha market, adding to their income. They had built more rooms on the other side of the courtyard behind their house and were able to rent them out. For the times and their backgrounds, they were prosperous. Papa knew he would have to send his son and his nephew to secondary school, so he tried to put away money for the coming expense.

Papa continued his leadership roles in Onitsha and the village. He also assumed a stronger position in the church. Like other traders who had been successful, he attended St. Andrew's Anglican Church in Onitsha with his family. For Sunday services he sometimes put on a proper British-style suit. He looked very distinguished, with his handsome face, even features, and stern expression. Other times he wore native dress, a flowing robe made of a heavy cotton fabric with a hat like a jester's cap of the same or similar fabric. He always stood straight as an arrow.

"You are too late to enter—you must wait for the next hymn," he said to those arriving after the service had begun. No one could enter when there were prayers, readings, or a sermon underway. He looked frightening enough that he was not challenged. As a respected church leader he was invited to serve on the vestry committee, a role he relished.

Becoming part of the new religion was another way of moving on and embracing the new life. When I first learned of Papa's conversion and dedication to the Anglican Church, I thought he might have been conforming to advance his and then his sons' prospects. But as I came to know him, I realized that his Christianity was sincere. He was an early adopter of all the new ways brought by the colonizers. Like the boys in Cubs, and like others, he assumed many of the British practices while keeping hold of Igbo traditions.

Nigeria was in a state of flux. Papa's life illustrates the changes well. The old ways of demonstrating commitment to one's community were not available. Already when Papa was a young man in training for his initiation, Igbo men no longer had to fight other villages or capture slaves to show their prowess. Papa and the others had been left with wrestling to display their physical strength. Young male initiates were expected to show bravery by enduring the facial marking stoically, another way to demonstrate their fitness as Igbo men. When Papa ran from the experience, his father was ashamed. But within a few years that custom had faded too. No one thought about cutting the faces of Papa's children.

Skill at farming was still highly regarded in the 1940s and having a successful yam harvest was important to people in the village, but as Papa recognized, working in the white man's world provided a higher level of status and could lead to higher income. The change in position would benefit more than his immediate family. For an Igbo man, the whole family, the clan, and even the village and town would benefit when his children moved ahead. Everyone's prestige would rise as the children advanced.

Over decades, immigrants have come to the United States to give their children more opportunity in life. Papa was not emigrating, but the intent was the same: move to the new way of life and ensure a Western education for his children and nephews. There is a major difference, however. For the immigrant, the improvement is primarily for the children. The parents will probably benefit too, while the family left behind will be happy but gain little. The profit for Papa and others like him was for the whole community, including those still to come.

Life seemed settled. Mama and Papa were respected, attended church, worked hard, and enlarged their family. They had their old house in the village and their own new house, with rental property, in Onitsha. Their children and their nephew were getting the white man's education.

But major challenges were looming. Leprosy, disputes over land, the death of a child, and evil spirits were on the horizon.

# 8

# A YEAR OF DISASTERS

*"O GINI NE ME NNA ANYI?* What is wrong with our grandfather?" ten-year-old Clement asked his grandmother Nogem before she began her storytelling one evening during the break in the rainy season, August 1943. Clement was in Nanka with his parents and siblings during the school holidays. He was now enrolled at Central School Onitsha for his final two years of primary education.

"He has a sickness and has to stay by himself," she said. "He does not want to give the sickness to anyone else."

"But you go to take him food. Will you get the sickness?"

"I will not if the ancestors protect me," said Nogem. "Stop asking so many questions or I will not tell tonight's story." Clement could not risk being the cause of missing a story. His siblings and cousins would have been very angry at him!

Clement's grandfather Ogbungwa had leprosy, the dreaded disease that, along with tuberculosis and other tropical illnesses, was endemic in southern Nigeria in the mid-1930s. The disease carried a stigma. Clement's grandmother did not name it, nor did others call it by its name.

British missionaries had begun taking an active role in studying and treating tropical diseases in their colonies. The annual report of the colony of Nigeria for 1938 says, "It is estimated that there are some 200,000 lepers in Nigeria—about 1 per cent of the total population—and that of these nearly 6,000 are in voluntary segregation."[4] T. F. Davey, editor of *Leprosy Review* and a Methodist missionary, wrote, in 1957, "During the past 20 years massive yaws infection in a dense rural population has been accompanied by an outbreak of leprosy of unusual magnitude."[5]

"Dense rural population" describes Nanka precisely. The compound where Ogbungwa lived with his wife, and where they raised five sons and one daughter, was approximately 200 feet by 120 feet. By the time of Papa's return from Sapoba, Ejike had married and was living in the compound with his wife and young children. The other four sons, Ejike's younger brothers, including Papa, all shared this compound. Although the space seemed large to Clement when he was a child, it certainly fit the definition of dense population. Other families around them lived in equally tight quarters. Land was scarce. Each time a father divided his land among his sons, more people lived in the same amount of space. Occasionally the town gave uninhabited land to someone deserving whose father had insufficient land to share. But there was constant pressure for space for dwellings and for farming.

Ogbungwa was not the only one in the family to suffer from leprosy. Three of his children—Papa, Papa's youngest brother, Obi, and their sister, Nweli—contracted the disease. Papa recovered on his own, without going to one of the leprosy clinics that had recently been established. Obi, on the other hand, stayed at the clinic for months at a time. He was away at the clinic in 1952 when Clem was departing for the UK. Obi returned home when he was finally healed. His daughter Georgina wrote about the illness in her biography of her father in the 1990s. She would still not name the disease; the shame persisted.

Nweli spent weeks in the clinic. She returned home when the progress of her disease was halted, and she was said to have recovered. However, she bore the physical scars for the rest of her life. She bore the emotional scars too. She was never fully integrated into the community again. I remember her from my early days in the family. She came to family events and brought her own tiny stool. Unless one of her daughters came with her, she sat alone at one side of the gathering.

No matter what befalls an Igbo family member, he or she still belongs to the family. Once Ogbungwa's condition was recognized as permanent, he lived alone, in a house behind the obi. As far as the people of Nanka knew, leprosy was passed from person to person by touch, and once the rash had spread, no one dared make physical contact with the infected person. From 1939 until his death, Ogbungwa was isolated, cared for by his wife. Clement barely remembers him. He was warned not to go too near and saw him only briefly when Ogbungwa walked around the compound on rare occasions.

While Papa's father was suffering from the unnamed disease of leprosy at home in Nanka, another tragedy struck. After the family had moved to Onitsha from the logging camp with two small boys, Mama gave birth to two daughters, Monica and Edna. Like other Igbo women, Mama nursed each baby for seventeen or eighteen months. Then she began to wean the child and resume intercourse with her husband, so children were usually spaced at intervals of two to three years.

The fifth child was another son, born in 1943. He was called Sunday for the day on which he was born. He was a delight, charming his older siblings with his frequent laughter and attempts to walk. One Sunday in 1944 the family was leaving St. Andrew's Church in Onitsha to return home to St. John's Cross.

"*K'n kulu ya*. Let me carry him," Monica said, reaching for her youngest brother as he tried to walk beside their parents. At the age of seven, she was frequently given the task of caring for her siblings, especially the youngest. She loosened the wrapper she wore, leaned forward to place Sunday on her back, and tightened the cloth again, fixing him securely in place.

She bounced as she walked, knowing how the movement made him giggle. Halfway home, she turned to her mother.

"He's not laughing," she said. "He feels warm."

As they reached home, Sunday began shaking. "Take him, Mama," Monica said, loosening the wrapper. Mama grabbed him. Her heart pounding, she cradled him close and listened to his labored breathing. His eyes closed, and he seemed too still.

"Call Okeke's mother," she said, referring to one of their tenants. "Her son had this illness; she'll know what to do." Monica raced to the tenant's door while Mama rocked her baby.

Okeke's mother called out as she approached. "Keep him warm. Take him near the fire," she said. "Rub him with palm oil."

Mama moved quickly to sit on the low stool near the fire where one of the tenants was cooking. Eleven-year-old Clement ran to the area where Mama kept her cooking supplies and returned with the bottle. "Pour the oil into my hands," she said.

"What's wrong with him?" he said. His eyes grew wide as his mother held the child near the fire and rubbed him all over with the sticky red oil.

Godwin, age nine, reached out to touch his little brother. "He's too hot," he said. "Take him away from the fire."

The two little girls burst into tears as Mama hugged the weakening baby. *"Chukwu nyerem aka, o na anwu!* God help me, he is dying!" she cried.

When he became limp in her arms and she could not revive him, she wailed. Papa, a proper Igbo man, had never entered the cooking area. But he came quickly when he heard his wife's desperate cries. Okeke's mother and other tenants came out to stand around her and weep with her.

"How could you let this happen to our son?" Papa said when he spotted the lifeless body.

"God has chosen to take him," an older man who attended church with them said. "You must not blame her. Mama did what she could."

By evening, the priest from St. Andrew's had come. They buried their baby in the compound not far from the fire where Mama had tried to save him. Mama wept all night. Papa did not know how to comfort her. Nor did he, an Igbo man who was supposed to be brave and not show his sadness, see this as his role. Instead, by morning he spoke harshly.

"It's time to stop crying," he said. "You have other children to care for." She roused herself, bathed, and put on a clean wrapper. Still she mourned for the week, crying silently each night. She held the other children closer than ever before and comforted them when they cried for their lost sibling. On the next Sunday she and Papa led their four children to St. Andrew's again. They prayed for their lost baby.

Infant death was common in the 1940s. Most families had lost at least one child. But that did not make the death less painful. It was a blow to the whole family. Mama was heartbroken, and Papa was angry. He began to wonder if there was something evil at work.

Papa spoke to other Nanka men at their next meeting. "You know Nnaji's baby died in the same way some time ago," one said. "Then the next baby died, and another after that."

"Do you think our baby could have been *ogbanje?*" Papa said. "What if the next child dies, or one of the older ones?"

In Igbo tradition, ogbanje were children who would die within a few months or years of their birth and then return in the body of another child, only to die again. The ogbanje were said to hide a totem or charm somewhere in the family's compound or nearby, to show the way for their reappearance. Naturally the cycle of birth and early death brought grief to the families.

Though the Anglican Church by this time was telling its members that the curse of ogbanje was not real, and that children died of diseases, not because of evil spells, Papa knew better. He had seen the effects. He knew how Nnaji's children seemed healthy at birth and for their first few months, but then sickened and died suddenly.

Sometimes a family who lost several children got angry and took severe action. There were instances when the body of the child was mutilated to discourage its return. There were even stories of babies born bearing the scars or signs of the cutting that had been done to dissuade them from coming back.

The cure for ogbanje was to find the totem or charm that the child or its evil spirit had hidden. Once the item was found and identified, it could be destroyed. That almost always broke the cycle, and the parents would be spared further tragedy.

Usually parents only suspected ogbanje after the death of more than one child. But Papa was unwilling to wait. He decided he needed to consult a *Dibia* to ensure the next babies would not meet the same fate. He also wanted to be sure that the existing four children were not ogbanje.

Papa's decision did not mean he was insincere in his Christianity. But the new religion did not provide a solution for this problem. Rather than ignore the chance for an end to this tragedy, he thought it was better to take advantage of the traditional remedy provided by the Dibia. After all, customs that had existed for ages did not disappear when Christianity arrived. He did not need to tell the priest about visiting the Dibia.

"I'm taking the children to Nanka," he said to Mama two weeks later. "You will stay here." He had the name of the Dibia whose specialty was dealing with the babies who kept dying and coming back. He did not tell his children why they were going. After all, if one or two of them were ogbanje, they might try to hide the fact when the Dibia came. Instead he said they were going to see about his father's health, whether the unnamed disease was worse, and to see Nogem, his mother and the children's grandmother.

As always, Nogem welcomed them. She even had a story for them that evening after she had taken food to her husband in his hut.

"Hold out your hands," the Dibia told the children, lined up in front of their uncle Ejike's obi the next afternoon. Clement and Godwin wore shorts. The girls, who were seven and four years old, were naked. "Let me see your palms."

The Dibia grasped Clem's trembling hands, stared intently, and traced lines on the boy's sweating palm with his forefinger. After a minute that felt to Clement like a day, he dropped Clem's hands. "You can go," the Dibia said. Clement rushed to Nogem's side, having a hard time holding back his tears.

Godwin held out his hands. The Dibia lifted them closer to his face. After just a few seconds he shouted, "This child is full of wickedness."

"Don't let him die!" Nogem said.

The Dibia pulled Godwin by the ear. "Tell us where you have hidden your charm," he said.

Godwin broke into tears. "I didn't hide anything," he sobbed.

"You will be happier when you confess. Tell the truth. If you don't, it will be hard for us to search and cure you. I will leave you until I examine the others."

Godwin, shaking with fear, fell to the ground as the Dibia moved to Monica, next in line. "You can go," he said after he inspected her palms.

But Edna, like Godwin, was declared an ogbanje. The Dibia addressed the four-year-old girl. "You can show us right away where you have hidden your totem," he said. "Or you can make your parents search. They will not be happy!" Edna refused to speak.

The Dibia went back to Godwin and with gentle words persuaded him to assist. "There," Godwin finally said, pointing in the direction of the goat shed. Papa fetched the shovel and handed it to the Dibia. After forty-five minutes of digging, he called Godwin over.

"See what I have found," he said. "Do you recognize this?" He held up a smooth, crescent-shaped stone. Godwin had stopped sobbing. He looked at the stone.

"I played with it when we came to the village for Christmas last year," he said. "I liked the shape. It reminded me of the biscuits they give us at church."

Edna still refused to say where her ogbanje charm was hidden. But she had gone to sit on the ground next to her grandmother's cooking shed. The Dibia decided to dig there. A half hour later he recovered what could have been the head of a small wooden doll. "That looks like her doll that she lost many months ago," Nogem said when the Dibia showed it to her.

He held the two items up and prayed to the ancestors to remove the curse from the children. "I will burn the doll and break up the stone. You will not be disturbed again," he said.

Nogem cried with relief as she watched him depart. Papa took the children back to Onitsha the next morning and described the visit to Mama. He assured her she had nothing more to fear. Still, for the next few years, Mama and Papa worried. She had three more children, a boy, Geoffrey, and two girls, Grace and Nebechi. Geoffrey was treated with extra care. Until he was three, his parents and the older children thought he might not survive. They still worried, though less, with Grace.

All seven children were given English names by Papa. The first four were given their Igbo names by Papa's father. The last three were given their Igbo names by Ejike, since Ogbungwa died before they were born. All except the last were called by their English—or as Mama said, Christian—names. Their Igbo names were reserved for official documents, such as school registration. I never learned why Nebechi was an exception, called by her Igbo name, which means "look toward God" or "waiting for God." Perhaps Papa suspected that she would be the last, and he wanted a public affirmation of the traditional Igbo culture stamped on one of his children.

Today some medical professionals say the children's deaths ascribed to ogbanje may have been a result of sickle cell. Others have suggested SIDS, or sudden infant death syndrome, as the cause. One scholar suggests that a mother's belief in ogbanje may have resulted in her not seeking appropriate medical help when, with the right care, the death could have been prevented.

There is less talk of ogbanje today. However, it has not disappeared entirely. Though most Igbos are Christian now, this newer religion is laid on top of traditional beliefs, just as it was for Papa; it has not entirely replaced them. For those who believe in spiritual powers that are beyond our knowledge, the explanation of the Dibia may suffice: children can die from an evil spirit who has come to torment the parents. The evil spirit must be driven away by destroying the totem!

The explanation of ogbanje for their children's deaths was a way for parents to deal with the tragedy. As medical care improved over the years, the reliance on tales of ogbanje decreased. Yet even today Nollywood movies use stories about ogbanje to advance their plots. Enough people find these stories credible to make the movies popular.

Other people in southern Nigeria also had a tradition like ogbanje. The term *abiku* is used among the Yoruba for children who die and are reborn. Like Igbos, Yoruba parents were not shamed or ostracized for having these child deaths; rather, the community united around a family that suffered.

Ogbungwa died later that year, toward the end of 1944, Clement recalls. He said, "Even though he had been isolated for his leprosy in his later years, he had been a person of distinction. He was so well known and esteemed that the funeral lasted for seven Igbo weeks, twenty-eight days." People flowed into the compound from all over Nanka and even farther away. Mama's family, the in-laws from Agulu, came. Townsmen who lived in Onitsha made the trip home to Nanka to pay their respects.

"Every day there was a new set of masquerades, dancers, and drummers," Clem told me. "They shot guns in the air. In one case the gun misfired and wounded the shooter!"

"What happened to him?" I said. "Did he die?"

"No, he was so full of palm wine that he barely noticed his injury. The others led him to a bench and wrapped the wound with cloth. After an hour he got up again to join the others! I've never seen such a variety of dancing coming from all parts as I did during those days," Clem said.

Nogem had been physically separated from her husband for years because of his leprosy. Nevertheless, on his death she had to fulfill all the Igbo traditions required for a widow. On the day he died, his female relatives, the umuada, performed the ritual removal of her hair. Her head was shaved with a blunt razor. Then she was made to sit on the ground outside her hut. A few of her own relatives came to sit with her as soon as they heard the news. The other women were seated on mats, but the widow had to remain directly on the ground. She was not allowed to bathe for the first two Igbo weeks following her husband's death, though her own relatives wiped her body during the night when no one else was around.

No one was to see her eat. Her own people spirited her away from sight to eat and relieve herself as necessary. She wore only rags. She could not see her husband's body.

There were other rituals from which she was spared. In some villages, a widow would be forced to drink the water used to wash her spouse's dead body. Widows were occasionally stripped naked or made to bathe in public. Nogem had five adult sons who protected her. They were able to persuade the umunna, the men of the family, to direct the umuada to administer less harsh treatment.

As visitors came, they first approached Ogbungwa's sons and any other male relatives who were present. Then they went to Nogem where she sat on the ground. Women wailed and pulled at their hair or clothing to show sympathy. Men sometimes put a few cowries, the traditional money, or even a few pence of the modern money in a bowl kept by her side. Many visitors brought jugs of palm wine in tribute. Others brought pieces of cloth, which were strung along raffia ropes behind the men's seating area.

Groups of visitors were shown to benches in assigned areas after offering their condolences. The ndi anutara di, the women married into the family, were kept busy preparing food for the visitors. The guests were served pounded yam, cassava, and soups. The women also made sure that Nogem and her own female relatives who surrounded her had their food. After all, Nogem was one of them.

The customary burial spot for men is in their own compound, in an unmarked spot behind the obi. But because he had died with leprosy, a disease that carried shame, Ogbungwa could not be buried there. Instead his body was taken to a place far from the village.

No one has been able to tell me where he was buried. But my informant,

Clem's cousin Chinedu, said his body would have been near a burial place reserved for those who had been afflicted by evil spells or spirits. In earlier days, twins, regarded as unnatural and thus malevolent in Igbo tradition, were buried in this place if they did not meet the fate of being simply thrown into the forest to die. Ogbanje were buried there, as were people with mental illnesses. Once the missionaries came, they endeavored to convince the Igbo people not to stigmatize twins or those with wicked illnesses. Not completely won over, the villagers often gave these former burial grounds to the newcomers for their first churches.

# 9

## PAPA'S DREAM COMES CLOSER TO FULFILLMENT

AS THE PRIMARY SCHOOL DAYS were ending, Papa warned his son. "You have to come first in the entry exams for secondary school. Make sure you concentrate and do not get distracted," he said.

"I will do my best," Clem said, looking uneasily at the stick his father held.

The two leading secondary schools in 1945–1946 were Dennis Memorial Grammar School, or DMGS, and Government College Umuahia. Clem took the entrance exams for both. DMGS was his father's choice. It was not more than a mile from their house in Onitsha. But Government College, about seventy miles away, was Clem's choice.

"Why did you want to go to Umuahia?" I said.

"Maybe I wanted to get away from home," Clem said. "But that doesn't seem right after the years away with the catechist. I really don't remember."

"Did you know someone there?"

"I must have," he agreed, and added, "To my delight I was invited to an interview at Umuahia."

But the choice was not his to make. DMGS offered a full scholarship that completely covered his tuition and boarding. Papa would have to pay only for books. Umuahia also offered a scholarship but for less. That settled the issue.

Somewhat disappointed, Clem got ready to enroll at DMGS. Now, with this scholarship secured, Papa in his role as the forward-thinking brother insisted that his nephew Okoli attend DMGS also.

He met some opposition. "Why does he need to go to secondary school?" Ejike, Okoli's father, said. He had resisted sending his son to primary school years earlier, though he had finally given in. He had not changed his opinion in the intervening decade. "He does not need more book learning. He needs to learn to farm."

Even as he said it, Ejike knew he would lose the battle. Okoli was eager to continue. He had never come first in his exam results, as his cousin Clement had, but he was a decent student. Papa would pay his fees. The cousins entered DMGS together in September 1945.

They were placed in different dormitories and in separate "streams," or classes. Just as they had been in the final two years of primary school in Onitsha, Clem was in the A stream, for the better students, and Okoli in B. They saw each other frequently but did not share daily life or classes. They did, however, walk back to the house on St. John's Cross on days off and travel together to Nanka when they had holidays.

Papa was vigilant in monitoring his son's and nephew's behavior. At the end of their first school year in May 1946, Clem and Okoli went home to 5 St. John's Cross. They would go to the village in a few days. Both boys were looking forward to seeing their grandmother Nogem again. They were getting too old for her stories, but they anticipated the pleasure of relaxed village life.

The next morning, Papa called his son. *"Bia ebea!* Come here!" The command held no option for refusal. Clem went to the sitting room, where his father was standing, holding something behind his back.

Clem approached his father, dragging his feet. What had he done? "I hear that you are playing big man with cigarettes," Papa said. He pulled a packet of cigarettes from behind his back. "You want to smoke cigarettes? Here, smoke." Papa handed his son the cigarettes, one after another, and made him light and smoke them.

"I only tried one cigarette, one time," Clem said between fits of coughing and retching. But his father was not interested. When the pack was finished, he grabbed his son by the arm and threw him under the bed in the adjoining room. The lesson took hold. Clem never had any interest in cigarettes, though he did not speak to his cousin for several days for tattling.

During the second year, Clem came home over a holiday weekend with a request. He had seen other boys in the dormitory with tins of Ovaltine, a well-loved chocolate drink, and he had watched jealously as they enjoyed their beverage in the evening after studies. He approached his mother, but she sent him to his father.

He was so frightened to make the request that he waited until the Monday morning when he and Okoli were to return to school. By the time he had the courage to ask, his father had left for the market. Clem followed him and approached him at the entrance to his palm oil stall.

"Excuse me, sir, but Mama says I should ask you for six pence to buy Ovaltine."

"You want to buy what?" his father said. "You need to get back to school and pay attention to your studies. Don't bother me again for money." Clem ran from the market and did not stop until he was near DMGS.

Twice more when he was at home, Clem made his way to the market to ask his father for the money. Each time he was trembling as he approached. But he was determined. On the third attempt, Papa reached into the pocket of his trousers and handed his son a six-pence coin spattered with palm oil. "Do you know how hard I work to earn this money? You have to understand the value and you must not waste it."

Clem's future course in life was set during his long vacation after his third year at DMGS. He was spending part of his holiday in Enugu at the home of a Nanka man.

"I had been out to see a friend from DMGS who lived nearby. I was walking back to the house and took a different way," Clem says. "I heard a racket coming from a building along the side of the road. I stopped and looked through the gate, trying to see what was making all the noise."

I've heard the story more than once but still enjoy Clem's pleasure at telling it! "Suddenly a big Nigerian man in a uniform, a guard, appeared at the gate. I ran!

"But before I'd gone far, a white man from inside the building came out and called me back. 'Come inside,' he said. I hesitated, but he motioned to me to follow him. We went past an office and into the inner part, where the sound was so loud I could barely hear him.

"He said, 'This is the equipment that creates electricity. It must turn this huge wheel. That's why it makes so much noise.' He let me watch for at least a half hour! It was the diesel generating plant for the town's electricity.

"He told me he was an electrical engineer. He had gone to university in England to study engineering. He could run this equipment."

Clem was hooked! From that day on, he was determined to be an electrical engineer, and he never wavered in his decision.

A year later Clem and his cousin, who by now had taken the name Jonathan and given up the "native-sounding" name of Okoli, stayed at the home of a townsman who was loaning money to Clem's father to help with Jonathan's fees. Nathanial, called Natty, the townsman, was earning a salary as an employee of the court in the colonial structure. It was a special treat to visit his home in Aguata, the district headquarters near Nanka.

In 1949 each district headquarters had a court. A British magistrate traveled from town to town, staying two or three days in each, to hear cases involving land disputes, theft, or harm to individuals. Few of the British colonial officials made any effort to learn the local languages. The people who brought their grievances to the court usually spoke no English. A translator was required.

Figure 9 Clem during his years at DMGS

Each court had the all-important court messenger, or "Courtma," a person from the area who spoke English well enough to interpret his native language for the court. On the days when cases were to be heard, petitioners would come to the Courtma's home in the early morning. They brought gifts of yams, kola nuts, even goats to persuade the Courtma to speak in their favor before the judge. Once in the courtroom, they would state their case in Igbo in front of the magistrate. The magistrate would turn to the Courtma for translation, and the testimony would be translated as the successful petitioners had requested.

The magistrate would take notes. He might ask questions, which the Courtma would translate for the petitioners, then relate the response to the magistrate. The opposing side's statements would be "translated" to make the case favorable to the person who had won the Courtma's attention in the early morning. Those who lost had little recourse, for they did not know what the Courtma had said. They had no idea what to refute! If a person was found guilty, he was arrested on the spot.

Clem and Jonathan stayed for several days with the Courtma and his family. They ate well, enjoying the bounty of the gifts.

The Cub Scouts, the system of the Courtma, and the whole educational structure were creations of the colonial power. Another visible sign of the prevalence of British rule was Empire Day. Every year during his days at DMGS,

Clem participated in the annual May 24 ceremony. Just as Clem had loved the Cub Scouts at his elementary school and the opportunity to march in formation around the school, he was thrilled with the parade for this special day.

Onitsha, as the capital of the province, had its own resident officer. He and the other leading colonial officers dressed in white trousers and jackets with gold buttons, pith helmets, and polished boots for the parade.

"Be quiet and stay in your place," the teacher told his restless students as they waited to sing and march. "Listen to the resident's speech; I will test you later on what he said."

"Honorable guests, it is my duty and privilege to raise the flag for this Empire Day 1949," the resident may have said as the flag was raised over the field and the band played "God Save the King." The young people joined the rest of the assembled crowd to sing. With the sound coming through a tinny loudspeaker, the resident would have continued, "We have celebrated Empire Day since early in this century. It is our opportunity to salute you as members of the British Empire.

"I bring a message from King George. He sends his greetings and reminds you that you have an opportunity but also a responsibility as members of the empire. You are urged to work hard to develop this great country."

He may have invoked the name of James Griffiths, the secretary of state for the colonies, as another well-wisher. "Nigeria has made progress over the past year. More medical doctors are now present in the country and the health facilities are improving" could have been part of his speech.

The boys like Clem were not interested. "When can we start marching?" Clem whispered to his friend Eugene, standing beside him.

"Just wait. We have to sing again," Eugene said. The band began "Jerusalem" as he spoke. He and Clem joined in.

The resident finally concluded his speech and the band struck up marching music. The boys saluted proudly as they passed the reviewing stand.

Clem remembers one other song usually played and sung on Empire Day.

Brightly, brightly, sun of spring upon this happy day
Shine upon us as we sing this twenty-fourth of May
Shine upon our brothers too,
Far across the ocean blue,
As we raise our song of praise
On this, our glorious Empire Day.

That evening there were fireworks to honor the British Empire.

At the time when Clem and Jonathan were participating in Empire Day in the late 1940s, there were Nigerians beginning to urge a sense of national identity and the end of colonial status. A few of the students at DMGS were politically aware, but Clement and his cousin, proud to be part of the empire, simply enjoyed the loud speeches, the cheering, and seeing lots of police and soldiers in uniform. He had little interest in the British Empire on which the sun never set.

By his final year at DMGS, Clem was thoroughly dedicated to his goal of becoming an electrical engineer. But the path to a higher education was littered with obstacles. There was no possibility that his father could send him to England, and certainly not to the US, where a few Nigerians were attending university. Even though the education of young men from Nanka was a concern for the whole town, not just for Clem's father, no one had the money to assist.

Suddenly the British Empire became personally relevant. He knew that his only hope for fulfilling his dream was a scholarship from the Colonial Office. The colony's education ministry was charged with finding the promising young men—and a few women—who would be sent to England to study.

In 1951, his final year, Clem took the dreaded "Cambridge school certificate exam" to determine his eligibility to proceed to university within the colonial structure. A few students who excelled in the exam were sent to England and placed in British A-level schools and then in universities under the care of the Colonial Office.

He also took the entrance exams for the University College, Ibadan (UCI), the only advanced institution in Nigeria. Far more children completed primary education than were able to get places in secondary school, and the same was true for the students completing secondary school getting entrance to university.

The students taking the entrance exam were divided into two groups, those doing arts and those doing sciences. The year of Clem's exam, the rules were changed to say that students had to pass the English exam from the arts section, as well as other subjects, to be accepted at UCI.

Clem excelled in the science subjects, coming first in the country! But he did not get the pass mark of 50 percent in English, so he was not admitted to UCI. He was crushed. There was a limit of five students admitted for engineering. Those five had not matched him in the science results, but they had clearly passed the English part of the exam. With the hope of performing better the next year, he stayed on in the postsecondary course at DMGS. But within a few weeks he received a cable that he was to come to UCI after all.

"I couldn't believe it," he said. "There were already five students in the program, as far as I knew. Of course, I went, and it's a good thing I did.

"They had a conscience," Clem said. "That made them admit me. I had come first in the science exams, and the rule had just been changed that year."

"But they already had the five that were allowed," I said.

"When I arrived and told the other students that I had come for engineering, they said it could not be true."

It all seems a little haphazard. But this was colonial life. The people affected by the decisions were like pawns, placed where the colonial bureaucracy wanted them. After a restless night, he saw a Mr. Braithwaite in the Admissions Office. "I found out that one of the five students selected for engineering did not show up. That's how I was invited," Clem said.

He was comforted but concerned. He was not offered a scholarship, so for two more years, Papa had to borrow. An achievement like this garnered support from the whole town, and people came forward to loan him the necessary funds.

At least Jonathan, Clem's cousin, no longer needed financial help. He had decided to become an Anglican priest. "God has spoken to me," he told Clem. "I have spoken to the principal, and he has agreed that I can follow this path. I will take over your bond, and you will be free to continue your education when we finish at DMGS."

The bond was a feature of many scholarships in Nigeria. When Clem was given the scholarship to DMGS, he had committed to teach for three years at a primary or early secondary level to pay off the obligation. For the Colonial Office, it was an effective method to ensure enough teachers in the primary and early secondary years while encouraging students who were eager to advance.

When Jonathan completed his service he would attend seminary, supported by the Anglican mission. The cousins were on very different paths, but both headed for success in the new world of Nigeria as it drew closer to independence.

In 1952, during his second year at Ibadan, the Colonial Office notified Clem that he would be going to the University of Leeds in England on a government scholarship. He would be enrolled for a degree in his desired electrical engineering to begin in September that year. He was ecstatic and wrote immediately to his parents. His father spread the word to the relatives in Nanka, and soon the whole town knew their son was going to England. They prepared a send-off party in Onitsha for family and friends.

The speechmakers praised him for his achievements. Unlike in the US, where academic results are private, students' exam results were public knowledge in Nigeria, and he was congratulated for coming first in many exams. The elders cautioned him. "You must continue to work hard. Do not let yourself be distracted. The whole town is counting on you," he was told. Others warned him not to come home with a British wife. His mother reiterated that message to him in private.

I love the photo from around the time of that party, taken in the prevailing custom of the day. The whole family, with cousins and uncles in attendance, is in front of their house in Onitsha. Clem is seated near the center in the light gray suit, between his father and his sister Monica.

Mama is on the other side of Papa, wearing a wrapper with British colonial symbols—a large pound sterling sign, the crown of British royalty, and the scepter. She has on a white lace blouse, a pendant around her neck, and an elaborate head tie, a three-foot length of stiff cotton or satin in the style of the time. Her watch and wedding ring, signs of status, are visible.

Both Papa and Ejike wear native dress, a thigh-long top with embroidery around the open neck and matching trousers. Papa's hat is like a jester's cap, made of the same fabric as the rest of his clothing. Ejike has a porkpie hat of velvet or heavy cotton. The third brother is standing behind, wearing what we later called a safari suit.

Figure 10 Family gathered to commemorate Clem's departure for England

Ejike's second son, Nwosisi, who was living with the family in Onitsha, and Clem's brother Godwin are also standing at the back, wearing ties. Monica is sporting a large hat. Jonathan, on the other side of Monica, is wearing a tie and jacket. Everyone looks extremely solemn, almost frightened, except Edna and Jonathan, who have small grins on their faces. Edna, in a dress, is at the right end of the row of younger people seated on the concrete floor.

The three youngest are beside her, looking miserable in matching print dresses for Grace and Nebechi and native dress, like his father is wearing, for Geoffrey. At the left end are two cousins, Isaiah, whose father had died, and Edwin, son of the third brother, in shorts and white shirts.

I asked Clem why Obi, Papa's youngest brother and the one who reported to their father that Papa had absconded on the day of the facial scarification, was not in the picture. "He was in the leper colony at the time of the party," Clem said. I wondered why they would not have asked his wife to be in the photo to represent the family. Then I realized that was impossible. Women like her, married into the family, had no status for an event like this. The only women are Papa's wife and daughters.

Mama and Papa accompanied Clement to Lagos to see him off. They stayed with friends from Nanka for several days while Clem went to the Colonial Office to sort out his travel and documents. He would go by air, a two-day journey at the time, with an overnight stop in North Africa. On the day of his departure, his parents were able to follow him right to the steps of the plane where it stood on the tarmac. As Clem mounted the stairs, he turned back to look and wave.

"I saw my mother crumple into a heap on the ground, crying," he says. "I knew she wanted me to pursue my dream, but it was all I could do not to turn around and go to her." Nine years later that image was in his mind when he was finally persuaded to return to Nigeria.

The Colonial Office settled him into the home of an elderly couple as a boarder for his first year at the University of Leeds. "They gave me money to cover my expenses. It was so cold! I used most of the money trying to warm my room. I kept putting coins into the heater," he said. "Then I would get into the bed and cover myself completely, and still shiver all night!"

Though a few other Nigerians were at the university, there was no one else from Nigeria or even from Africa in the engineering department with him. The man and woman who put him up as a boarder were not outgoing or particularly interested in helping him adjust to life in a strange place. It was a lonely beginning.

For the first time, he was living apart from all family, clansmen, and countrymen. He attended events organized by the Colonial Office, mainly dances in a formal setting, where he could briefly interact with young ladies from town who came to entertain the foreigners. He met Wole Soyinka, who became a noted playwright and poet, but only at events. In his second year he moved into Devonshire Hall at Leeds. "This was the most desirable residence hall," he said. "Getting in was competitive. I don't know how I managed!" The change made his life much more pleasant, and he was able to remain in Devonshire for his third and final year.

"I missed getting a first-class degree," he said, "because my lab work was poor. Still, I received my BSc engineering degree and was recruited by the Central Electricity Generating Board (CEGB). There I was soon recognized as a talented engineer.

"I read about the head of the CEGB. He contributed papers to scientific and scholarly journals," Clem told me. "He wrote about electricity generation and transmission issues in England and other countries. I wanted to be like him, so I decided I would do the same."

He also enrolled in an economics course at the University of London. "It was tough! I worked a full day, then went home to study," he said. "But I knew I needed this added degree to give me complete credibility in not just engineering but also management. I was as proud of the economics degree as of the engineering!"

During his nine years away, he occasionally wrote letters to his family. He heard from his parents a few times. But correspondence was not easy. Mama could understand parts of what he wrote. But to be sure they understood, his parents had to get one of the other children to read his letters or take the letters to someone in the market. To write to their oldest son, they again enlisted a son or daughter, who by this time barely remembered their oldest brother, to write for them.

By 1960 he felt completely at home in the UK. There had been several girlfriends, including one he especially liked. He had been promoted again at the CEGB. His flat in Manchester, not too far from his office, was comfortable. He considered buying a house. The pull of home, frequently so strong among Igbos, had faded for him. Maybe he would never return to Nigeria.

Just before Christmas 1960 he received a call. "I am phoning from the Electricity Corporation of Nigeria, London office," he said. The person on the other end of the phone line spoke with a cultivated British accent but was clearly

Nigerian. "We are beginning to look for Nigerians to take up senior positions in Nigeria now that the country is independent."

"When did that happen?" Clem asked. He had not noticed the major festivities of Nigeria's independence ceremonies on October 1, attended by Princess Alexandra, who represented the royal family. The caller explained. "We now have Nigerians as prime minister and head of state. You should be proud."

He continued, "Your name has come to our attention because of your work at the Central Electricity Generating Board and the papers you have written. We would like you to consider a position in the senior management."

"You said you are from what company? Did you say the Electricity Corporation of Nigeria?" Clem said. "When did Nigeria get its own electricity corporation?"

"ECN was established in 1950," the caller said. "The general manager, the chief electrical engineer, and other senior people have always been from England. But it is time that we Nigerians show leadership. The chief engineer could leave as early as next year. If you were to come now as his deputy, we would expect you to take over as chief electrical engineer after one year."

"No wonder I had never heard of it. I left in 1952," Clem said. "But I am not interested in returning at this time."

A second caller from the ECN London office rang Clement two weeks later. He too spoke about the importance of having Nigerians fill key positions in the now-independent country.

"But I already told your colleague that I like my position here. I do not intend to leave," Clem said. He thought the matter was finished.

However, unknown to him, ECN traced his parents to their home in Onitsha and told them about the job offer and their son's refusal. Not long after the second call from the ECN London office, Clem answered a knock on the door of his flat in Manchester to find his cousin Jonathan.

"How did you find me?" Clem said after they embraced. They had not seen each other since the farewell party nine years earlier.

"People in the London office gave me your address," Jonathan said.

"I didn't know the Colonial Office had my address," Clem said.

"No, there is no longer a Colonial Office. The London office of ECN is the one that told me how to find you." By the time Clem was telling me this story, he knew that his parents had sent Jonathan to urge him to return. He believed that ECN had even paid for Jonathan's visit to England and helped him get to Manchester.

"We had some good times at DMGS, didn't we?" Jonathan said.

"We did. I remember when you told me to come with you to the far end of the athletic field during our fourth year. I thought you were going to beat me up! Instead you said that you wanted to become a priest. I thought you had lost your mind!" Clem said.

"We've followed different paths. I'm now the assistant priest in a parish. You are an electrical engineer, just as you wanted."

Jonathan introduced the topic that had brought him to Clement's door. "Your father is very proud of you. He knows you have an important job here in England. He understands that you are settled here. But he would be even more proud if you were the deputy chief electrical engineer in Nigeria."

Clem nodded but made no reply. Jonathan continued. "Your mother really needs to see you again. She says if she dies before you return home, her death will be on your head."

Clem leapt from his chair. "Is she ill? Why didn't you tell me?" His eyes filled with tears as he remembered lying beside her on the mat in front of the house when he came home from the catechist's.

"No, she's not ill. Sit down," Jonathan said. "But she wants to see you while she is still healthy and active. She wants you to get married but not to a foreign wife."

He could imagine his mother's embrace. In his mind he could hear his father telling others about his son, the electrical engineer, returned from England! He recalled how close he and Jonathan had been when they were in school. There were six siblings and many cousins whom he had not seen in nine years, and the village and community were calling to him as well.

"Maybe I should go back," he said as Jonathan stood to go. "I will call the ECN office and tell them."

What Clement did not reveal to Jonathan was a further reason for leaving. In addition to his job in the electricity industry, Clement was running a bar with two friends. His name was on the documentation for the business. One night when they had stayed open past the legally required closing time, the police raided the premises. Clem had to go to court. He called a lawyer, who advised him to plead to the court that he had a high-level appointment awaiting him in Nigeria.

The plea was successful. The court stipulated that he would receive no fine or imprisonment if he departed the United Kingdom within sixty days. So that, coupled with Jonathan's intervention, made leaving an attractive option.

A few days after Jonathan's visit, Clem called the ECN office and accepted their offer. They booked his return to Nigeria on a passenger ship, so he could take a few belongings with him. As he prepared, his excitement grew. Though he had Nigerian and British friends and congenial work colleagues, there was no sense of community in England like what he had known growing up. Had he become so immersed in his studies and then his work that he had completely forgotten his origins?

Would he fit in at home again in Nigeria? Or had he become too much of a stranger?

# 10

## THE SON RETURNS;
## PAPA BUILDS A HOUSE

"IT WAS THE BIGGEST HAPPINESS of my life to see my parents and Geoffrey waiting for me at the wharf," Clem said when I asked about his return. "I had not realized how much I missed them."

Mama had wept with sorrow when her oldest and favored son left for England. Now she shed tears of joy as she watched him disembark from the ship and come to her. Her fondest dream of the last few years was fulfilled. Her oldest son was home again. Contrary to her greatest fear he had come back without a foreign wife.

Papa too was overjoyed to have his son back home. He longed to share Clement's achievement with the people of Nanka. There had never had an engineer before. The whole town would be thrilled with this milestone.

His family was not the only group greeting Clement when he returned. ECN had its own delegation at the port. "You must be so proud," said an Igbo man who came forward to shake Papa's hand. "I am ECN's head of personnel. We are very happy to have your son join us."

"Thank you. Yes, we are proud and happy," Papa said. "I did not know there is another person here who speaks our language." He gave the man's hand a second shake.

The head of personnel introduced Clem's parents and brother to the other senior men of ECN who had come to welcome their new deputy chief. The public relations officer took several photos of Clem and his family. Then he led them to a car that had been arranged to take the family to a hotel for the night. ECN requested Clement's presence in the office early the next morning. Then he could depart with his family. He should return to Lagos and "resume duty," in the British phrasing, in two weeks' time. ECN would provide a house for him and arrange for his belongings to be stored there. They would also give him a car and driver for his first month on the job.

ECN gave Clement an advance on his first month's salary. Instead of boarding a crowded lorry packed with passengers and their chickens and goats, the family traveled back to the East in a newer and more expensive Peugeot 404 station wagon, which held just seven passengers. On the full-day trip from Lagos to Onitsha, where they would spend the night before going to Nanka, Papa brought his son up-to-date on the land in the village.

"You remember the stone house where we lived when you left? It was not far from Ejike's obi," Papa said.

"Of course, I remember. That's where I painted the picture on the wall," Clem said. "Is the picture still there?"

"It's there, faded, so you cannot recognize the figures," Papa said. "But now I have land of my own where I can build. We will be able to have a proper house."

"Did you not own the land where that stone house is?"

"No, that is Ejike's land. He had to let me stay since I had no place of my own. For many years I have asked him to give me my own land. But he refused."

"Why do you need land?" Clem said. "Are you planning to move back to the village? I thought you and Mama liked living in Onitsha and wanted to remain there."

"Have you forgotten our traditions? Every Igbo man must have his own land in his village. He can then pass the land on to his sons. My father's land was large enough. It could have been divided among all five of us sons. But he never spoke about the land."

"Why didn't he say how it should be divided?"

"I don't know. Perhaps because of his illness the last several years of his life, or perhaps because he was isolated with the disease. Ejike is the oldest, so he inherited the land. He should have given each of us a portion. Instead, he kept it all for himself and for his sons."

"Can't you go to court to sue him for the land?" Clem said, thinking of the case he had avoided in London.

"Do you think you are still in England?" Papa said. "No, our courts don't interfere in land matters in the village. Our tradition allows the oldest son to keep the land if his father does not tell him how to give it out. No one can force Ejike to share the land."

Papa continued, "He couldn't be forced to give me land. But he also could not require me to move out. For all these years I've stayed. My two brothers were given land down toward Atama, a couple of miles away, by another relative. You know one has died, but he had a house there, now owned by his son. The other is settled with his wives and children. Obi, the youngest, took a small plot from the edge of the compound and built a hut. Ejike let him keep it."

"You said you now have land. How did you get it? Where is it?"

Papa said, "One day I was asking Ejike again, as I had so many times before. When Ejike refused to listen, I shouted. I told him he was being unreasonable. I thought he should see that I needed a place of my own."

"What happened? Did you fight?" Clement said.

"We didn't fight. Ogbungwa's senior brother, my uncle Nwafor, heard us shouting. You know his compound was next to ours. He called me to ask what was happening. When I told him, he gave me a piece of land from his own compound," Papa said.

"I can see the land tomorrow, can't I?" Clem said.

The family reached Asaba, on the west bank of the Niger, waited for the ferry to cross the river, and were finally in 5 St. John's Cross, their house in Onitsha, when it was already dark. The next morning, Papa sent Geoffrey to the lorry park to find a taxi to take them to Nanka.

I asked Clem about seeing Nanka again after so long. He said, "The first day I was in Nanka I felt like a stranger. I remembered Papa's brothers, the three uncles who were still alive, and some of the cousins. There were many people I didn't know or didn't remember. But everyone knew who I was!"

The family stayed in the old stone house with the legacy of Clem's artistic ambitions on the wall. The land that now belonged to Papa was immediately adjoining, and Papa proudly walked all the way around it to demonstrate the size. Ejike had already begun constructing a stone wall to separate the two properties.

"Why is he building a wall?" Clem said to Papa. "Is he afraid you will encroach on his property?"

"It is customary to have a wall between plots of land that belong to different people, even to different brothers within a family," Papa said. "There's nothing evil about building a wall. There will be an opening, a gateway to go back and forth. And I want to attach the new house to the old one, so there won't be a wall where they join."

Papa was right about the opening. We still go through it today. There is a step about a foot high, and a lintel no more than five feet high, so one must duck and climb simultaneously. Traditional Igbo gates and doorways were always made to force entrants to lean low and step over a raised portion. I have asked but the answer does not seem easy to come by. My guess is that the step was partly to prevent rain water from entering, partly to keep out unwanted animals, and party to make people arriving show respect. never learned the reason of course you know – to keep out evil spirits!

"When was the 'welcome home' party for you?" I said to Clem.

"Papa and his three remaining brothers held the party four days later in the church hall at *Afor Udo.*"

"Wasn't that the same place where you attended your first year of primary school?" I said.

"Yes, that's where I went to school when I lived with the catechist across the road. And that's where I ran from when I spotted my mother during her visits to Nanka."

Now Papa's son was not only an engineer, Nanka's first, but he was deputy chief engineer for the Electricity Corporation of Nigeria. The leading men of the town spoke of the honor Clem brought them. His achievement was for the whole town of Nanka, not just for himself or his family.

Clem said, "I wasn't asked to speak at the party in my honor! Probably just as well, as I was not accustomed to speaking in Igbo."

Papa's dedication to his son's and his nephews' education had paid off handsomely. For Papa the goal was never just his own or his relatives' welfare, but rather the prestige of the family in Nanka. He was forward-looking and had recognized during the 1930s and '40s, the middle years of colonial rule, that the earlier forms of prestige no longer held. When Papa was young, recognition came to the man who grew the most yams and filled his yam barn to overflowing at harvest. There had been a time when being the strongest or cleverest wrestler brought honor. Even earlier, the warrior who defeated the greatest number of enemies or brought home the most slaves as captives was a hero.

Now education and the Christian religion were the keys to status. Clement's rise was an example of what was possible in the British colony with academic excellence. He had returned from the UK in 1961 as the deputy chief electrical engineer. A year later the British chief engineer departed, and Clem was given the position, as he had been promised when ECN first contacted him. Papa was filled with pride and loved telling others that his son was the chief electrical engineer of Nigeria's Electricity Corporation.

During the civil war, 1967–1970, Clem was responsible for the Coal Corporation as well as the breakaway country's electricity utility. He was also made executive chairman of the Biafra Airports Board. Late in the war he became chairman of the Panel on Post-War Reconstruction. Papa did not know all the titles or roles Clem held, but he knew his son was responsible for important activities on the civilian side of Biafra.

Several years later Clem started his own engineering company, providing yet more opportunity for his father to rejoice in the way his son had taken advantage of the British system of education. Nigeria had adopted the former colonizers' definition of progress, and Clem was a clear example of success.

Meanwhile, his cousin Jonathan was moving ahead with his fervent embrace of the religion brought by the British. He was already a priest when he visited Clem in Manchester. In 1975 he became bishop and then archbishop of the Diocese on the Niger. His own father, Ejike, who had resisted having his son attend school, eventually became a Christian and took the name Mark. Papa showed equal pride in his nephew's achievements.

Isaiah, the other nephew for whom Papa had paid school fees, was able to attend university in the US on a scholarship. He became a civil servant, then an academic. All three owed their careers to Papa's determination. His huge effort to raise the profile of the family was successful.

The day after the welcome home party, Clem walked around the old house where he had spent so many nights. It would be strange to have a new house next door. But there was no rush, he thought. He and his parents could still stay in the old place when they came to the village occasionally. And he could make it look better. People in England decorated their homes with flowers and bushes. He dug up a couple of plants from the new compound and brought them over to replant outside the old house.

"Ejike stopped me," Clem said, "and tore out the bushes. He told me to leave the place alone. The next thing we knew, Ejike had knocked the old house down and extended the wall the length of his compound."

Customs like ownership of land are powerful and can keep the system working well, but when a step is missed, such as Ogbungwa's not sharing out his property before he died, relationships can become fraught. If Papa's uncle had not intervened, Papa might have gone to the *umunna* to complain. They could have asked Ejike to give Papa land, or they could have decided not to intervene. They might have advised Papa to buy land elsewhere in the village. Most likely they would have found a compromise and asked other relatives to give Papa a space. The result could have been the same. But the bitterness about land has carried into the next generation, with Clement still harboring resentment for Ejike's lack of generosity, though Ejike and Jonathan have been dead for years.

Like most Igbo men, for Papa the importance of owning land was followed closely by the need to build a house on that land. Now that his son had returned, and Papa had his land, it was only natural that he should build a house. Clem, on the other hand, understood how his father felt about owning land but was unaware of the significance of building on it right away. Their differing expectations led to a surprise for Clem three years later.

With his return to Lagos after the welcome in Nanka, Clem settled into his new house. Soon he began sending money home to his parents every month. He knew how hard his father had worked to put him and his cousins through school. Now it was his turn to fulfill the common expectation that a son, especially the first son, would help to provide for his parents when he was able. It was not a large amount but what Clem thought they needed. Then Papa started phoning to ask for additional money. Clem could not understand what they were doing with this money.

I was the one to reveal the mystery!

# 11

## TWO-YEAR ASSIGNMENT, LIFETIME COMMITMENT

CLEM AND I MET IN the latter part of 1963, during my second year as a Peace Corps volunteer. Clem had been the chief electrical engineer for a year. We began dating casually. In mid-December I told him that I would be going to the Eastern Region, his part of the country, during the Christmas holidays. Peace Corps asked us volunteers to be useful if we could during school vacations, taking just two or three weeks during the year for our own break. I had arranged to assist in a day camp in Enugu, the capital of the East, run by a friend.

"I will ask my cousin Isaiah to take you around," Clem said. "He studied in the US and he'll be happy to meet an American. He can show you an Igbo village and introduce you to a family, so you'll see more than other Peace Corps volunteers."

"Most volunteers live in villages, so they experience more than I do, living in Lagos," I said. "But I would be grateful to have Isaiah take me to a village and to meet a family." In my naïveté, I did not realize it was Clem's family I would meet and his village I would visit.

On my first Saturday morning in Enugu, Isaiah picked me up from the hostel where I was staying. He looked a lot like Clem, with the same round face and even, straight eyebrows. He led me to his Volkswagen Beetle in front of the hostel. "We'll drive to Onitsha," he said. "That's where Clem's parents live."

"Tell me about them," I said. "Were they educated? Why did they send Clem to England?"

Isaiah filled me in on their background as we drove out of Enugu and toward Onitsha. "Mama is from Agulu," he said as we passed that town.

"Why do you call her Mama? She's not your mother."

"My own mother died when I was little, and she was a sort of substitute," Isaiah said. "But everyone calls her that. You can too.

"This is the secondary school, DMGS, where Clem studied. I was there a few years later," he said, pointing to several buildings on a corner of a busy Onitsha street. "It's what you would call a high school."

Two minutes later he parked in front of a one-story stucco house on a street full of similar houses. I had to walk across a four-foot-long wooden plank over a gully to reach the veranda and up a couple of concrete steps to the door. There were open wooden shutters on the windows. "This is Cathy, a friend of Clement's from Lagos," Isaiah said.

"Welcome," Mama said, reaching out her hand to shake mine. "Please sit." She pointed to a worn armchair against the back wall of the small room. Isaiah took a place on the equally old sofa. The sitting room walls were drab, either unpainted or completely faded. Bits of fabric hung over the windows.

That was the extent of what I could understand. Clem's parents were a little guarded but polite. Papa broke kola nuts for us, offering what appeared to be a prayer. I chewed a small piece. It was bitter, though I managed to swallow it. He sent one of Clem's siblings across the road to buy soft drinks for us. Geoffrey and a sister, Grace, as I learned were their names, brought out straight chairs from an inner room and sat with us. I tried to engage them in conversation, but they were shy and answered with as few words as were polite.

After an hour or so we departed. "Clem told me I should take you to Nanka, our hometown," Isaiah said as he drove. "You'll meet Ejike, our oldest uncle, and his wife Obele. You may be surprised to see that they live in separate houses, as is our custom."

I was introduced in Igbo this time and had no idea what was said about me. Ejike was leaner than Papa, and a little shorter. He wore a knit cap, a kha-ki-colored shirt, and shorts, with nothing on his feet. He invited us into his hut.

"*Wete kola,*" Ejike called out, turning to a woman standing in front of a smaller hut.

"*Wete* means bring or get," Isaiah said. "This is Obele, Ejike's wife," he added as she approached with the nuts on an enamel plate. Ejike spoke what seemed like an invocation, just as Papa had done a couple of hours earlier in Onitsha, before breaking the nut for us. This time I didn't chew it; I hid it in my pocket.

Occasionally, Isaiah would interrupt to translate as he and Ejike spoke. "He just told me that one of our clansmen's wife died," he said, and later, "The yams are not growing as well as usual."

Then we left Ejike and went through the gate to the compound next door. "This is the foundation of the house Papa is building," Isaiah said. "Clem hasn't even seen this yet. He'll be very surprised!"

When I returned to Lagos and told Clem about it, he was not only surprised but disappointed with his father's decision. He had thought the money he had been sending to his father was to help with his parents' living expenses. "Why is he doing this?" Clem said. "We don't need a house in the village. I know it's the tradition, but can't that wait?" I had no answer.

Clement also told me on my return that two days after my visit to Onitsha, his mother had phoned him to say, "Who is this American lady?"

"She's just a friend, Mama. I assure you there is nothing." Like mothers everywhere, she understood more than her son admitted, even to himself, and certainly to me—not yet!

During the next three months, Clem and I continued seeing each other, and our dates became more frequent. We grew closer. I began spending nights at his house. In late March we were on our way to a Sunday night dinner at Bristol Hotel in downtown Lagos. I turned to him. "Why did you ask Isaiah to take me to your parents and your village?"

"If you must know, because I want to marry you," Clem said. As soon as the words were out of his mouth, he seemed surprised at what he had said!

"Don't you think you should ask me first?" I said, smiling.

He could not see my smile and did not hear the happiness in my voice. "Don't worry, I won't raise the issue again," he said.

I protested. "I did not say you should not raise the issue—I just said you should ask me before assuming!"

As I have learned in more than fifty years of marriage, Clem has a hard time seeing between extremes. For him my question in response to his statement about marriage seemed like a complete rejection. We had a most unpleasant time over dinner, speaking only when necessary. We went back to his house but stayed far apart in bed and did not talk until the next afternoon when we had both returned from work.

It took us a few days to recover. I finally made him understand that I was pleased with his non-proposal. He made something close to a real proposal, and I happily accepted! Although we had known each other only a few months, we loved each other. Despite the obvious differences of race, culture, upbringing, and height (I am taller), we believed we could have a wonderful life together. Perhaps the differences even contributed to our love.

We recognized our dissimilar temperaments. I tend to see the world with a more positive outlook, and I am outgoing. Clem is less likely to expect good from others or from experiences. He is an introvert. We talked about these differences and how we complemented each other.

He was authoring a book about industrial planning in Nigeria, often waking in the middle of the night to write for an hour or two. I offered to proofread and make corrections. I sometimes discussed my teaching with him and valued his suggestions.

At the end of March 1964, we shared the news with friends. I told the Peace Corps country director that I would return to Nigeria after leaving the country at the end of my two years; at that point I still had two and a half months of Peace Corps service. I approached the two schools where I was teaching to ask if they would hire me to come back as a private teacher. The smaller school offered me a contract and I accepted. We set our wedding date for December 26 of that year. We would marry at the Anglican Church where Clement took me when we started dating seriously.

I wrote to my parents. They were sad I would be so far away, but supportive. In June I concluded my Peace Corps service and returned to the US for the summer. Mother and I went shopping for a wedding dress and the accessories. I used the money Peace Corps had deposited for me during my service. "Will you bring the dress, shoes, and veil when you come in December?" I said to my mother. I was stopping in Europe on the way back and did not want the extra luggage.

Clem informed his parents too. They were not supportive, not at first. His mother's suspicion had been proved right and they doubted the wisdom of his choice. He assured them that I would not take our children away, as one foreign wife in Onitsha had done.

When I returned to Nigeria at the end of the summer, I moved in with Clem. We became closer and at the same time more understanding of our differences. My Igbo language ability improved. Clem's parents were still opposed to our marriage, so Clem decided on a plan. He invited them to Lagos in late September when I had a few days off from school and he was at work. I was able to have simple conversations in Igbo. I took them sightseeing around the city. With three days of close contact, I won them over.

We reminded them how adamant they had been when Clement was leaving for England years earlier, directing him not to come home with a foreign wife. Since he found me in Nigeria, he did not exactly disobey; we even joked about that with them!

Before they returned to Onitsha after their brief visit, they gave us a ceremonial broom. "Hold the handle together. Use your right hands," Papa said. "This broom is for you to keep. You should use it to sweep away any disagreements," he said. He and Mama assured us they were looking forward to our wedding and meeting my parents. They also asked us to visit them in Onitsha before the marriage. We agreed to come over the October 1st Independence Day holidays.

There was one more tradition Papa wanted us to share. We drove the three hundred miles from Lagos as he had asked. But no ceremony was held. I was wondering if we had misunderstood, or if it was secret and we did not know when it took place.

But when we were about to head back to Lagos, Clem's father asked us to sit down in the parlor. I was curious. Papa, as I always addressed him, called out, "Mishus!" This was his usual method of getting his wife's attention. She came out from the kitchen, wiping her hands on her wrapper. "Wete mmanya. Bring the palm wine."

She brought out a brown ceramic gallon jug and placed it on the floor beside her husband. "Wete tumbler," he demanded. She carried a tray holding one glass and set it on a small table he had pulled near him. He turned to us and spoke about the importance of marriage as a union between two families, expressing regret that my family was not present. He asked me to write to my parents to relate his message, and I promised to do so, also reminding him that he would meet them in Lagos in a few weeks.

He lifted the jug, tipping it to pour a little palm wine on the floor, saying in Igbo, "I give this wine to honor our ancestors." Then he filled the tumbler and asked me to take it from him and kneel in front of Clement. "Take one sip, and hand the remainder to him to drink," he said. "When you give him the wine, you are showing that you accept him to be your husband."

I was not pleased with kneeling in front of Clem. After all, Clem had not knelt to ask me to marry him. I did not want to establish a message of subservience in our relationship. But I could see how important it was to Papa, and I did as he asked. Clem, looking rather sheepish, accepted the glass and drained its contents. He returned the tumbler to me with a kiss and I gave it back to Papa.

Over the years I learned that Papa didn't often show pleasure with a smile. But our performance of this ritual brought out a big grin. Even without my family, Papa and his son Clem had symbolized knocking on my parents' door to ask for my hand in marriage. I had completed the essential process of showing that I accepted Clem as my husband. And I had a new experience to add to what I was learning as I knocked on the door of these treasured Igbo customs.

We were married on December 26, 1964, at St. Saviour's Anglican Church in Lagos. My parents had arrived two days before and stayed with American friends. Clem's parents had also arrived two days ahead. They and Clem's siblings Monica and Geoffrey stayed with Clement. I had asked Monica to be my bridesmaid, since my sister was not coming. We had also assigned Geoffrey the task of recording the ceremony.

In the 1960s it was not considered proper for a woman to stay with her intended husband. I moved out of Clem's house to stay with my friend Anne Uzochukwu and her husband, Ben, Clem's friend, who lived nearby. My father picked me up there to take me to the church. Our team of three men, our "wedding planners," had arranged the car, the police band for the reception, and all the other details of the wedding and reception later.

Papa and Mama dressed in native attire, he in *buba* and she in wrapper and head tie, all made from the same lovely print cotton fabric. In our wedding photo that appeared in *Life Magazine* in January 1965, Papa is to my mother's left with his hand hooked through her arm. Mama is between her son and my father, smiling shyly at the photographer.

Figure 11 Picture that appeared in Life Magazine, January 8, 1965

Our reception was in the spacious grounds of Clement's house, the official residence of the chief electrical engineer. The police band played, a well-known Lagos businessman was our master of ceremonies, and our several hundred guests—including staff and management of ECN, Nanka people in Lagos, and friends—enjoyed the food and drink. Apart from the near collapse of the wedding cake, the event was warm and wonderful. My father, not known for his oratory or willingness to speak in public, gave a delightful speech praising Clem's parents and the other people they had met.

In the evening after the wedding and reception, we gathered with our two families in Clem's house. Papa asked Mama to bring out a package. His request reminded me of the time they had presented us with the traditional broom to signify our pledge to sweep away disagreements! When she brought the roughly wrapped bundle, he stood.

"You are welcome in Nigeria. It is good that you made the trip here to see your daughter marry our son," he said in Igbo with Clem translating. "You did not ask us for any bride price, and we did not bring palm wine for you. But we have brought a small token for you to take back home." My parents removed the wrapping to find a wooden table, fourteen inches high and nearly two feet long, with an elephant and palm tree carved in the center and geometric designs around the sides.

They were surprised and pleased with the gift. They were a little embarrassed that they had not brought a gift for Clem's parents. "You are the parents of the bride, so it is right that you receive gifts and not give them," Clem assured them. "We ask the parents of the groom to pay a bride price. You didn't have to do that!"

Figure 12 Gift from Clem's parents to mine

My parents returned to the US the day before New Year's Eve, taking the table with them. It was in their home for many years; after their deaths I brought it to our house. We have it today in Connecticut.

What a contrast between our marriage and that of Clem's parents. Their marriage was arranged by their families. They had little choice in the selection of their partner. Either one of them could have refused at the time of the carrying of palm wine, but no one would have supported their refusal or understood such a totally unexpected development. They had barely spoken a sentence to each other when the marriage was concluded, and the new wife left her family and her home for life with her new husband.

How did our wedding, indeed the whole marriage arrangement, appear to my parents-in-law? First, Clem's family was not involved in any aspect of the selection of his bride. Though his parents met me briefly, and his mother had suspicions about his intent, he never asked their opinion, much less asked them to find his bride for him! During the months after he returned from the UK, his sister Monica had sent prospective brides to him. He rejected them all. On his own he arranged to meet me. He informed his parents about his decision, rather than consulting them. He did spend a few days with my parents before we married, but certainly not to ask for their daughter's hand in marriage!

The most significant difference, I believe, is that our marriage did not unite our families. Our parents enjoyed meeting one another during the days surrounding the wedding. My parents appreciated the gift they received, and certainly were able to tell many tales about their time in Nigeria to their friends at home. But they felt no ongoing relationship to Clem's family. They lived continents apart and with different languages, so a close bond would have been impossible. There could have been letters and photos back and forth if my parents had wanted to create a connection. It did not occur to them, or to me, to establish such a link, so they simply heard news about Clem's family from my letters.

I did become a part of Clem's family and worked hard to fit in, speak the language, and accept the customs. Though my parents were never close to Clem's family, I had the opportunity to introduce my sister to people in the village two years later, and I was overjoyed.

But before my sister, we introduced our first child! Our first trip to the village together was for this major event, the naming ceremony of our son, Chinaku. Papa was bursting with pride from the moment we arrived in the village the day before to the day after the ceremony when we returned to Lagos. His son Clement, whom he had labored over to make sure he got the best education, was now the chief electrical engineer of Nigeria's Electricity Corporation. He had a prestigious car, a white American wife, and now a son!

As custom dictated, Papa and his senior brother, Ejike, had provided the name for our son—Chinakueze, or "God is the one who creates kings." "When are you coming for the naming ceremony?" Papa had asked in a phone call when the baby was two weeks old.

Clement had looked at me as he repeated the question. We chose a date a few weeks later. I was thrilled that we were not abandoning this custom that I knew would tie our child to his ancestral home. But I was hardly prepared for the emotion that I felt.

"Nno, welcome," Mama said as she hugged me and took the sleeping baby in her arms. With her warm greeting and obvious joy at seeing my baby, I felt closer to her than I had before. I was now part of the family and I belonged here.

Emma (pronounced ē-MAH) Clem's oldest cousin, had slaughtered a goat earlier in the day and placed it over a fire to burn off the hair. When we arrived in the evening, the smell of the singed goatskin was heavy in the air. But that did not deter us from enjoying the pounded yam and okra soup Mama had prepared for us. Soon we were in bed with the baby in his yellow carry-cot beside us. We could hear the women, the *ndi anutara di,* who were busy in Obele's compound cooking for the celebration that would take place the next afternoon. The goat was in the pot, and the aroma of the soup had replaced the acrid smell from earlier.

When we woke, the air was fresh. I sent Rosa to prepare a bucket of warm water for me in the enclosed area near the kitchen where we took our baths. After bathing I carried Chinaku around our compound and took him next door to greet the women who had returned to finish preparing the food. They all adored the baby and took turns holding him. We ate our *akamu* and *akara* for breakfast and greeted visitors who dropped by ahead of the ceremony.

"Do I look all right?" I said to Clem, pirouetting in my favorite fitted dress of red, blue, and green *Akwete*. He approved with a kiss. He put on a white shirt and tie in honor of the occasion. I asked Rosa to dress Chinaku in his blue kimono with an embroidered flower pattern and put on her best dress. As guests began to arrive, we went downstairs and found Mama in a blue print wrapper with matching blouse and head tie. Papa looked dignified in his long gown of the same fabric. He had added a dark blue felt cap and a walking stick.

Chairs for the family had been set up in front of the house, and benches for the guests. Ejike stood up. *"Ndi be anyi, kwenu.* My people, shout." The guests shouted, "Yah." He turned to his left, then his right, with the same greeting. Each time, the response was louder and Chinaku began crying. I rocked him in my arms. "Don't worry. You're safe here."

Ejike continued. "The ancestors have honored us. Our son Clement has returned from England and is now chief engineer. He has married and now has a son. We thank our ancestors."

Obele had placed a tray of kola nuts in front of him. Now he held up one nut. "I thank our ancestors for this kola," he said. "Kola brings life." He broke the kola nut into three pieces, took one himself, and placed the rest on a plate. Several young relatives came up to pass the other trays of kola nuts to everyone present, men first, then the women.

After the kola, jugs of palm wine and bottles of Star beer were brought out and served. Most men had their own calabash gourds with them. Some, I suspected, had started their drinking earlier in the day. Chinaku stopped crying. After a few more minutes, Ejike took Chinaku from me and held him up before the crowd.

"We have given this child the name Chinakueze." He poured a libation of palm wine onto the ground. The baby was handed around to all the senior men. Then the women took turns holding him. He was passed back to me as the women brought out and served the food. After everyone had eaten their fill of jollof rice, garri, pounded cassava, and okra soup, a men's dance troupe performed, accompanied by drums, the high-pitched wooden Igbo flute, and maracas. Then the women who had cooked and served the food began to dance in a circle formation. This was my group! One of the women came to pull me up to join them. I danced around the circle with them to the laughter and enjoyment of the guests.

As the dancing ended, Ejike asked me to bring the stump of our baby's umbilical cord. Clem had told me to save it when it fell off a couple of weeks after Chinaku's birth and to bring it along. Holding the dried cord, Ejike said, "This cord binds Chinakueze to Nanka, to our compound, and to our people forever. Whenever he returns he will know that he belongs here. When he is away, he will always know that part of him is here." He placed the cord in the small hole that had been dug earlier. I felt an incredible surge of emotion for the family that had embraced me, and now my baby, so warmly with this powerful sign of belonging.

I returned to Lagos the next day, leaving a tiny part of my son behind in his father's village. Would he feel this connection? I knew that I did; it was now my village too.

At the end of that year, 1965, we went to the village again, this time to celebrate the Christmas and New Year's holidays. My sister, Beth, had come to Nigeria to visit us in mid-November. We had celebrated her birthday on November 21 and mine on December 13 together. Of course, she came with us to Nanka. We also had our baby, Chinaku, his nanny, Rosa, and our cook.

"This is my sister, Beth," I said to Papa when we got out of the car in Nanka. He and Mama had come a couple of days earlier to get ready for our arrival.

"*Nno*, welcome, Bett," Papa said. "How your journey dey?" I understood the Pidgin English perfectly.

"He's asking how the trip was," I said to Beth. "You can say it was fine, or long."

I saw Mama emerging from the kitchen and repeated the introduction.

"You are welcome," Mama said to Beth. I said a few more sentences to Mama, asking her about other family members, and nodded at her replies.

"How can you understand that language?" Beth said to me. "It's so strange."

She watched me with a look of bewilderment while I spoke to several other family members who came from their surrounding homes to greet us.

I was becoming more adept at Igbo and loved using the language. I spoke it at every opportunity and translated for her whenever necessary. What I could not do was teach Papa and others how to say her name. The *th* sound is not part of the Igbo language and was impossible for them. The closest they came was Bett or Betty, as also happened with our daughter later.

She didn't care. Apart from being baffled by the language, she connected well with family and friends in Nanka. She is warm and outgoing and easily became friendly with one of Clem's cousins, Pius, who spoke English. For Clem's extended family, seeing my sister provided a sense of relief. They knew that only my parents had been present at the wedding a year earlier and felt sad for me that I had no one else around when I married.

Our last day in the village, I took Beth to a corner of the compound. "Do you know that we buried Chinaku's umbilical cord here?" I said.

"Ooh, that's gross!" she said, as I had guessed she would.

"We had a ceremony, with drinking, eating, and dancing. You would have loved it!"

"I guess the drinking and eating would have been great! I'm not so sure about the dancing," she said. "Did you dance?"

I assured her I had and showed off a bit of how Igbo women move in a circle.

Clem no longer resented his father's use of the money to build the house in the village; rather, we appreciated his taking the step when Clement would not have done so. Two years later our gratitude was multiplied tenfold. When the country was engulfed by civil strife, and eventually a civil war, the house and the village became our refuge.

# 12

## WHEN NIGERIA BREAKS APART, I BECOME AN INSIDER

NIGERIA'S FIRST COUP TOOK PLACE early in 1966. It was followed by another six months later, and by 1967 Nigeria was in turmoil. Northerners had slaughtered thousands of Igbo people living in the North. Even in Lagos, the capital, where we lived, Igbo people had been killed. The government was in the hands of the military, with each of the country's four regions led by a high-ranking officer.

The single entity, Nigeria, that the British had put together in 1914 was falling apart. Many factors contributed: differences in religion, tribal affiliation, education levels, political structure, and opinions about sharing the country's oil revenue. Resentment of the apparent success of Igbo people was an issue. The Eastern Region, the home of the Igbo people and a few smaller ethnic groups, was threatening separation.

Starting in late January 1967, Papa and Mama called us from their home in Onitsha, the largest city in the East, at least once a week. "When are you coming home?"

The next time it was "Did you not hear about the slaughter in the North?"

Then, "Why are you still in Lagos? Don't you know it is dangerous for Igbo people?"

We did hear rumors about Igbo people, senior government officials, who were not sleeping in their own beds but moving around among friends' homes every night, fearing assassination. We knew that Igbo military leaders were at risk.

"What are you doing about this situation?" my American friend Carol, married to an Igbo man, said to me when I visited her in mid-March.

"We don't know what to do," I said. "Clem hates to give up his position at ECN. I love my teaching job at the American School. What about you?"

"Walter has already gone to his home in the East," she said. "I'm waiting to hear from the head of a school in Ghana. If they have a job with housing for me, I'm going."

Two weeks later she was gone. That scared me.

In late April, nine weeks before our second child was due, we packed up our belongings. Suspicion among Igbo people was rife, and Clem was concerned that he might be targeted if he announced his departure. He could be thought a traitor for abandoning his role as chief electrical engineer of the Electricity Corporation. He did not notify the general manager or anyone else that he was leaving. He urged me to be cautious as well.

I was the fourth-grade teacher at the American International School. On my last day, I finally told the principal and my students that I was departing. We fled to Enugu, the capital of the Eastern Region , where Clem became the head of the electricity and coal corporations. The major general in charge, Odumegwu Ojukwu, declared secession as the independent Republic of Biafra on May 30, 1967. We rejoiced with everyone else in the city, imagining the possibility of a bright future but aware of the huge risk. We knew Nigeria would not accept the secession easily and had greater force at its disposal. War was the likely response. Our daughter was born in Enugu, in the newly created country, on June 25.

Clem called his parents in Onitsha to announce the birth and ask for a name. It took just three days. "Papa has given her the name Ijeoma," Clem said after answering the phone in our new home in Enugu. Of course! The verb *ije* means to go, and *mma* is an adjective or adverb meaning good or well. Ijeoma means "safe travels," clearly chosen in thanks for our safe return from Lagos.

"It couldn't be more appropriate," I said. "But I want her first name to be Elizabeth, and I want us to call her Beth like my sister and my aunt." I was prepared for battle, but Clem was happy to oblige. She became Elizabeth Ijeoma, and we called her Beth.

Three months later the civil war, the Biafran War, was underway. Nigeria was determined not to lose the breakaway territory. Their troops were approaching Enugu, and we had to escape again, this time to Clem's village, where the house was waiting. With our three-month-old daughter, our two-year-old son, and our nanny, we set up housekeeping in Nanka.

We would have been stranded without the house. Clem's parents came in November 1967, when Onitsha fell to the Nigerian army. Once she arrived, Clem's mother took over. No matter whose money was used to build the house, it was Papa's house for as long as he was alive. His wife was the person in charge. The next month Clem's brother Geoffrey came home from his university in northern Nigeria, and two sisters arrived.

In keeping with Igbo tradition, all family members were welcome. There was never any doubt that we would make room for whoever came home. Clem's salary had to stretch to cover all the expenses.

Our life settled into a routine. I had two small children to care for. Our cousin Rosa was their nanny and my helper. Basic tasks consumed our time. There was no running water. Every morning, Rosa and Clem's cousin Georgina, the daughter of the youngest uncle, Obi, went to the stream with their pots and buckets. They poured the water they carried back into large clay pots in the room we used as an indoor kitchen. I had brought our water filter and a two-burner gas stove from Enugu. We filtered and then boiled the water to drink. I did some cooking. Usually, we shared in what Mama cooked in the shed next to the house. Sometimes I helped her with the food preparation but never became adept at cooking over an open fire.

"*I g'eje afia?* Are you going to market?" Obele, Ejike's wife, or Mercy, Obi's wife, would ask on the morning of every *Afor,* the town's primary market, every fourth day.

"*Anam eje.* I am going," I said. If I was driving, one or both would often ride with me. Other times one of us would not be going but would ask another a favor. I came to love the Igbo phrase *K'n tue gi ife*—"Let me ask you to buy something for me." Then the person requesting would specify what was needed and count out the money to hand to the buyer.

Sometimes Mama went to market with me. Shopping with her was hard.

I was accustomed to bargaining and considered myself an active negotiator in Igbo. But she was relentless. I found that I became impatient when we were bargaining as one. Eventually, I found that we could divide up what we had to buy rather than attempt to do it together. That was a more peaceful experience.

As the war went on, prices rose and inflation worsened. It became more and more challenging to buy basics. I was in the market one day when Dora O. approached me. "Mrs. E. and I are thinking about purchasing meat together. Would you like to join us? We could buy a larger cut and get a better price, and then share it out."

"Yes, I would like that," I said. "And either one of you can probably get a better price than I can."

Even though I was well known in the village, sellers were likely to raise their prices when the only white woman for miles around was the buyer. We cooperated on our purchases of meat, rice, and garri several times.

We did not have electricity but used lanterns. Each evening, one of us had to check that the lamps had enough kerosene. I worried that Chinaku or Beth would get burned, but they never did.

Mama's mother, Eye, also stayed with us during part of the war. Soon after the civil war started in 1967, and we had fled to the village, Clem and I went to see her and her son Okeke with our son and baby daughter. We knew they were not finding the wartime easy. We asked her to come back with us, but she wanted to stay in her home. A few months later, however, we took Mama along, and she persuaded her mother to come to Nanka with us.

Eye was often cold during the rainy season, which started in May, nine months after we had arrived in the village and two months after she came. One morning she was sitting by the fire in the outdoor kitchen. There was a kettle of water on the tripod, just starting to boil. She tried to stand up too quickly and fell against the pot and the fire. Her leg was severely burned. The nurse, Osisioma, cared for her as best he could when there was little medicine available. She had been sharing Mama's bed upstairs. We placed a bed for her in the downstairs sitting room, so she could see all the activity going on, and Osisioma could visit her easily.

When I left in September 1968, she was still recuperating. When I returned, I learned that she had become a casualty of the war. Once her leg healed, she insisted on returning home. Clem drove her when he was in Nanka one weekend. Two months later the Nigerian army approached Agulu and seemed likely to enter and take the town, which they eventually did. Eye and her family fled on foot. She couldn't keep up and begged them to leave her along the way. They refused, and her son carried her. But when he could no longer keep up with her on his back, and she seemed near death, her family made her comfortable at the side of the road. They promised they would return for her, but she and they knew her end was near. They left her and never found her body.

Mama exhibited the same tenacity and stubbornness as her mother. In mid-1968 the war had been going on for nearly a year. Food was becoming somewhat scarce, and the Biafran currency was losing value as inflation hit. It was difficult not only to find what to buy but to get the right change to pay for it.

One morning Mama announced that she was going to Aguleri, about thirty miles away, north of Onitsha and on the Niger River, to buy fresh fish. We knew that the Nigerian army—the enemy—was between us and the Niger. We all protested her idea, Papa most loudly. But she insisted. I admired her courage and her persistence. To see her in operation as the one who acted made me feel somewhat inadequate. What was I doing except looking after my children?

She went, leaving before dawn the next day. She returned two days later, triumphant. The fish she brought back sold well in the market, and we had our share, a treat in those days.

Now as I write about Mama, I again admire her tenacity, her determination to make the most of her family and hold everything together in the face of hardship. When Clem and I decided that I should leave Biafra with our two children, she wept.

"We may die before you come back," she said. "But you are doing the right thing to take your children away from this war. Write to us and tell your parents about our struggles."

"I will be back, Mama," I said, holding her close.

During my twelve months living with my husband and his family in his village, surrounded by other Igbo people, I learned in my bones what I had known in part or in principle. Hierarchy, structure, and obligation are critical determinants of Igbo family life. I was familiar already with the sense of duty. I knew that Clem helped support his parents from the time he arrived back from England. When I met Clem, his nephew Edwin was living in one room of the boys' quarters, servants' housing behind the main house. Other relatives came occasionally, and it was Clem's responsibility to take care of them.

Learning and accepting the overarching structure of the town and the importance of place within it was a challenge. I had to adjust my thinking about what family means. What we in the West call the family is composed primarily of one set of parents and their children. Grandparents, aunts, uncles, and cousins may be considered extended family, but they are not the core. An Igbo family never exists in isolation. The family is part of a larger kinship group, the extended family, who have the same name and come from a common grandparent or great-grandparent. Several families share a common ancestor many generations back and together compose a clan, *umunna,* or "children of one father." Many clans make up a village, and together several villages form a town.

I learned about the structure of our family, clan, village, and town from Clem and his cousins Georgina and Chinedu. I also benefited from the knowledge of our friend Samuel Ogbuju, the editor of *Nanka News.* Sam has drawn a complete chart of the town of Nanka with its seven villages, and each village with its several

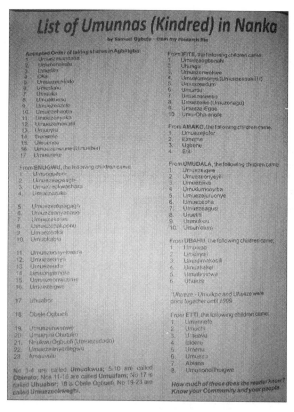

Figure 13 List of Umunnas in Nanka, from Samuel Ogbuju

clans, as part of his work for his PhD in geography at the University of Lagos. He named the document "List of Umunnas (Kindred) in Nanka."

The heading of the first list is "Accepted Order of Taking Shares in Agbiligba."

"What's the meaning of 'accepted order of taking shares'?" I said after serving him a soft drink when we were together in our downstairs parlor during the 2016 Christmas holidays.

"Think of it within a family," Samuel said. "The oldest son will get the first share of the property when his father dies. For the town of Nanka, Agbiligba is the 'first' village, so it gets the first share of anything the town has to divide."

I wanted to ask what the town might have to divide, but Sam, always on the move, was out the door to speak to our cousin Christian.

The other six villages are headed with the words "From [village name], the following children came," reflecting the awareness of a common ancestor whose identity is no longer known. Our village, Enugwu, is the second of the seven. The names of the first, third, fourth, and fifth are like music: Agbiligba, Ifite, Amako, Umudala. I have never heard of the sixth, Ubahu, and only rarely of the last, Etti.

Within Enugwu there are twenty-three clans. Ours is number seven, Umuezekesiri, or "the children of Ezekesiri." Below the list of Enugwu clans, Samuel wrote that there are several subgroups; ours is Obinato. I was familiar with that name, but I do not recall ever hearing the clan name Ezekesiri. When the men want to gather for a meeting of the clan, it is Obinato, the subgroup, that gets together.

I know people from several other families who are part of our clan. Across the road from us in Nanka is the family of Nnadi. Another family, Ezento, lives less than a quarter mile down the road. Benji, from that family, came to our son's traditional wedding in 2005. We attended his daughter's wedding years later. We are all related as part of the same umunna, or clan. And I continue to meet more!

During the Christmas holidays in 2016 I ventured out for a walk along a path I had never taken before. I was less than a mile from our house when I passed a girl who looked to be in her late teens.

"Good morning, Ma," she said. "You are just passing our home." She pointed to a small cement-block house with a tin roof just off the path. "Please come to visit."

*"Nno, ogo anyi.* Welcome, our in-law," her father said as she led me to a chair he was bringing outside. "We are part of the same *umunna.*"

"I'm sorry I did not recognize you," I said. "Thank you for telling me."

"We have nothing to give you," her father said. I assured them that was all right; they had not been expecting me after all. But I could see he was bothered. He instructed his daughter to fetch a plate of something like *agidi,* made from ground corn and steamed in banana leaves. I ate a little and they insisted I take the rest home. The next day the daughter came to our house to greet me. We are kin.

No one knows who the first Onyemelukwe was, even less the first Ezeke-siri, the founder of the clan. The oldest name that I have heard in our extended Onyemelukwe family is Nwafor, also called Ezeofor, the older brother to my husband's grandfather Ogbungwa.

When I became part of the family, Ogbungwa, his wife Nogem, and one son had already died. The Onyemelukwe family that I joined consisted of Papa, his three remaining brothers, and their children. Among these children were two men, Ejike's two oldest sons, who were older than my husband. The oldest brother, Ejike, was automatically the leader. On his death, leadership passed to the next oldest brother, Papa.

These relationships are fixed forever. An Igbo man cannot move away and become part of another village or clan. He is tied to his town, his village, his clan, and his family. He can certainly move to another town, even another part of the country, or a different country altogether. He may even be born outside Nigeria and not visit his home. But that does not change his identity. Just like he cannot "give up" his Igbo tribe and become a Yoruba or Hausa, he cannot give up his uniqueness as a person from a certain umunna, village, and town.

At the single-family level, the roles are fixed. The person in charge, the head of the "nuclear" family, is the father. His wife or wives and his children should respect him as the head. They should obey him and not challenge his authority. His dominance is shown in small matters: he is given his food first, he is the one who can call a family meeting, he leads the prayers, and he breaks kola. His dictates are not to be questioned. His wife or wives and children should not disagree without risk of severe punishment.

"You are my wife. You have to listen to what I say," Clem sometimes ex-claims when he is frustrated with my independence. He usually accompanies his dictate with a smile, knowing that I accommodate him now and then, but usually follow my own path.

Within the extended family the roles are also set. The oldest son of the oldest son has rights that others do not. He also has responsibilities. The most senior male is the head of the extended family. He represents the family in meetings of the umunna. Though these rights and responsibilities are usually fixed, they can be modified on occasion. Once, long ago, the rules were bent to make Papa the leader, though Ejike retained the nominal leadership. Today the same happens with my husband assuming leadership.

Similar reasoning was behind both. Even though Papa did not have formal schooling, his experience traveling and working outside the village gave him a broader and more forward-looking approach than Ejike. He became a Christian early, and he was dedicated to education for his children and his nephews. Even though he quarreled with Ejike, who refused to give him land, he became the effective head of the group of brothers. Still, Ejike was consulted as the ultimate authority. Only he could speak for the family in a meeting of the umunna, but he usually did so with Papa by his side.

My husband's role today mirrors that of his father. Within the extended family Clem's cousin Emmanuel, or Emma, should be the head. But because Emmanuel did not get an education, Clem has become the leader. He chairs the family meeting held every year when we are in the village, and he is called on to help settle disputes. Still, the ultimate voice is Emmanuel's.

Among his siblings, Clem has always expected, and usually received, obedience. One of his younger brothers has died; it is Clem's responsibility to oversee the brother's family. He reiterated the whole framework in phone calls with his nephews recently. The older nephew has a good job in Lagos. He pays rent and other costs for his mother, a younger brother, and one sister. He called to tell my husband that his mother and younger brother had moved out in anger, taking just the clothes on their backs, and gone to stay with friends. Clem spoke to the mother, who referred to her two sons as colleagues, and Clem told her that was unacceptable. "They are not colleagues, there is a hierarchy, and they must observe it," he said.

My year in the village gave me a deep inside view of family, clan, and town relationships. And I had more than a privileged view—I became part of the structure as I was drawn in and held close by all the relatives and townspeople. My great respect and love for these close ties grew out of that year. The sense of belonging, being part of the community, is central to an Igbo person's identity. An Igbo man or woman has confidence about his or her place in the world. My ties continue to be strengthened with each visit. I never feel awkward or out of place, though I am so clearly an outsider.

The difference between our Western customs and those of Africans shows clearly in family structure and how family members behave with one another. I never saw my father assert his authority in the way that Papa did. My father, and many other fathers in the West, did not expect us to show deference or respect in the same manner as Clem's father.

I stayed with my parents in Madeira from September 1968 to May 1969, when I left them to go to the US. They reminded me, in the way they behaved toward Chinaku and Beth, that they had always wanted and expected each of us children to develop our own personalities. We were to learn manners and morals from them, but not regard them as authorities to be obeyed. They did not wish to tell us what to think or how to act. Instead, they encouraged us to think for ourselves, make decisions ourselves, and be responsible for those decisions. Individualism was highly valued.

This difference was, and sometimes continues to be, a source of conflict between Clem and me. When our children were little, and even more now that they are adults, I did not tell them what to do. Clem believes he can command them to act as he thinks appropriate and is unhappy when I will not concur with his demands.

True to my promise to Mama, I returned after the war ended. I had been away for a year and nine months. Again I had to adjust my thinking to accommodate African practices and make them fit my life. But I have always followed most of the customs about raising children that I learned in my own upbringing. Blending these disparate traditions is one of the challenges of our bicultural marriage.

Our son Samuel was born in March 1971. We resumed our regular visits to the village during the Christmas holidays. Papa continued to demonstrate his authority, and in 1974, when we went to Nanka, Clem told me a story about his mother's defiant side.

# 13

## PAPA THE AUTHORITARIAN AND MAMA THE REBEL

*"WELU NWANYO.* TAKE IT EASY," Papa said. "You are disturbing everyone with your noise." He shook his stick out the window of his special room over the gate and shouted to the girls playing in the compound. They were skipping, clapping, and singing in their game of *igbu-oga,* or *ten-te.* Two players face each other a couple of feet apart. With rhythmic steps and chanting, they reach out and try to tap the other's hand, each attempting to avoid being touched.

They became quieter for a few minutes, but soon the chanting and hand-tapping sounds were back to their previous level. It wasn't disturbing anyone, not even Papa. He just wanted to make his presence known and remind people that he was the head of the family. Not that anyone would question his authority! He was a handsome man, still five feet, eight inches tall, sturdy, and sharp at around age sixty-six. His voice was deep and commanded respect. He did not smile easily.

It was December 1974, four years after the war ended. We had come from Lagos to Nanka for the Christmas holidays, as we did nearly every year that we lived in Nigeria. The targets of Papa's shouting were our daughter, Beth, and two other girls, all around the age of seven, who had played together when they were babies. I was sitting on the veranda of our house with Clem, watching the girls and listening to Papa. Our sons, ages nine and three, were with other children in the village. I knew they were safe. Mama was in the kitchen preparing our lunch.

Papa with his stick reminded me that for a Nigerian man, respect is of the utmost importance. It is his right; he does not need to earn it. When he shakes his stick and commands silence from the children, he is asserting his role as head of the family. He can do the same even with his grown children. If he wanted to tell them to be quiet, he could do so, no questions asked, and they would obey! They would dare not insult him by answering back.

Now, four years after the war, I saw Papa as a figure of strength, the enforcer of discipline, and a teacher of family relationships. I had grown accustomed to his gruff manner and knew that a warm heart beat underneath. He was a model of the hierarchical structure, with his deference to his older brother and the respect he received from his younger siblings.

He enjoyed his private space, reached by steps at the side of the compound entrance, where he commanded a view of our house and yard. From the opposite window, he could watch people passing in front of our compound. If they were going uphill, to his left, they were heading to the market and center of town. If they were on his right, following the road downhill, they were returning from the market or on other errands to their homes farther along the way to Atama, our town lake.

Visitors often came to see Papa. He entertained them in his room over the gate, occasionally bringing them into the house so Clem could greet them as well. He took advantage of those times to demonstrate the importance of reverence for the ancestors. When Papa broke kola for guests, he focused on the Igbo custom, holding the kola in his raised right hand and thanking the ancestors for their protection. He did not, however, ignore his Christianity and ended with *"N'afa Jisos* – in the name of Jesus, amen," before breaking the nut to share.

From my first day of meeting Clem's parents in 1963, I sensed that Papa wanted people to know he was the power in the family. But as I came better acquainted with them during the year before Clem and I married, more closely during my year in the village, and in the years after the war, I recognized that Mama could hold her own quite effectively. I learned that she was the core of the family, the substantial force behind Papa, and a warm and loving presence to her children and many other relatives.

In their early years together, Papa was making his mark in business, in town affairs, and in the church. He was also educating his children and other relatives. But Mama was the leader in the home. Like any wife, in almost any culture, she knew when it was necessary to deceive her husband to maintain peace and harmony.

I learned about her love of snails early in my marriage to Clem. During the visit in 1974, he told me how she would prepare them when Papa was away. I recount the scene as I imagine it would have happened when Clem was about fifteen.

"Bring the big pot," Mama said as she lifted her purchases from her head and placed them on the ground in the shed that served as the kitchen. "I bought the snails at the market."

"They are still alive," said Monica, eleven, her oldest daughter, as she peered inside the basket before dragging the largest pot from the back corner. She removed the dead spider inside.

"Fetch water for the washing," Mama said. Edna, two years younger than Monica, ran out of the shed. She carried a bucket to the tap halfway between the kitchen area and the main house, forty feet away, and came back with the full bucket on her head. Mama removed six large land snails from the basket and placed them on the ground. Five-year-old Grace picked one up and shrieked as it wiggled its feelers.

"Get more wood," Mama directed her second son. "I need a big fire." Godwin, at thirteen, was proud of his strength. He carried in several split logs to add to the fire under the tripod where the pot was resting.

All the children had been urging her to buy the six-inch-long land snails, ejuna in Igbo. They had a small window of time while Papa was away. Papa hated snails. He hated the earthy smell when they were cooking, the rubbery feel of the meat, and the musty taste. He even hated the remnants of cooking them, the telltale line of scum near the top of the pot! Whenever he left their home in Onitsha on his bicycle to visit the village twenty-four miles away, his family took advantage of his absence to eat the delicacy. They had to leave no trace. And they were never sure when he would return. Usually, he stayed away from Friday afternoon until Sunday evening, but he sometimes came back on Saturday evening instead.

"Godwin, break the shells," Mama said. Godwin was ready with the hammer. Hitting the shells until they broke open was his favorite part of the preparation.

"Edna, you help Monica wash them. Look carefully to make sure there is no more sand."

She checked the pot to see if the water was close to boiling before inspecting her daughters' cleaning efforts. Then she continued with her rapid instructions.

"After you wash off the sand, rub them with the alum." Mama pulled two-inch-long pieces of a gray metallic rocklike substance from the market basket and handed one each to Monica and Edna. Nebechi, age three, joined her sisters.

Monica held her youngest sibling's hand and guided it over the snail's body. "Rub hard," she said. "We don't want any of the sliminess to remain, do we?"

"Are you sure Papa won't be back tonight?" Clement said as he watched, remembering his father's punishment when he had learned his son had smoked cigarettes and not wanting to invoke more wrath.

"Don't worry," his mother said. "The snails will cook in a few hours. We'll be done eating them and cleaning up before he returns."

And they were! Papa was never the wiser.

One way that African mothers instill a sense of belonging in their children is by insisting they help take care of the home. The girls are taught from an early age how to inspect rice to clear it of small stones, how to pound yam in the large wooden mortar, and how to fry plantain. Both girls and boys are responsible for caring for younger siblings. The idea that parents would pay a child to perform tasks in the house, or to babysit for a younger child, would cause Igbo parents to laugh with disbelief.

I have seen mothers in the US worry about letting their daughter or son handle a knife in the kitchen. An Igbo mother will behave in the opposite way. She will demand that her child use the knife, punish her if she cuts herself, and expect her to cut the food well. If there are only sons of the age to help, they will help.

Mama followed this tradition when her children were young. But Clem, the oldest, was never much of a caregiver or helper. Instead, Mama gave him special treatment. When he wasn't away at school, she pampered him. Sometimes in the evenings, Mama would lie beside him on a mat on the veranda and tell him stories. She made sure he had the most substantial piece of meat when there was meat in their evening meal. Little was asked of him in the household chores. She brought a nephew of hers to assist in the house, making it even easier to relieve Clem of tasks. She didn't ignore the other children at all; she just made clear to everyone that her oldest was exceptional.

In addition to caring for the family and the home, Mama joined Papa as they became avid churchgoers in Onitsha. Although Papa presented himself as the leader in the family's religious life, I suspect Mama was more influential than he acknowledged or perhaps realized.

She devoted herself ever more seriously to church in the days when her children were growing up. The nearby Anglican Church, St. Andrew's, welcomed her and her husband. It was not only her spiritual home but also a prominent social gathering place. She became a leader in the women's guild. She made sure her growing brood of children and the relatives living with them were clean and neatly dressed every Sunday as they accompanied her and Papa to the service. When they were in the village, they attended St. James, the church opposite the market.

Despite the time I spent with Mama, I never fully understood her relationship with Papa's family, her in-laws. On the surface, she seemed to get along with them, but I can count on one hand the number of times I saw her in Ejike's compound, next door to ours. She did not even go there to spend time with Obele, Ejike's wife, who outranked her in seniority in the family, while I was at Obele's often. I suspect she carried a lifelong resentment toward Ejike for being the older brother who had refused to give land to Papa.

That was not her only grudge. One day while we were in the village during the war, she surprised me with a bitter comment about Jonathan. He had been in England when the war started, and several people had advised him to remain there. Mama thought he should come home to help. Toward the end of the war, he did come back to Biafra. As a priest, he was asked to help with relief supplies for the refugees in the town. Mama believed he could have given her a more significant share from his stock.

Her bitterness toward Jonathan went further back, I learned. In her mind, he never expressed enough gratitude for Papa's support in educating him. After all, Papa was the one who had insisted Jonathan attend school against the wishes of his father. Papa had paid his primary and secondary school fees. When Jonathan became a priest, married Beattie, and was posted to a church in the hinterlands of Onitsha, they took Clem's younger brother Geoffrey as their servant, cementing family ties, as Mama saw it.

Clem filled me in on the story. "Jonathan's mother died when he was young. His father, Ejike, and his stepmother, Obele, were not educated or adventurous. They would not have traveled to visit him. My parents treated him like a son when he was younger. Once he married, they visited him from time to time, taking yams and other gifts."

"What was wrong with that?" I said. "Weren't they subsisting on a beginning priest's salary? Surely they could have used the help."

"I think Mama's attitude as the person 'in charge,' acting in place of Jonathan's mother, annoyed his wife, Beattie, who said they were coming to spy!"

In 1975 Jonathan was consecrated as a bishop. Clem and I went to Onitsha for the event and to the Anglican cathedral with Clem's parents. After the service, Mama did not say that it was fulfilling to see our relative become a recognized leader in the Anglican Church of Nigeria. Instead, she commented that Jonathan had not mentioned Papa when he thanked those who had helped him. Clem believes that this event—together with the deterioration of the relationship between the two women, Beattie and Mama—contributed to Mama and Papa's decision to leave the Anglican Church and join an evangelical religion.

Mama continued to be my teacher and mentor in Igbo ways, although we sometimes quarreled over my commitment to Western customs. She thought it strange that I wanted the children to sleep on their own in a separate room from us while they were still little. Today I believe she and others have the right idea. It no longer makes sense to me to isolate small children. But in *the 1960s and early '70s I was committed to* Dr. Spock's Baby and Child Care, the "bible"

for new mothers in the US. I read it faithfully.

She took me to meetings of the *ndi anutara di*, or women married into the family, and made sure I knew how to behave. One day during the Christmas holidays in 1974, we were on the veranda at the side of the house. She was grinding *ugu* to remove the thin shells so that she could cook the delicious *ugu* porridge. "Did you know that Isabel's husband died? She's one of our ndi anutara di. We will call on her this afternoon."

"Where will he be buried?" I said.

"Where else?" I was surprised at her answer; clearly, she thought it was obvious. "He was already buried in their compound."

"Will you be buried in our compound when you die?" I said. I remembered reading or hearing that a family will sometimes return a woman's body to her home of origin. I thought her body might be taken to Agulu; my question was in earnest.

"Of course," she said. "And so will you."

I had endured the lack of electricity and running water during the war a few years earlier. But now it was getting on my nerves even though we stayed for only a couple of weeks at Christmastime. "I don't want to be buried where there's no light and no water. I will ask our children to take me somewhere more comfortable."

"You won't have a choice," she said, though she smiled at my attempt at a joke.

Later that day we went to the home of the bereaved woman. I put on my best dress and shoes. Mama wore a brocade wrapper, white blouse, and elegant satin head tie.

She led me along the path to the house of mourning. We had an idle conversation. But as soon as anyone in the grief-stricken compound could see us, she began crying. I realized this was a show and nearly smiled at her ability to be sad on cue! However, I had to follow suit. I did not cry—that would have been excessive for me—but I did put on an expression of sadness. We entered the compound and offered our condolences to the widow, seated on a mat in front of the house. We spoke to the man's brothers who were sitting nearby. One of the mourners directed us to the *umuada,* the women of the family, who kept a few of their members present during the mourning period. Then we greeted the ndi anutara di, the group we shared with the widow.

At each step, I imitated what Mama said and did. Finally, we took our seats with others who had come to observe the occasion. We were each given a drink, and after half an hour, Mama said we could go. She showed no sign of sorrow as we walked back home. She was an excellent teacher in many Igbo customs for me, including how to behave at the home of a newly widowed woman!

# 14

## PAPA'S DEATH

JUST FIVE YEARS AFTER MAMA had instructed me on the proper behavior for a widow, she became the widow. In 1979 Clem and I were in London with the children for a couple of weeks' holiday. Two days before we were due to return, Clem's cousin called.

I handed the phone to Clem, surprised at a call from Jonathan. Clem was on guard immediately. I watched his face as he listened. When I saw the stricken look, I took back the phone, which he was holding away from his body.

"Cathy, I called to tell Clement that his father has died," Jonathan said. "You have to come back right away. We cannot make any decisions until you are here."

I was able to change our flights, and we returned to Nigeria that night. We drove to the village the next day. "Do you remember the first question Mama asked when we arrived from London after Papa's death?" Clem said when I asked him to help me remember these events.

"No, I don't. What was it?"

"She wanted to know whether Jonathan should be the one to bury him. 'He appeared from nowhere and expected to conduct the funeral,' she said. 'I said we had to wait for you. But I do not think he should be the one, not after the way he treated us.'"

Clem reminded me of his reply then. "There's no question about it. The religion Papa was following when he died, that religious leader will bury him." Clem had spoken quickly and made the decision seem natural. But he had replied in the heat of the moment, and he, a devoted Anglican, wanted at least part of the service to be the familiar Anglican ritual. Could he persuade his mother to accept a role for Jonathan, who was, after all, a bishop?

The question of which religious leader should perform the funeral was only one of a series of difficulties that confronted the family. Other customs were in contention, fueled by religious differences. The evangelical church that Papa and Mama had joined told its followers that widows should not shave their heads. Mama was refusing to let the umuada carry out this tradition.

"My pastor says I should not follow this pagan custom," she insisted. But the umuada, keepers of tradition, proved to be stronger. "We will not allow anyone to enter the compound for this funeral if she does not follow our tradition," they said. I left the village for a few hours, and when I returned, her head was shaved.

Just as her mother-in-law, Nogem, had done so many years earlier, she had to sit on the ground for twenty-eight days, seven Igbo market weeks, to show her sorrow. Her townswomen surrounded her. She was not allowed to see her husband's body even when it was lowered into the ground. People came to commiserate with her, but otherwise, visitors were not to see her eat, sleep, or relieve herself. Strange and cruel customs, I thought.

At first, Clem supported Mama's wish to have her evangelical pastor perform the service. Clem's brother Geoffrey and his sister Grace were determined to bring their own evangelical preachers for the funeral ceremony. Then, on reflection, Clem decided that the funeral should be a traditional Anglican service. In the end, it was a combination. The evangelicals preached from their religious beliefs, Grace sang a song from her church, Geoffrey spoke, and Jonathan performed the last rites over the body as it was buried in our compound.

The funeral and surrounding events were a microcosm of the trends and influences circling in Nigeria at the time. Christianity had made tremendous strides, educating millions of Nigerian children, including Clem, his siblings, and his cousins. There was improved health care, and leprosy was much less of a threat. Papa had died of heart failure, a more "modern" disease.

Earlier customs that affected some widows included expulsion from her husband's home or a forced marriage to a younger brother-in-law. But with the passage of time and the influence of the churches, these practices had become rare. Besides, Mama was past the age of being wanted by a younger brother. With her grown sons, no one dared to think of threatening her with dispossession.

As I reflect on Mama and her hostile attitude toward Jonathan and Papa's other relatives, I wonder if there was a competition long ago over whose relatives would get an education. Perhaps she wanted Papa to pay for her relatives to attend school instead of his nephews. I also wonder if she remembered that Jonathan had been their emissary who persuaded Clement to return home. She might have dropped her grudge had she recalled that.

A few days ago, I was telling Clem what I had written about Mama's early schooling. He had forgotten that she'd gone to school as a child, but he reminded me of what I had forgotten. "When I came back from the UK, she was more assertive, more confident, and a leader in the church women's group in Onitsha," he said. He attributed the change to literacy classes that she had attended while he was away.

Mama was also a force at the annual church bazaar in the village. She would leave early in the day to help in the preparations, which included setting up chairs and tables, awnings, and sound systems. There was also cooking. "Open the plate" was the phrase used for paying for what one of your relatives or friends had cooked. When we arrived at the bazaar later in the day, and the bidding was underway, I would bid on a few items that appealed to me. I bought some lovely George cloth at the auction one year, and I always had to "open the plate," that is, bid on the items cooked by Mama and Obele.

Then three years after Papa died, Mama succumbed to cancer. She had begun complaining about a pain in her stomach or abdomen. Clem asked her to go to Iyienu, the well-run hospital nearby, which had been started many decades earlier by missionaries. She did go, but the doctors did not diagnose her cancer. A few months later, she went back. This time they found the tumor. Clem encouraged her to go to Benin, where Grace, the next-to-last of the seven children, lived. She had become a nurse, or as Nigerians say, a nursing sister. Mama went to her, but Grace, supported by Geoffrey, the brother just senior to her, encouraged prayer as a solution to her pain.

By the time the cancer was advanced, Geoffrey, a professor of medicine at Ahmadu Bello University Teaching Hospital in Zaria, northern Nigeria, admitted her there.. When I spoke with him about cancer, he intimated that he thought someone had put a curse or used witchcraft on Mama. "She has cancer. That's what is wrong with her, not a curse," I said.

"But we don't know what causes cancer, do we?" he said. "It can be witchcraft, sent by someone who wants to harm her, that makes cancer appear."

"Did you hear what Geoffrey said?" I was not sure my husband had heard his brother's words.

"Yes, I heard," Clem said. "I guess being a professor of medicine doesn't give you all the knowledge it should!" But my brother-in-law Geoffrey is by no means alone in his opinions. Even today, there are frequent stories in the Nigerian media about what witches have done to their victims.

Mama's funeral was quieter than Papa's had been. All our umunna came to mourn her. We had an evangelical preacher again, at the behest of Godwin, Geoffrey, and Grace. Clem still insisted on Jonathan being the one to administer the final rites, and Mama was laid to rest next to her husband.

Our children remember her with affection and Papa with a mixture of fear and fondness. More important to my husband is that they know they are part of the chain of the Onyemelukwe family, of the umunna, the village, and the town. He reminds them from time to time of the meaning of the name Onyemelukwe.

Of equal importance to Clem is that they understand the significance of owning land and being able to pass it on. He finds it nearly impossible to imagine that our sons do not seem bothered about property in the village. They know they will inherit the plot where we now have our house. But will they have to share it? Will they ever go to the village when we are not there?

In the mid-1990s, we thought we had found a solution to the problem of dividing a small space between our two sons. It arose from events that had occurred many decades earlier.

# 15

## THE CURSED LAND

ONE MORNING IN APRIL 1944, Papa took his machete and hoe to his new plot of land a half mile from his house. It was the start of the rainy season and the time for planting. With proper preparation, enough care, and the right amount of rain, he would have plenty of yams this year. Even though he did not stay in the village, he would be there often enough to check the progress. His younger brother who did stay at home could look after the crop when he was away.

The land had lain fallow for at least two years. His first task was to clear the area where he would plant. Then he would build the three-foot-high mounds, three feet apart, where he would place the seed yams. He used his hoe, a metal blade attached to a wooden stick, and dug, pulling out the weeds covering the ground. As he worked, he thought about whom he would ask for the extra seed yams he'd need. He would be able to repay the loan after the harvest.

He thought about the chief of the town, Igwe Ofomata, who had given Papa this large plot, nearly an acre, because of Papa's support during the chieftaincy selection a year earlier. Another family, from another of Nanka's seven villages, had wanted the chieftaincy for their own, but they had been unable to rally enough followers in the contest. Yes, that's the person he would ask for the seed yams.

Though Papa was a Christian, he silently praised Ani, the Igbo god of land, and asked for her help as he loosened the soil. He stopped every few minutes to wipe his brow and shake off the sweat from his hand. He had worked for nearly three hours when the rain clouds appeared. The first drops of rain hit the ground. He kept going, determined to clear at least one more row.

Out of the corner of his eye, he spotted a cloud of mist rising from the rows he had cleared. He had never seen anything like it before. Was Ani sending him a message? The mist grew denser and seemed to follow him. He dropped the hoe in horror as he remembered the words that had been hurled at him a few days earlier.

"The land is not for you. If you try to farm this land, you will die."

A younger half-brother of the chief had threatened Papa, proclaiming the land was cursed. Papa suspected the younger man wanted to give the land to someone else.

He grabbed the hoe and ran. He looked back once. The mist was still there and was growing more significant as the rain fell harder. He increased his speed and did not stop until he was far from the field.

When he reached home, his wife said, *"O gini?* What has happened? You look frightened."

*"Onwero.* It's nothing. I came home because of the rain." He could not explain that he had been frightened by a mist. Nor did he tell her he had left his machete in the field.

The rain stopped overnight, so the next morning he ventured back to the field, trying to put out of his mind the strange haze that he had seen the day before. He prepared more rows, stopped to eat the lunch his wife had sent with him, and went back to work. An hour later the rain started again. Soon the mist appeared, denser than the prior day's. He grabbed his hoe and machete and fled.

He would not go back. Convinced that the curse was too high a threat to his life, he gave up his dream of a more abundant harvest. He and his family would make do with the small plot of land behind his house. He would supplement what he grew there with what they could buy or trade with his proceeds from the palm oil business in Onitsha.

The field returned to its fallow state. Five years later, when he walked by the area on his way to a traditional wedding, he noticed that someone was cultivating yams in part of the field. He asked members of the Igwe's family about the land.

One of the younger half-brothers answered him. "We have given the land to Ralph. He served our family for many years, and we gave him his freedom and the land."

Remembering how frightened he had been by the strange mist, Papa did not argue.

When Papa died in 1979, he took the mystery of the land and its curse with him. We would never have known about the property if not for an offhand remark by Clem's cousin Jonathan.

One morning during the Christmas holidays in 1994, we were with Jonathan, seated upstairs in the parlor of his house in the village. It was a grand edifice, as befitted his role as bishop on the Niger in the Anglican Church. He and his wife, Beattie, had furnished their village home with overstuffed armchairs, side tables, and a coffee table. An impressive illustrated Bible and at least a dozen event invitations were on the table. It was the day before New Year's Eve, a rare day of rest for the bishop, who had many weddings, funerals, and other events at which he would officiate during the holidays.

"What are you doing with the land your father left?" Jonathan said.

"What land?" Clem said. "All the land Papa left me is gone. He told me to give my two brothers their own plots. I've done that. We have our compound, just beyond the wall, which will go to my sons."

"Your father had another piece of land by the chief's compound," Jonathan said. "It's large, and you should take possession of it."

The addition of a new piece of land would solve the problem Clem and I face with two sons. Land is the most valuable commodity in densely populated Igbo territory. For countless generations, fathers have passed land down to their sons. By the time Jonathan told us about the large plot of land that we apparently owned but had not claimed, I had become enough like an Igbo wife to understand the need.

Without land, an Igbo man is incomplete. By custom, he may stay in his father's compound until he has his own place. He can never be evicted, but no Igbo man wants to live forever in the shadow of his father or older brother.

Land has spiritual significance as well as material. It "serves as a link between the living, the dead and the unborn . . . that binds generations past, present and future together. The living members of African societies hold that ancestral land handed down to them by the dead in trust for the future members. . . . That is why every Igbo man struggles to own land."[6]

"Can you take us to see it?" I said.

"We can go now," Jonathan said. We called our driver, climbed into our Mercedes, and off we went. I knew where the chief's compound was, of course. But Jonathan directed the driver to turn left on an unpaved road just before it. Less than a quarter mile along the way, Jonathan told the driver to stop.

"It's here," he said, pointing to the plot on our right. We got out and walked onto a field mostly filled with weeds. There were no buildings, though we could see that someone was farming a small portion of it. It was more than twice as large as the property where we have our house. It would undoubtedly alleviate our problem of dividing land between our sons. There was no fence or other marking of ownership.

That afternoon Clem sent a message to Japhet, a son of the chief who had given the land to Papa. In the evening Japhet came to our house. I brought out the required kola nut to welcome him. Then I offered him a cold Star beer and called the steward to bring it out, take off the cap, and pour the first glass.

Clem explained that we had just learned about the land that very morning. "My cousin Jonathan remembers that the land was given to my father many decades ago. But Papa never farmed it or built on it," Clem said.

"Yes, we know the land belongs to you," Japhet said. "I remember that my father told me the story. But we could not give it to you because there is an ongoing dispute within the family over the ownership."

Japhet explained that his father, the chief, had several wives. As often happens, the sons of the different wives quarreled over ownership and inheritance. Since Papa had not farmed the land or demonstrated his ownership, one of Japhet's half-brothers had given the property to the former slave called

Ralph. "Ralph's son is now farming on it," Japhet said.

He poured a second glass of the beer. "We are suing Ralph's son to re-claim the land," he continued. "We are sure the case will be settled soon, and the land will come back to us, and we can pass it on to you. But we are stalled right now because it is proving difficult to pay the lawyer's fees."

I wondered why he had never contacted us if he knew the land belonged to us, as he said. I decided this was not the time to ask him whether he would ever have told us about it if we had not learned the story from Jonathan!

"Send your lawyer to me," Clem said. "I would like him to tell me about the case." Japhet finished his beer and said he would contact the lawyer the next morning.

The next afternoon the lawyer came with Japhet to our house. After in-troductions, the lawyer pulled a stack of soiled papers from his battered brief-case. He explained the status of the case.

"I have presented the case, and it is before the district court," he said. He expected a hearing in the next few months. He suggested Clem join the case as a litigant and sign an agreement with Japhet stating that when the case settled, the land would be ours. Japhet asked if Clem could take over paying the law-yer. It seemed clear we had little choice if we wanted the land, and we agreed.

We told our sons about the land. Clem went so far as to ask our older son, who had first rights, to decide if he wanted our current compound or the new property. He chose the existing space. Clem told our younger son the new land would be his.

A few months later we heard that the case was decided in our favor. We were ready to erect a small wall around the property. But our excitement was dampened when Ralph's son filed an appeal. Again, Japhet and his lawyer were sure our side would win. And we did. But Ralph's son filed another motion. The case is now before the Supreme Court. It has been there since 2006.

Jonathan had not known why Papa never took possession of the land. During conversations with Japhet and others in the chief's family, we learned the story of the curse and mysterious fog. Papa had decided the land was not worth his life. He was so frightened he never even told Clem that he owned the land. Perhaps he had forgotten about it.

When I told a friend in the US about this case, she said, "Isn't there a deed?" Funny how a standard question seems so abnormal in the setting of a Nigerian village.

There was no deed. But there are traditions that govern land matters. Among the Igbo, land exchange is accompanied by *ntu na ogwugwu,* or "gathering of witnesses." When land is passed from one family to another, people from each side must be present. They may be family members, but there will also be elders and clan leaders. The chief is told and may be present. There are speeches, stories, laughter, and drinking. Gifts of palm wine, yams, and goats are offered by the family receiving the land. The collective knowledge that the land exchange took place is the "deed." Anyone present can be called upon to testify that the transfer took place. And their descendants are also responsible for holding the knowledge.

Jonathan had told us and the lawyer that he was present at the ntu na ogwugwu as a young person. His brother Emmanuel was also there. "Then why wasn't their testimony enough to convince the court?" I asked. "How could an appeal be allowed?"

"Because the other side also claimed to have held an ntu na ogwugwu when they acquired the land. And they had witnesses too."

When we examined the documents, we were convinced that ours was the earlier claim and should have precedence. But the fact that it was earlier was still not enough. Since Clem's father had not taken over the land, the other party claimed, the property was still in possession of the chief's family. The dissidents in the family could and did give it away to Ralph. No one with knowledge of the ntu na ogwugwu stepped forward to prevent it, Ralph's son claimed.

We held a strategy session with the lawyer during our 2008 Christmas holidays in the village, fourteen years after learning about the land. Clem's cousin Emmanuel, the other living relative who had been at the ndi ogwugwu, was with us. This time we sat in our parlor, in our own overstuffed armchairs. We had run the generator in the morning, so we had cold beer. Now the electricity was off, and the fan was idle. But with the Harmattan, the heat was not extreme. Emmanuel drank half his Star beer and then revealed a hitherto unknown fact.

"Ralph's son says he owns the land because the dissident faction of the chief's family gave it to his father," Emma said. "He names witnesses who were present at the ntu na ogwugwu ceremony when the land was turned over to them."

We nodded in agreement—that was what the lawyer had told us.

"But this proves his case is false," Emmanuel said. "Ralph was osu, from a slave family. When owners gave land to a slave, there was no ntu na ogwugwu ceremony. It is like giving land within the family. His claim cannot be true."

I was excited about this valuable new knowledge. "This proves Ralph's son is lying," I said. "Surely now we will win."

"I do not think it is wise to use this evidence before the Supreme Court," the lawyer said.

"Why?" I asked.

"One of the judges may be from an osu family and could be offended at having this information presented."

Understanding the layers of the case is like peeling an onion. There was never a deed; such documents did not exist at the time. The ceremony by itself is insufficient because the opponents also held one. We cannot use the truth about who performed the ntu na ogwugwu ceremony because one of the justices may be osu.

"But there is a law from even before Nigerian independence that forbids discrimination based on osu, isn't there?" I said. I recalled looking it up once.

"Yes," the lawyer admitted. "There is a law. But a law cannot remove prejudice. In fact, that law could be used as a basis to forbid using our evidence about the osu status."

Will we ever get the land? I give it a 50 percent chance. Yet land ownership is such a significant part of Igbo life that we cannot give up. It feels as if we are repeating the struggle Papa faced with his older brother over the land question.

Land continues to be both a uniting and dividing factor within families, clans, and villages. Today Igboland has a population density of 350 to 1,000 people per square mile, and "could be the most densely populated area in Africa after the Nile Valley."[7] No wonder the land question is of critical importance. A man's inheritance, his land, solidifies his place in the community. Because he has land, he has rights and dignity. His land ties him to his home. An Igbo man without land is like a man without a home.

We are reasonably sure that our sons will never live in the village. But I have come to agree with my husband that they should have their own land. They are Igbo men after all. For Clem, even though he's now American, westernized, and educated, there is no doubt that land ownership is critically important.

And what about the mysterious mist?

Recently, with the internet to provide answers, I found what could be the truth. The compound carbonate, when it interacts with water or other liquids, gives off bubbles. Think of bicarbonate of soda, or our fizzy carbonated drinks. Whoever did not wish Clem's father to own the land would have placed carbonate in the soil, probably following the advice of a native doctor, who would have known the effect. When Papa began planting in the rainy season, there was the frightening mist!

# 16

## NIGERWIVES AS A LIFELINE

"YOU SAVED MY LIFE." An American woman of about forty with short brown hair, wearing a little eyeliner and mascara, was addressing me. "I met my husband eighteen years ago. We married a year later. He wanted to return to his home in Nigeria and I came with him. I had no idea what I was getting into. I was going crazy in the first year. I nearly left," she said. "Then I got pregnant."

I reached out to touch her arm as she continued. "One day, before my first baby was born, I met Brenda in the market, and she brought me to Nigerwives."

"What's your name?" I said, leaning forward but still unable to read her nametag without my glasses.

"Michelle. I've met so many friends here. They're like family to me. They've even helped me understand my husband. I'm glad I stayed."

It was Saturday, January 7, 2017. I was at the monthly meeting of Nigerwives, the organization for foreign wives of Nigerian men. The day before, I had returned to Lagos after spending Christmas and New Year's in my husband's village in eastern Nigeria. I had called my friend and co-Nigerwife Millicent on Saturday morning to confirm the time and ask her the location.

"Yes, the meeting is the first Saturday of the month at two p.m.," she said. "Have you really forgotten?"

"I've been away a long time," I said. "Where is it? Are you going?"

"It's at Corona School, Ikoyi. I can't go today but I'm sure Doris Fafunwa will be there," Millicent said. "She'll be very happy to see you!"

I asked the address, told our son, in whose home we were staying, that I would need the driver, and contemplated my wardrobe.

Most of my clothes were still in the suitcase, many in need of washing. I did not bother to unpack since I was leaving the next evening to go back to the US. Maybe the red "lace," as the industrial embroidered fabric is called in Nigeria, I had worn for our fiftieth anniversary three years earlier? It was festive. No, I thought, too flamboyant. Should I wear the white pants, white silk blouse, and red linen jacket with a mandarin collar that I had worn to the Anglican cathedral before Christmas? Or the dressy black-and-sparkly-gold skirt I had put on for the chieftaincy installation for Clem's brother and his wife? I finally decided on jeans, a green-and-white-striped cotton blouse, the tan fitted jacket I had bought at the Westport Woman's Club Clothing Sale, and a green paisley silk scarf.

As I was checking my handbag and getting ready to leave, Millicent called. "I've just learned that the meeting is not at Corona School. There are repairs going on," she said. "I don't know if it's taking place somewhere else."

"I'm all dressed and ready to go!" I said. "I'll just drive over there and see if anyone else shows up. Even if we can't get into the school, we could find someplace to gather." I made sure I had plenty of my bookmarks and cards to give out.

Hyacinth, the driver, knew the way to Corona School. Like many roads in the former capital, Queens Drive had been renamed. Now it bore the name of a former Oba, traditional chief, of Lagos.

I was familiar with the area too. When I was a newly arrived Peace Corps volunteer in 1962, I had attended a cocktail party at the home of the minister of education, Igwe Aja-Nwachukwu, on the corner of Queens Drive and Awolowo Road. Passing the location filled me with memories of Peace Corps friends. I knew Dave had died and I had seen Bob at a recent reunion, but what about my good friend Art? I wondered about my students from long ago—where were they? Scattered around the world most likely. I knew only two, one who works for my husband in Nigeria, and another who is an architect in Lagos.

The driver pulled over by the high steel gate of Corona School. There were no cars around. The gate was padlocked. It was barely two p.m., so I waited five minutes, thinking other women might drive up. No one did. I rattled the gate. "Hello! Anyone there?" I shouted several times. Hyacinth got out of the car and called too. We were about to give up. Then a sleepy-looking heavyset man in a uniform walked slowly toward the gate.

"I'm looking for the meeting," I said when he reached us.

"The school repair nevah finish," he said. "Dem cancel meeting. Dem say go this place." He held out a scrap of paper through the bars of the gate.

"Hyacinth, can you read this?" I said, not having my glasses on.

"It's in Ikoyi," he said. "On Raymond Njoku, not far." We climbed back into the vehicle. Hyacinth turned around and we were on our way, relieved to know there really was a meeting!

More memories flooded in as we drove. Several friends had lived on Raymond Njoku in the 1970s and '80s: Mike and Norma Briggs, Richard Gamble and his wife, Fran, her sister Mary Rowe and her husband, and Tondalaya and Ron Gillespie from TechnoServe. In 1977, our daughter, Beth, had prepared a play at a friend's house on Raymond Njoku. When I arrived late for her performance, she was in tears. I felt miserable.

Around two thirty Hyacinth dropped me off near the entrance. Clearly plenty of people had known where to go. At least twenty-five women were crowded into the living room of the hostess. I introduced myself to a couple of women who were standing near the door. Doris saw me from across the room.

"Hey, Cathy, I'm so glad to see you!" she said. "I didn't know you were in the country." I made my way to her. We exchanged news about our children and grandchildren. I said with a sheepish smile, "I nearly did not come! Millicent called me just before I left the house to say Corona School was not open and she didn't know whether or where there was a meeting."

"How did you find us?" Doris said. I explained. "Isn't it typical?" she said. "We keep telling new Nigerwives not to give up too easily! You're such a good example." Indeed, one of the factors that bind Nigerwives together is how we learn to respond to obstacles.

The president stood to start the meeting. I felt completely at home as I listened to the announcements. "The election for new officers takes place in February," she said. "Be sure to come to the next meeting, which we expect to be back at Corona School, so you can vote."

She continued, "The annual Small World fundraising event is on February eighth. We need volunteers to cook, serve, and take tickets. The annual general meeting of Nigerwives from the twenty branches all over the country will be in Ibadan in March. Women from Lagos need to be present to represent us. Members of the Ibadan branch will host guests overnight."

Doris stood to add a comment. "Past general meetings have been wonderful, with entertainment and programs. The hosts usually find speakers who are local celebrities or government officials. Last year we had an excursion to interesting sites."

This was exciting news! Twenty branches, and an annual general meeting, the most recent of many! When my friends and I founded Nigerwives in 1978, we had not known it would survive and thrive to be so strong. When I left Nigeria for the US in 1986, there were five Lagos "area" groups and branches in three or four other cities. I was proud of the organization I had helped establish.

Then Doris rose again to speak. "I want to introduce someone," she said. "Cathy is visiting from the US. She was one of the founders of Nigerwives thirty-eight years ago. She drafted our first bylaws."

I stood up and addressed the women in the room. "Doris was also one of the founders," I said, putting my arm around her. "I'm so pleased to be here today. I'm really thrilled to see so many of you, including a few women I remember!" I pointed to two women seated in front of me on the sofa who looked familiar.

After the announcements, women stayed to socialize. I spoke with several others besides Michelle. "Nigerwives has been really important in helping me learn how to adjust," one said. Another told me, "I would not have stayed in the country if not for Nigerwives." Their words reminded me again of the importance of Nigerwives in helping foreign women become part of Nigerian society and part of their husbands' families. The organization was clearly fulfilling its mission, stated in every newsletter and on the website: "to assist the integration of foreign wives [of Nigerians] into the Nigerian society."

Jean Obi, the third of the co-founders of Nigerwives, was not at the January 2017 meeting; she was in England spending the holidays with her married daughters. But her presence was felt. In the 1970s, when she worked at the Nigerian Exams Council, she had become aware of the plight of blind students. There was no accommodation for them to take the national school certificate and university entrance exams, but many were eager to advance their education. Jean learned Braille, convinced the Exams Council to administer Braille tests, and coded the tests herself.

In the years since, the project has grown and thrived, just like Nigerwives. There is now a Nigerwives Braille Book Production Centre, with many Nigerwives assisting in book production and distribution. Members of Nigerwives participate in reading to visually impaired students. In their adoption of the Braille book project, individual Nigerwives behave like members of a Nigerian village or tribal group. This is our own. We must support it. We will give it our energy and our commitment to make it succeed.

Unlike the Braille project, which Jean created in response to the needs of disadvantaged Nigerians, we created Nigerwives to serve our own needs. As I saw at the 2017 meeting, Nigerwives continues to fulfill its mission to be a resource and support system for foreign wives of Nigerians. Our original focus, however—what drew us together to start the organization—was financial.

There were restrictions on buying foreign exchange. A person could not convert Nigerian pounds to dollars or another currency in unlimited amounts. If you were traveling overseas, you could take your ticket and passport to the bank, where you could buy a limited amount of foreign currency. Employees of foreign companies in Nigeria had portions of their salaries paid in their home countries. Peace Corps did this, so when I concluded my service, I received a payment at home.

After Clem and I married in December 1964, I followed the Nigerian rules that allowed foreign wives of Nigerian men to remit 50 percent of their income to their home countries. When I went to the US for a year during Nigeria's civil war, the funds I had sent were helpful. When the war ended I returned to the reunited Nigeria and to my job at the American International School and resumed the foreign exchange transfers.

In 1977 the government faced a financial crisis with a drop in the price of oil. They searched for any means of preserving foreign exchange. Someone in the Ministry of Finance decided that foreign wives of Nigerian men were an easy target. We were suddenly told we could remit only 10 percent of our salaries to our home countries. I was furious. This was completely unacceptable!

During the next few months Jean, Doris, and I began planning. We were soon joined by Josephine. Soon we had an organization and with the help of influential husbands we achieved our goal of restoring the 50 percent home remittance.

We did not forget our mission—to help foreign wives integrate in Nigerian society. How we raised our children was a frequent topic of conversation. In 1983 we decided to hold a seminar about rearing our children in Nigeria. Doris and I agreed to organize it. We decided that the best format would be a panel of speakers with a range of opinions and experiences.

"Who should be on the panel?" Doris said.

"We want a mix of countries that the women are from, don't we?" I said. "And perhaps a mix of our husbands' tribes? We could start with you, an American with a Yoruba husband, and Josephine. She's British, and her husband is Hausa. We could ask Jean, also British and married to an Igbo, and Joan, who is herself West Indian, married to an Igbo."

We thought about questions the panel members should address. "How different is your approach to discipline from your husband's?" could be a question, I said.

"Is there anything you experienced growing up in your own country that your children do not get here?" Doris suggested. "And the opposite. What do your children learn here that they wouldn't get in your own country?"

"I wonder what the children would say," I said.

"Maybe we should ask them."

"Maybe they should be the panel members!" In a few minutes we had changed our focus. Our children were the ones who should be discussing the issues, not us mothers. One or two mothers could be the interviewers, inviting opinions from four or five of our children. We made a list of children between the ages of eight and eighteen who we thought would be good.

We asked two other women to join us for a second meeting to select the children we thought would be the most articulate and give us a range of gender, age, father's tribe, and mother's country of origin. We wrote out a list of questions. Then we thought about a title for the panel. "Lessons from Our Children" seemed right, but we wanted a descriptive word for the children. Mixed-race was wrong—many children had two Black parents. Double nationality was too cumbersome. Besides, a few parents had not given their children passports from the mother's country. Someone said, "'Half-caste' is what I've heard children called. But it sounds so hateful and demeaning."

"Let's get the children together and ask them what they call themselves," Barbara suggested. We divided up the task of contacting the mothers whose children we hoped would participate. We were able to gather five children two weeks later for a last planning session before we needed to get our publicity together.

"We've been debating what name to give you as a group," I said to the five children and teens. "We want to announce the title of the panel as 'Lessons from Our . . . Children.' How do you describe yourselves?"

They did not hesitate. "We're half-castes," they said. So that's what we called our seminar, "Lessons from Our Half-Caste Children." We had already secured a space to hold the event. By this time we had a newsletter, so we put an announcement in the next edition. We also sent notices to our two branches, in Onitsha and Kaduna, and invited their members to come.

The children were outspoken advocates for the advantages of being multicultural. Not one felt he or she had lost anything by being in Nigeria with parents from two different traditions. On the contrary, they believed they were richer for the experience of drawing on two backgrounds. They were clear that being half-caste was a mark of pride, not a derogatory term as we mothers had thought.

The latest newsletter I have is from May 2000. On the front page it says, "The President . . . is already planning this year's 'Nigerwives Annual Seminar!'" This issue also congratulated Jean Obi on the birth of her granddaughter and Doris Fafunwa for her travel to Vermont for her fiftieth high school reunion.

I found two other noteworthy announcements from perusing past Nigerwives newsletters. I had forgotten that I had sent a notice after our daughter's wedding! There it was, in the January 1993 issue. "Congratulations to Cathie [sic] Onyemelukwe and her husband, Clement, on the marriage of their daughter, Elizabeth, to Kelvin Raynard Garner," it says. "Cathie sent us a note with a clipping from the *New York Times* announcing the wedding which took place at the end of August last year at the Harvard Memorial Church. . . . The bride's uncle, The Rev. Jonathan Onyemelukwe, the Anglican Bishop of the Niger Diocese, officiated."

And there's more about our daughter's wedding! "Sheri Fafunwa [daughter of my co-founder Doris] and her husband, Okey, attended the wedding with their baby son Chibuike, as did Lamar Akpan, another 'Nigerkid.'" I recently reminded Okey, now a well-known author living in the US, that he and Sheri came to the wedding. He had forgotten, like I had! The connections we formed through Nigerwives are valuable and irreplaceable.

Also noteworthy is an announcement inviting Nigerwives to an event. "The President said she had received an invitation addressed to Nigerwives to attend the conferment of chieftaincy titles on our member, Megan Olusanya, and her husband [Professor Gabriel Olusanya] by the Ooni of Ife, at Ile-Ife, on Friday 18th September. It is hoped some members would be able to attend to support Megan." Several other Nigerwives have been given chieftaincy titles as well.

As we formed and fostered the organization, we were adapting some of the norms of Nigerian culture to our own situation. We had begun even in the first year to attend one another's important family events, such as children's christenings, baptisms, or naming ceremonies. Members continue to support one another at joyous events, such as weddings and chieftaincy conferment, but also at funerals, always providing a sense of community for foreign wives. During meetings and in gatherings outside our regular meeting times, we have supported each other with conversation and consolation. We all enlarged our circle of friends and acquaintances.

I had remained active in the American Women's Club (AWC) as we started Nigerwives. I persuaded a few other Nigerwives to attend AWC meetings, but the interests and needs of the two groups were not alike. I thought frequently how different my life was from those of most AWC members. They were in Nigeria for two or three years, sometimes longer, but would always return to the US. They were there to accompany their husbands. I wrote a few columns for the AWC newsletter about Nigerian customs, eager to share what I knew to help others feel at home. At one AWC meeting, I was complaining to another woman about my recent visit to the immigration office. "It would be a comedy scene if it weren't essential," I said. "Officialdom run amok, for sure!"

"I'm so glad my husband's company takes care of that. Doesn't your husband do it for you?" she said.

"Well, he probably would if I insisted. But he has his own company to run so I don't ask." It was a point of pride for me and other Nigerwives to know we could handle the Nigerian bureaucracy. I often commiserated with my friends Jean and Doris about this experience, as we had earlier about the home remittance. We faced the degrading requirement of needing a letter from our husbands to vouch for us, basically to invite us back to Nigeria, whenever we traveled out. With the letter we could get a reentry visa for every return and a residence permit that had to be renewed every time we got a new reentry visa.

The frequent trips to the immigration office in Lagos were horrific. You stood in line for half an hour or more. Then the person at the counter might say it was time for a lunch break. You thought you had all the correct papers, but the immigration officer would find something wrong. Your husband had written the wrong date for your travel in his "invitation" letter, so it did not match your ticket. Or you had only the ticket out and not the return ticket. Sometimes your file was missing, and you were told to come back another day. If all your paperwork was accepted, you were still told to come back in a few days to get your documents. You had to leave your passport. After seeing the chaos in the office, leaving the passport with them was frightening.

In 1983 Nigerwives took up the case of our needing new visas and residence permits every time we traveled out of the country. Again, we enlisted our husbands to take our letter of request to the proper ministry. When we achieved our goal, I was surprised to find the official notice was addressed to me as president of Nigerwives. The people at the immigration desk at the airport were not always up-to-date on regulations. For years afterward, Nigerwives members carried a copy of the letter, addressed to me, stapled in the back of their passports, stating that the residence permit was valid for the life of the passport.

Gradually the difficulties of life in Nigeria began to outweigh the advantages. My children were mostly away. I had been running my clothing company, Trinity House of Fashion, for five years. Each month making payroll was difficult. Managing my staff, keeping a generator running, and finding outlets for the clothing were all challenges.

In the summer of 1985 I accompanied our older son, Chinaku, to the American embassy in Lagos to look at catalogs of business schools in the US for him. As I read the course offerings, I was intrigued. I was amazed that one could study these subjects about running a business. Why was I struggling on my own to figure out how to turn a profit at my clothing company? Would it not be fascinating to learn about management ideas and the financial structure of companies? Chinaku did not apply, but I did!

# 17

## TAKING UP A NEW CHALLENGE: RETURN TO THE US

AFTER TWENTY-FOUR YEARS OF LIVING in Nigeria, the pull of community that had drawn me in and held me grew weaker. My husband was spending far more time out of the country than I was, yet it was his country. His parents, who had provided the strongest ties to his hometown of Nanka, were both dead. Our children were away. Chinaku was finishing his degree at the University of Benin in Nigeria and would be embarking on his own career. I did not expect him to live at home any longer. Our daughter, Beth, had already entered Mount Holyoke College in the US, my alma mater. Sam, our youngest, was in boarding school in Jos, Nigeria, six hundred miles away.

So in September 1986 I returned to the US for the two-year master's in public and private management, MPPM, now called an MBA, at Yale's School of Management (SOM). I have never returned to live in Nigeria. I miss the sense of community and connection we had in Nigerwives and even more strongly in my husband's family, village, and tribe.

When I entered the graduate program at Yale University in New Haven, Connecticut, in 1986, I experienced "reverse culture shock." This phenomenon is familiar to all Peace Corps volunteers and others who spend an extended amount of time in developing countries, or what we used to call "third world." It comes with an overwhelming sense of too much. The pace of life is too fast; the stores are too full of a confusing variety of available goods; there are too many channels of communication and too many people speaking too fast. The feeling is of bewilderment, of not having one's feet firmly planted.

I realized that for Clem's parents, the culture shock of learning about, then accepting, an American wife for their son must have been as great as mine on returning to the US. When Clem returned from England without a British wife, they were overjoyed. They had expected him to come to them to help him find an appropriate Igbo wife, just as Papa had done many years earlier. Or if not for them to find the wife, at least for them to participate. They knew his sister Monica was sending candidates to him. They hoped he would accept one of these, inform them so they could check out her family's suitability, and then pursue the traditional ceremonies. In the end, they accepted me fully and with love. I could likewise reacquaint myself with and become comfortable in the US.

I began to ponder the disparities between the US and my adopted home. How did we live our lives in Nigeria in ways that fostered such a strong sense of belonging? And why did Americans fail to foster the same sense? I knew there was no overarching American culture in the same way there is an Igbo culture. But the differences were stark.

Most striking was the ease with which my fellow students at SOM had abandoned former places of work or school and lived far from their families. Their lives were fluid. They had no fixed home and seemed to have few attachments. I likewise had abandoned my former work and lived far from my husband and children. But I knew I had that grounding. I and my children still belonged to Clem's family and clan, even though we were far away.

"Do you have any idea what he was talking about?" The woman walking beside me looked as puzzled as I felt.

"He could have been speaking Greek," she said. I was relieved that at least one other person had been as mystified by the finance professor's lecture as I was.

She had short dark curly hair framing a round face. I guessed she was in her thirties, older than the average student but not close to my forty-six years. We paused as we turned the corner to Donaldson Hall, the social center of the School of Management, with one long wall of glass looking out on a courtyard. The other side of the hall was lined with a comfortable seating area. A few students sat chatting.

"They must be second years," I said. "They look like they belong here."

It was Wednesday, September 10, 1986, my first full day of classes at the Yale School of Management. I had returned eight days earlier from twenty-four years of living in Nigeria. I was thrilled to be at Yale and eager to embrace my new life as a grad student. But had I overestimated my ability? If I couldn't understand my first lecture, how would I survive two years?

In my first week back in the US, I had bought and furnished a condo, purchased a car, and driven my daughter to Mount Holyoke College, where she was a sophomore. I had taken my son to enter the tenth grade at a boarding school near Boston.

I had missed the pre-course math session, which had been recommended for me. I had also missed the first day of classes. Now I was in a fog about the content of the first finance class. It would get worse!

I had apparently performed well enough on the GMAT and was attractive enough as a candidate to be accepted. At the welcome event the day before, I was one of six students the dean profiled to let us know what a brilliant class we were.

He had described me as a fashion designer, making me squirm in my seat. True, I had run Trinity House of Fashion for more than five years, but I didn't design anything. I relied on commercially available patterns, which I gave to my manager. He used them to cut the clothes in different sizes. But I had created and run the business in the difficult environment of a developing country.

Our entering class, the Yale School of Management Class of 1988, was about 170 strong. We were nearly half female. The youngest was twenty-one, the oldest forty-seven. There was one other former Peace Corps volunteer. A few people already had graduate degrees. One was a medical doctor.

After the welcome the day before, we were divided into two groups for "community building." That was the introduction to the Interpersonal and Group Behavior class, or IGB. From ten a.m. until three p.m., with a lunch break, forty-eight of us were together with an instructor.

Dr. Bena Kallick was the professor of my section. She introduced herself—PhD in psychology, adjunct faculty here at Yale's School of Organization and Management. She said, "This class, Interpersonal and Group Behavior, may be your most valuable class at SOM. You probably won't think so during this semester but remember what I'm saying in four or five years!"

Then she drew a large square on the blackboard. "This is the Johari window,"[8] she said. "It provides a way to help you understand yourself and your relationships with others. It was created by psychologists in 1955 so it's stood the test of time."

| | Johari Window | |
|---|---|---|
| | Known to Self | Not Known to Self |
| Known to Others | Arena | Blind Spot |
| Not Known to Others | Façade | Unknown |

She separated the square into four sections. "The Arena is the public area where you know yourself and others know you too. We will talk about other sections later."

She continued, "Choose another person to form a group of two, called a dyad. You may choose anyone in the room. Take your time. When you have chosen, introduce yourselves to each other."

I had no idea what to do. Would anyone choose me? Should I choose someone else? Who?

I looked to my right and saw a man who was not quite white and not black. He appeared a little older than the majority and a little less threatening than the twenty-something white men and women. He was still in his chair and seemed equally at sea. I turned with a smile. "Would you be my dyad partner?"

"My name is Bruce King," he said by way of answer. "I am from Wisconsin. I'm Oneida."

I gave him a questioning look.

"The Oneida are an eastern Native American tribe. We came from New York State originally. But now we live in other states too." He spoke slowly and thoughtfully. This was good. Twenty-four years in Nigeria had made being part of a tribe seem completely normal.

"I grew up in the Midwest," I said. "But I've lived in Nigeria since 1962. My husband is Igbo, the third-largest tribe."

Should I ask if he was married? I was not sure of protocol. He said nothing further.

"We have three children. I just drove my daughter to college in western Massachusetts and my son to tenth grade in boarding school near Boston."

Still he volunteered nothing. "Our older son is still in Nigeria working."

Then Bruce spoke. "I'm married. We have two children."

Most other conversations sounded a lot livelier than ours. We were saved from further silence when Bena spoke. "Now think of the Johari window. Tell your dyad partner something in the Façade area. It should be something significant about you that other people don't know. It will be a secret between the two of you."

I turned back to Bruce. "I've come to Yale to explore my options. I've been married for twenty-two years," I said. "We've drifted apart. My husband assumes I'll go back after two years. But I am not sure I want to stay married."

Bruce's secret was the opposite. "I'm worried that being in grad school might harm my marriage. My wife came with me to New Haven," he said. "I'll have to study a lot. I don't know whether this student life will pull us apart."

After each dyad had shared secrets, we were instructed to join another dyad. "Each person should introduce his or her dyad partner. Share information from the Arena area, not the Façade."

We did as she instructed. "I'm introducing Bruce King. He is from Wisconsin and is a member of the Oneida tribe. He is married with two children," I said. Sarah, with shoulder-length brown hair and a perky smile, introduced Bill. Then the men introduced Sarah and me. Although the introductions felt stilted, within a few minutes we were chatting easily. We talked about what we had been doing before coming to SOM, and where we had worked most recently. But we didn't share our secrets.

Bena told us to join another group of four. Three men, Jonathan, Dan, and Whitney, and one woman, Barbara, walked over to us. We repeated introductions. This self-selected group of eight people was our IGB group, a crucial part of the first semester. Three times a week we spent the IGB class time together, undertaking assignments to help us understand the dynamics of working in a group. We had readings, lectures, and many discussions.

Every couple of weeks someone in our group of eight would make a refer-ence to a TV show, popular movie, or event that I had never heard of or hadn't seen. My colleagues were surprised each time this happened, at least for the first few weeks. They could not believe that I was not familiar with *Star Wars, All in the Family,* and *Saturday Night Live.*

"You're like Rip Van Winkle," Sarah, age twenty-two, said. She added hastily, "I didn't mean you're old." But I understood. I was out of touch. No doubt I really was old to her—I had a son her age.

Our readings and class discussions were useful, but the real learning came from our group experience. We went through the semester without a clear leader of our group of eight. We could have shared leadership around different tasks and assignments, or even on different days. But we did not seem to know how to talk to one another honestly enough to do that. We were unable to address the challenge directly.

Some IGB groups became strong support systems for their participants. They formed study groups, shared class notes, and worked on class projects together. Members of some IGB groups became and have remained good friends, attending one another's significant life events.

Ours never became a cohesive group. We barely socialized, though I oc-casionally accompanied Barbara to dinner with a couple of other women. We did not study together or share information about other classes we were in. We did the assigned group tasks, such as observing and reporting on interactions between members of another group, but usually without enthusiasm. When the same group reported on us, they noticed that we did not seem well con-nected.

The experience was as strange for me as my first days in Nigeria had been twenty-four years earlier. I was adrift. I did not know the language, and the customs were strange to me. In the organizations I had helped lead, I was part of a group that faced common problems or lived in similar circum-stances amid difficulties. The basis of Nigerwives was to help women new to Nigerian culture understand their husband's, his family's, and the society's expectations and how to deal with them. Members of the American Women's Club all faced the challenge of living in a country where the customs were new and strange giving us a common purpose of joining together to confront the unknown.

In the US, at the Yale School of Management, I was back in the culture that honored individualism above all else. I had been brought up in this society, so it was not new, but I had been away from living surrounded by it. I learned again that in Western culture the emphasis is on the individual. Children are taught to think for themselves, develop their own interests, and stand up for their own rights.

I had become accustomed to the emphasis on community and belonging during my years in Nigeria. The contrast was stark. The IGB group that could have served as my community, easing me back into the culture of individualism, did not fulfill that function.

As the semester ended, we each had to write a paper describing the experience and our own role in the group. Bruce told me that he concluded he and I had relinquished what should have been our leadership roles. "I didn't speak up enough," Bruce said. "You could have been a leader, but others didn't seem to listen to you enough."

I was accustomed to leadership. I had founded and been the local and national president of Nigerwives. The American Women's Club in Lagos had elected me president too. I had run my own company for more than five years. But being in graduate school in the US, with so many capable people younger than I, was unsettling. I did not know how to be a leader for this group.

I was surprised that he felt the same way, though I quickly realized I shouldn't have been. The Oneida, like the Igbo, believe that age gives one the right to lead and have others listen. We were the oldest people in the group and should have assumed our rightful places.

Would the others have listened if we had spoken out more often and more forcefully? I do not know the answer, but if pushed, I would say no. Even though Bruce and I believed that age gave one the right to leadership, the rest of the group probably did not. Neither of us tested this.

IGB and the other classes were only part of my learning experience during the first semester. The early months of the fall semester held other surprises. In my second month, when I was at a restaurant with three classmates, I offered to pay for us all. I soon learned this was not acceptable. "If you pay for everyone, then another time someone else has to do that. Most of us are on tight budgets," Barbara said. "It's embarrassing to have you pay." We had to share the cost, generally figuring out what each person had ordered and paying just for our own, with tip added in.

The greatest surprise, however, came a few weeks later. I traveled to Nigeria with our son and daughter for the Christmas holidays. We had two weeks together in my husband's village of Nanka. I didn't come close to making up my mind about my future during that time. I didn't even try. I just relaxed and enjoyed being with our children, other extended family, and clan members in a setting I knew well. The shock came when I returned to Yale at the beginning of the second semester.

In my mailbox I found the report of my first semester's grades. I had barely paid attention to what the grading system was. I looked at the results and found that I had received "pass" in three courses and "proficient" in two. That seemed all right to me.

I went to the first two morning classes of the second semester. When I went back to my mailbox in the early afternoon, I found a notice asking me to report to the dean of students. I was a little worried, wondering if there was a problem with payment. I was sure I had sent the check for the second semester, as my husband and I had agreed.

The dean asked me to sit down in his office. He said, "You probably know why you are here."

"No, I don't," I said. "Was there a problem with the check?"

"No, your payment was made and will be refunded. Your grades in the first semester do not qualify you to continue. I'm very sorry, but you will have to leave the program."

"What?" I said. "I don't understand. I had 'pass' and 'proficient' marks in my courses. Nothing said I had failed."

He tried to explain the system. "The grade of 'pass' in a core course does not qualify for graduation credit. Having three 'pass' marks now means you cannot qualify unless you get 'proficient' or better in all the other core classes." I tried to understand but it made no sense. I couldn't help myself and started crying. "'Pass' really means you did not succeed," he said. "I'm very sorry. We should be able to help you find a place in another graduate program."

Through my tears I explained that Yale was a lifeline and I couldn't go anywhere else. I revealed the secret I had told Bruce and said my husband wouldn't pay for any other school.

I was told not to attend classes while the faculty discussed my case. I wrote a defense, saying, "It is unclear to me how a mark of pass really means fail." I found that there were two others, a woman from Lebanon who had become a friend and an outspoken Black American man, in the same situation. After three days of torment, the faculty decided to let the other woman and me stay in the program. The man had disappeared. We were told we had to take other "core" courses, including Political Science and Production, and get "proficient" marks in those to have the necessary credits to graduate. By the end of my second semester, the faculty had changed the requirements and the wording in the student handbook, so it became clear what the marks meant and what was required for graduation. And I had learned that even in a prestigious institution like Yale University there could be errors in communications. I became a little more patient about mistakes in Nigerian documents.

After I was accepted back into the program, I discovered that another friend who was doing a joint degree with nursing was in the same position. She too had to take all the remaining core courses and receive grades of "proficient" or better. The three of us worked hard for the remaining three semesters. In one of the more difficult classes, Production. I learned about critical path thinking and cost/benefit considerations. The final exam two weeks before graduation was as much a test of perseverance as it was of the knowledge I had acquired. But I succeeded, and the two others did as well.

What a change from my first day, when I was described as an exemplar of the kind of student SOM attracted! I nearly became the example of how to fail to graduate!

My two years as a student at Yale's School of Management strengthened my mind and my emotional resilience. I can discuss finance with our son, an expert in the field. I understand the importance of branding. I can draw a reasonable decision tree. I was enriched by the friendships and am still in touch with a few people from my student days. I have since learned that being a leader comes to me naturally in many settings. Today I can look back and understand better why I did not lead in my IGB group.

Bruce and I had shared our secret concerns about our marriages during the first day of IGB. Bruce stayed happily married and went back to Wisconsin with his wife and children. My uncertainty about my marriage did not end for another ten years. Until that time, I stayed mostly in the US, with Clem coming for visits.

After graduation I stayed in the New Haven area. Clem and I spent little time together. He could not in good conscience urge me to come back to Nigeria since he was rarely there. He did not seem interested in my life in the US. I visited him in London from time to time, and we all went to Nigeria together for Christmas in 1990 and 1992.

I had decided to bill myself as a consultant to small businesses to help them with international marketing. I understood the European business culture from experiences in Nigeria. Asia was not yet big on the scene, so my lack of knowledge in that sphere was not a hindrance. I had business cards printed, joined the Connecticut Venture Group to meet small-business owners, and prepared a brochure.

A few days after graduation I attended my high school reunion. Elwyn, a brilliant mathematician, had founded his own company. We talked during the reunion. I told him I had just completed my MBA and was ready to consult on international marketing, and he hired me! Two weeks later I flew to California at his expense. I spent a day at his company trying hard to understand the product well enough to talk about it to potential European buyers. My trip to Europe to contact potential customers was timed just right—I was in Berlin when the wall came down! I had been there in August 1961 when it went up, so this felt like an auspicious moment for me.

About this time Eileen moved into the condo next to mine. We became close friends during the year that followed. In 1993 she took a new job that required relocating. She asked me to come with her as she looked at houses in Westport, Connecticut. I had been thinking I would like to live nearer New York.

Eileen is thorough; she had researched the towns surrounding her new job, and she'd chosen Westport for its beach, its reputation as cultural and artistic, and its large Jewish population. Her realtor had shown her a few houses. She liked one along the road leading to the beach, a recently built, attractive gray bungalow. Together we walked through the property. She imagined her furniture in the house. We concluded our tour. "I think I will make an offer," she said. When we had parked in the driveway I had seen a house directly across the side road with a "For sale by owner" sign.

"Can we just stop in there for a couple of minutes?" I said. The house was the opposite of the one Eileen was considering. It was rustic-looking, ivy-covered, with wood frame windows, and barn doors for the basement entrance. We walked up stone steps to a patio and found the door. I knocked. The owner showed us around.

I fell in love with the house immediately. It was slightly run-down, with a rambling living room, small dining room, and a kitchen that probably had not been updated in decades. There was a central stairway leading up to three bedrooms, and a front porch that extended the width of the house and faced the main road. Somehow it had the look of home to me.

I called Clem and told him that I had found a house I wanted. He liked the idea that it was nearer New York than where I had been in New Haven. The town had a beach and a club where we could play tennis. We agreed that I should buy it. I had the closing two weeks later. Eileen did not buy the house across the road but another house in Westport. We are still close friends.

Westport has been my home since then. I have found my tribe here. But when I say "tribe," I mean nothing like the Nigerian use of the word. I was introduced to the American concept by Mary, my brother's wife. We were speaking on the phone years ago. As usual we talked about our children. She had told me that their third son was having a difficult time in school. The academics were not bothering him, but the social scene was. When he was in the first year of high school, she said to me one day, "He's doing well now. He's found his tribe."

I was puzzled. "What do you mean, his tribe?"

"He has found people who are like him. They are interested in the same things. They like the same music and they hang around together." I understood immediately. I had found my tribe in high school but barely, and only in the last two or three years. At Mount Holyoke I had good friends. But I always felt a little on the outside. I realized that in New Haven, I had found my tribe among the foreign and minority students, even though I was not actually one of them.

During my twenty-four years in Nigeria, I also had found my place to belong. I am not sure I can say I found my tribe. Rather I found a tribe and setting where I was at home.

After I met Clem and we decided to marry I learned to speak his language, Igbo. I remembered that I had been eager to try out my limited Yoruba, learned in Peace Corps training, in the Lagos airport when I had first arrived. I have found that speaking the language is a major entry point in how I am accepted. Using Igbo helps me know I belong in my husband's village and tribe. Getting the tones right is important, and not many foreigners can do that. I can even fool an Igbo person who doesn't see my white skin into thinking I am Igbo.

Perhaps it was easy to be accepted as an outsider in Nigeria, and then in Nanka, my husband's town, because I was so clearly not one of the people who belonged. I was there because I wanted to be, not because I had to be. I was not trying to bring my culture to them, or to teach them to be part of my culture. I was learning theirs and adopting it.

Through the stories of people in my husband's family and village, I have shown you the customs and traditions that are part of daily life. Though I left Nigeria for the US in 1986, I return regularly for visits. The habits, traditions, and customs I came to know in the twenty-four years when Nigeria was my home are still part of me, my family, and my view of the world.

The Unitarian Church in Westport has become a place where I am part of a community. It has become one source of my feeling of belonging, being part of a tribe. I first attended in the summer of 1994 and was amazed to find a place of worship where no one said words that I did not believe. It was clear that there was a social justice component to the life of the congregation.

I had gone to hear a talk, "The Liberal Response to the Religious Right." It was given by Denny (Denise) Davidoff, now my friend and mentor. I did not even know I was going to a church service until I got there. I found that the summer services, like the one I happened into, were led by laypeople. The minister Frank Hall led a class, "Building Your Own Theology," for prospective members in the fall. I joined the class and the women's choir and signed the membership book by the end of the year.

The women's choir is like a mini-tribe. A few women have been members together for thirty or forty years, and I cannot match their closeness. But I have made friends in that and the two other choirs in which I sing. I know I be cared for in these groups should the need arise.

Soon after joining the church, I was voted onto the Endowment Committee. I was proud and happy to have this assignment. At my very first meeting, I learned that the chair was stepping down and I was to replace her. Immediately I had a role in the church, an important one! We had an endowment of nearly three million dollars to manage. My term lasted five years, though with only twice-yearly meetings I did not become close to other committee members. I serve as a board member and treasurer at the church today.

I joined the Anti-Racism Task Force, led book discussions, and was part of forming the Social Justice Council. I worked closely with another woman to develop the bylaws, or charter, for the council. We received a substantial gift from one of the members to hire a social justice director. Together we held interviews and selected someone who has been a major asset to the church for more than a decade.

My real claim to fame at the church has been holding summer services myself. I have led four. The first was in 2002 with my friend Cheryl and her South African friend, who provided music. We used African themes for our readings, and I spoke about Igbo customs. In 2006 I led the service with my husband, son and daughter, son-in-law, and grandkids participating. We reenacted a few Igbo customs for the congregation. I shared in presenting a service on Community in 2013 and presented my own sermon in 2015. The latter three talks are in the appendix.

My tribe takes many forms in Westport today beyond music and church. I am a member of TEAM Westport, the town's committee dedicated to multiculturalism. Our focus most recently has been on racism.

I belong to two book groups. Elizabeth Baker was the founder of a group called Baker's Dozen, which has been meeting since 1995. Today five of the original dozen members remain. I've been a member since July 11, 2012. I'm glad the group decided at the beginning to keep a journal. We're now on journal notebook #3. Each month, one of us takes notes on the conversation about the chosen book.

My other book group is organized by and for Mount Holyoke alumnae and based in the alumnae club of Bridgeport, Connecticut, north of Westport. Both groups are a source of learning, great conversation, and friendship.

I maintain relationships with other former, or as we say, returned Peace

Corps volunteers. I co-founded the group Friends of Nigeria and have been active in the Connecticut Returned Peace Corps Volunteers.

The UN is a continuing interest. Today I am a board member of the US National Committee for UN Women, another example of a group where I easily belong because of my international experience and interests.

Despite all the connections I have in the US today, there are times I feel my strongest allegiance belongs to Nigeria. Nigerwives continues to exert a hold on me even though I can attend a meeting only once in a year, or even less frequently. On our nearly annual trips to Nigeria, I relish being in the village for a week or ten days. The sense of belonging envelops me like nothing else I know.

# 18

## PALM WINE A PART
## OF ALL CEREMONIES

PAPA INTRODUCED ME TO THE custom of a woman indicating acceptance of her intended husband with a sip of palm wine. I performed the ceremony as he requested in 1964, kneeling and giving the cup to Clement after my taste. For us, it was not a full "knocking on the door" ceremony, the first part of a traditional Igbo marriage, but the best we could do without my family present. It was just a few weeks before our church wedding. Since then, I have seen and loved watching it many times. Usually it brings tears to my eyes.

The palm wine carrying is equally meaningful. Usually it takes place with the presentation of the bride price. We did not try to replicate this at our 1964 wedding although we held a lavish reception at Clem's home.

But we held a two-purpose ceremony for our daughter in Clem's village to make up for our own lapse. She and Kelvin had already been married for several years. Their lovely church wedding was in 1993 in Boston, at the Harvard chapel, and the reception at Four Seasons Hotel. In 1998 we held a ceremony that combined "knocking on the door" and the wine-carrying, modified as necessary. Her husband is American and, like me at my own sipping-of-the-wine ritual, had no family with him, although they already had a two-year-old son, who was present. We had invited friends, and all the clan members were invited by word of mouth. For the occasion we hired musicians and traditional dancers.

Beth entered the compound carrying a jug of palm wine on her head and surrounded by the unmarried women from her age grade and others who wanted to be part of the fun. They danced their way into the center of the assembled guests. Her husband followed with his own group of men near his age. Lacking his own family and others in his age grade, we "loaned" him Beth's cousins, other clansmen, and friends.

When the music stopped, Beth lifted the jug from her head and placed it in front of Clem. She and Kelvin took their seats near us while Clem poured wine into a cup for her to give to Kelvin. Since they were clearly already a couple, she didn't have to search for him, but simply took a sip and passed the cup to him. Clem's cousin Emma spoke about the importance of a wife obeying her husband, which no one bothered to translate. He was clearly out of touch with Western marriage practices. Even among his younger relatives, this traditional sentiment is usually flouted.

The dancers performed and brought Beth to her feet to join them. Soon we were all dancing. Palm wine flowed. We had hired a caterer, and she organized her people to serve garri, pounded yam, soup, and jollof rice to the celebrants.

Another important use of palm wine is when someone visits the *Dibia,* variously identified as the spiritual healer, rainmaker, or shaman. A visitor will not take it on his initial call. He will however be asked to include palm wine in his payment for whatever service the Dibia is able to perform.

When Clem's father, Papa, died while we were in London the summer of 1979, we returned to Nigeria immediately and drove to the village the next day. The wake and funeral were planned for several days later. Like most such events, these would be outside. We would set up tarpaulins as tents, but still, it was the rainy season and we didn't want a major downpour. I accompanied Papa's youngest brother, Obi, to visit the Dibia to ask his help in preventing rain during the time of the ceremonies.

The Dibia consulted the spirits and said they would help us if we brought the proper offerings. One jug of palm wine was one of the gifts we had to produce. Two days after visiting him, Obi and I returned with the gifts. Besides the palm wine we brought several yams, five kola nuts, a bottle of schnapps, a chicken, and about twenty-five dollars.

And true to his word, the Dibia gave Obi a calabash and instructions for what to do if rain threatened. Twice during the long night of the wake, Obi had to pull the calabash out from beneath his chair, rub it, and use the words the Dibia had given him to stop the rain that was beginning to fall. We had a few sprinkles, but otherwise we stayed dry.

Extended family and friends who came for the funeral brought condolence gifts of palm wine. It was served all night long, although I gave up and went to bed around three a.m. Again, the next day, after Papa's coffin was buried in front of our house, the palm wine was flowing. By that afternoon, the fermentation was well along, and several men became tipsy.

Palm wine has other roles to play besides appeasing the spirits through the intervention of the Dibia and sealing the marriage bonds between families. When a man builds a house, he must consecrate it with a libation of palm wine. He will call on the spirits of the ancestors to bless and protect his house and his family while he pours a little palm wine on the floor.

Clem's cousin Nwosisi, or Emma, loves the ceremonies and traditions. He has more than once poured palm wine on the floor of our house during an appeal to the ancestors or in thanks for something good that has happened. When Clem's mother was sick with cancer, Emma offered a libation of palm wine to seek help. The next time was our first visit after Chinaku had graduated from the University of Benin. Emma thanked the gods with the libation.

The death of an in-law is an occasion to take palm wine on a condolence visit, just as people had done for us years earlier, after Papa's death. In 2002, Clem and I were required to visit the in-laws of Clem's youngest sister, Nebechi. Her husband is from a town about sixty miles from ours. His mother had died a few months earlier and this was our first opportunity to visit. Driving there was miserable. We kept getting lost. Yet when we reached their compound at last and took in our gifts of palm wine, we knew we had done the right thing by coming. Our hosts shared the wine and the food they had prepared with us, we spoke our words of sympathy, and our spirits, after the arduous journey, were restored.

The palm tree and its product, palm wine, are part of the culture in Igboland and farther afield. I cannot describe its importance better than this, from HubPages.com: "In Africa especially West Africa the palm tree does not only have a reverent standing in the economic and social life but is highly integrated into the culture and traditions. [At many] festivals and special occasions like child naming, marriage or being honored with a chieftaincy title or just at social gatherings the wine is highly favored and loved."

It is all true!

In 2016 we celebrated our fiftieth wedding anniversary in Nanka. We hired caterers to prepare the food and drink for the hundred guests we expected. Tarpaulins were erected, not so much for rain—this was the middle of the dry season, after all—but for the sun. Chairs, borrowed from the church, were set out, with tables for the most important guests.

Clem and I sat at the head table, which was covered with a white table-cloth and held a massive cake. The chief sat with us. Clem's dear friend Dozie, who had spoken at our wedding fifty years earlier, came to be our MC. I recalled his words from our wedding when he said, "Now that Clement is out of the way, I can become the most eligible bachelor in Lagos!"

When the guests began arriving I was not surprised to find that several brought palm wine as their anniversary gift for us. Once more the importance of palm wine was affirmed, and I drank it with joy.

# 19

## IGBO NAMES, MEANINGS, AND SIGNIFICANCE

"A BRAVE MAN WENT OFF to battle. He returned victorious, and he proclaimed his triumph so loudly and boldly that even the defeated people in the next village heard." Clem, seated at his computer in our home in Westport, Connecticut, is telling me once again the meaning of our surname, Onyemelukwe.

When he and I had just started dating, Clem explained the name, relating the story of the battle. "All that in five syllables?" I had said.

"Today the name conveys confidence, perhaps even arrogance. We have moved on from battles."

At the time I first heard the explanation, I didn't know it would become my name too. But I was interested in Nigeria's customs and culture, like any Peace Corps volunteer. We were at the nightclub Bagatelle, on lower Broadway in Lagos. It wasn't easy to hear over the music, and we got up frequently to dance. In between I asked him to repeat the name. I knew that Igbo, like many African languages, is tonal. Sentences or multisyllabic words can sound like singing. He repeated the name for me, and I did my best to imitate.

By the time we married, I knew enough Igbo to have a short conversation. I could decipher many Igbo names. And I knew how to say my new name with the correct tones, or levels. For me part of fitting in anywhere is speaking the language enough to be understood and to say others' names correctly. Becoming a member of Clem's family was eased by my ability to do this.

When I meet an Igbo person for the first time and say my surname, he or she is surprised at how well I say it. The individual will sometimes follow up by asking if I speak Igbo. I always answer in Igbo, invariably bringing laughter and a shout of joy. If other Igbo people are around, the person will call to them to ask them to listen.

In late 2016 I was at the Africa Business Conference at the Wharton School in Philadelphia, Pennsylvania, with my husband. Clem gave a talk on electricity and the power industry. During the lunch, we sat at a table of eight. The woman on my right was struggling to read my nametag, which was hanging amid the ends of my scarf. I held it out, saying my name while I did.

"You say it so well," she said. "How do you manage to do that?"

"*A nam a su Igbo.* I speak Igbo," I said.

"*Ezeoku!* You don't say!" she said. Leaning in front of me, she called to the woman on my husband's left. "She speaks Igbo like a native."

"What's your name?" the other woman asked. I responded. She exclaimed, "You wrote the memoir! My sister just finished reading it." I was thrilled to be recognized. "I'm going to read it," she said.

A minute later she handed me her cell phone. "Say hello to my sister. She wants to greet you." I felt like a minor celebrity! After I hung up, we three continued a delightful conversation in a combination of Igbo and English, leaving my husband in the middle to finish his lunch unbothered by the chatter.

Many non-Africans cannot hear the tones, much less replicate them. Perhaps because I have a musical ear I have always been able to do this. During Peace Corps training, other volunteers couldn't understand how I could repeat the Yoruba words correctly. Today, though I rarely use Yoruba, the few words I do recall I still say with the correct tones.

When I explain the name and the pronunciation in my talks, I illustrate the levels of the tones with my hand—high, low, and mid-levels. "Repeat it after me," I say to the audience while the name is displayed on the screen at the front of the lecture hall or auditorium. I love explaining the pronunciation and encouraging people to try to say it. And I love to tell the story of the meaning.

Stories about Igbo surnames are passed down in families, the way Clem learned about the meaning of Onyemelukwe. They form a link that holds generations and families together. Often, they are whole phrases or even sentences. Like ours, they may refer to a battle or another event from many generations earlier.

We know there is another family from a different village with the surname Onyemelukwe. If we meet an Onyemelukwe who we don't know, we can assume the person is from Nnewi, the home of the other family. I have met some but have never asked the meaning of their surname. I wonder if they interpret it the same way as my husband does. I will ask, the next chance I get.

Igbo first and middle names are also often full expressions. And they frequently have current meanings. They are rich with references to events in the family, the village, or even the world. Clem had told me about his Igbo middle name, Chukwukadibia, not long after we decided to marry. "You know *Chukwu* is God," he said.

"Yes, and you have told me that the *Dibia* is the native doctor, healer, or mediator between humans and the divine in Igbo tradition. What is the word *ka* in between?"

I had begun studying Igbo by this time, but I did not recognize that word.

"It means 'greater than,'" Clem said. "God, the Christian God, is greater than the Dibia."

"That's an odd name," I said. But as he explained, I realized it was not odd at all. I remembered the story about Clem's mother, Mama, or Grace, as she was known when she was growing up. She had become a Christian after attending school for three years. Her father had been angry that she had converted, but he had assumed that when she married, her husband would set her right. Then she married Clem's father, who had also become a Christian. Her father cursed her, saying she would never conceive. And it took three years for her to have her first child, Clement. When her father was notified about the baby, he proclaimed the Igbo name Chukwukadibia. It was just right.

Some first names are a single word referencing an event. Our niece Comet was born in 1986, the last time Halley's Comet was visible to the naked eye from Earth. I do not know whether her mother, Clem's sister, consulted others about the name, or simply chose it herself. I wonder how Comet will celebrate in mid-2061 when the comet returns, and she will be seventy-five.

Names may also contain hopes for the future. Soon after our marriage we knew we would need a baby name a few months later. Before Clem departed on a business trip, planning to be back before the baby's birth, he told me about the tradition that said his father would provide the name for our child. He wanted to follow this custom. I admired the practice and was happy to follow Clem's wish, clearly part of uniting family members over generations. I felt it would help cement my sense of inclusion in the Onyemelukwe family.

As it turned out, the baby didn't wait. Our son was born nearly a week before Clem's return. I had already notified Clem's parents that we had a boy before my husband came back. While I lay in the hospital bed, knowing we would hear from Papa with recommended names in the next few days, I began to think about names from my family. Should I not have some part in naming? Although I embraced the tradition and had no wish to oppose Clem's father's role, maybe I could insert a name that reflected my origins.

Two days after Clem came back and we were home again with our new baby, his father called. "I consulted my brothers. We have chosen the names Chinakueze Iwenofu," he said. Clem repeated these to me.

"That's a lot of name for a baby," I said. "What do we call him? And what does it all mean?"

"We can call him Chinaku," Clem said. I tried it out a few times. It still seemed long.

We figured out the literal meaning of the first name quickly. *Chi* is another word for God and, like *Chukwu,* is part of many Igbo names. *Eze* is king. With the verb in between, we had "God is the one who creates kings." It was a way to praise God and to signify high expectations for this honored first son of Papa's first son.

The second name, Iwenofu, was a puzzle. We concluded that the literal meaning was "anger should go away or be thrown away." But what was the significance?

"Hasn't Mama been quarreling with your cousin Jonathan?" I said. Papa had paid for Jonathan's secondary school education at DMGS. Mama especially, and Papa in concurrence with her, thought that Jonathan had not properly appreciated this when he became a priest. We confirmed our theory with Papa a few weeks later. Our son would bear a name that showed the hope of a future without the quarrel left from generations before.

Although I was thrilled with this way of giving a name, and welcomed

Papa's choices, I did ask that we add my mother's maiden name, Danforth. I reasoned that our son could use "Dan" if he ever wanted an English-sounding name. Clem agreed. Our son was christened at the Anglican Church, St. Saviours, where we'd been married, as Chinakueze Iwenofu Danforth Onyemelukwe.

The naming ceremony for our first child marked the beginning of a new name for me too. I was, and still am, addressed as *Nwunye* Clement, which means "Clement's wife." But from the day we arrived in Nanka for the naming ceremony, I have had the added distinction of being known in the village as Mama Chinaku.

One day when we were in the village, I said to Clem, "Isn't it demeaning to be known only as the mother of someone?"

"It's an honor. Why wouldn't you want this?" It didn't take me long to realize I would not be able to make Clem understand. Clem's siblings and a few friends in the village know my real name. His parents knew it but never used it. Otherwise people in the village have no idea what my name is.

I am also called by another name that surprised me at first. I was in the market, *Afor Udo,* the day after our son's naming ceremony. A man I had never seen before, or at least didn't remember seeing, came up to me. "*Nwunyem, kedu?* My wife, how are you?"

Who is this? I thought. Why is he addressing me like this? I was still new to the Igbo language, though I understood the words he was using.

"*O di mma.* I'm fine," I said. But I'm not his wife. What does he think, addressing me so familiarly?

Several women were grouped around Obele, Clem's aunt, who was seated on a low stool with the ground tobacco she was selling on a small tray in front of her. "*Nwunye anyi, nno.* Our wife, welcome." Of course, I smiled and replied. But when I got back home, I asked Clement.

"What do they mean, calling me their wife?" I said.

"They are telling you that you are part of the village and part of our family now," he said. I relaxed and enjoyed the greeting. Soon I learned that in Igbo custom, we say *nna anyi,* our father, to speak to an older male in the village, whether directly related or not. And we speak to children with a similar phrase, saying "our child" or "my child," again whether the child is a direct relative. We all belong to one another in the village.

I am now comfortable with all the names I've been given. *Nwunye* Clement is the most straightforward. But so is Mama Chinaku. *Nwunye anyi,* our wife, and *nwunyem,* my wife, feel like my name too.

In 1970 I returned to Nigeria after Biafra's defeat and the end of the civil war. Within a month I was pregnant again. Our third child was another boy, and Clem insisted on naming him after his father, Samuel. We were breaking tradition in using the name of a living relative. But we still asked Papa for a middle name.

He chose Chukwugekwu, meaning "God will speak." I believe the name reflected his disappointment over the loss of Biafra. Perhaps he was even hoping for another chance at an independent nation for the Igbo people.

Another custom I love is giving a name that denotes the day a child was born. I have known boys and men named Sunday, the most popular, and Monday and Friday. For some reason Tuesday, Wednesday, Thursday, and Saturday are never used. And only boys are given these names.

The Igbo names Nwafor, Nwankwo, Nweke, and Nwoye are all crafted from nwa, meaning child, and the names of the four Igbo market days, *Afor, Nkwo, Eke, and Oye.* These names are also more common for boys, though I have known one woman named Nweke. One of Clement's aunts was named Mbafor, meaning born not just on the market day, *Afor,* but during the hours when the market was underway.

Many Igbo names have a reference to God, often in praise, sometimes in supplication. Traditionally the god of reference would have been the Igbo deity Chukwu. But since the incursions of the Christian missionaries in the late nineteenth and early twentieth centuries, the reference is more likely to the Christian God. Clem and our two sons have names that are examples of using *Chi* or *Chukwu* as part of the phrase that makes up the name.

Our grandson's name is another. Clem was thrilled when Beth and her African-American husband, Kelvin, asked him to name their first son. He chose Kenechi, which means "praise God" or "thank God." *Kene* is the word for greet. When a friend is going to see someone you know, you can say, *"Kene ya.* Greet him or her."

Chimamanda, the first name of Nigerian author Chimamanda Ngozi Adichie, means "my God will never fail." Another lovely girl's name is Chidimma. The *mma* at the end is a version of *oma,* or good. So Chidimma means "God is good."

Many names do not refer to God or to events; they are just beautiful name Uzoamaka means "the way ahead is good or beautiful."

Adanna is a very popular girl's name. *Ada* means daughter, and *nna* means father. It is given to the first daughter, so if you meet an Adanna, you know she has that family role. Our friends' daughter Adanna is Clem's goddaughter.

Ifeoma is my sister-in-law. Her name means "something good." One of our cousins has a daughter named Akaoma. The literal meaning is "the hand is good." I asked her how she interprets her name, and she said it means good fortune.

With succeeding generations, will the significance of names be lost? Today our son Chinakueze, called Chinaku until recently, has shortened his name even further and calls himself China, pronounced like the country, for brevity. Beth and Sam have never used their Igbo names.

Igbo names are a treasure of meaning and significance. For me, they are an unending source of delight. My name, though not Igbo, has been given to me as part of Igbo custom. I've embraced it in its several versions, with the most common being Mama Chinaku. I am known throughout our village of Nanka by people of our generation, and our children's, by that name. I know it signifies my belonging to the family and the community.

# 20

## A WEDDING, A SECRET, AND A FUNERAL

"WE WERE SHOCKED TO HEAR about Benji's death," I said to Clem's cousin Emmanuel soon after Clem and I got to Nanka on December 22, 2008. "He was so pleasant. What a loss!"

Our luggage had already been carried upstairs to our bedroom at the back of the house. Mathias, our cook and steward, was in the kitchen, putting away the food and utensils we had brought with us. Clem and I sat on the front veranda with Emma.

"I've been looking forward to his daughter's wedding on the thirtieth," I said, pulling the invitation with its gold engraving out of my bag. "Is it still taking place?"

"They will have the wedding. Those plans could not be changed," Emma said. "The daughter is coming to Nanka tomorrow to prepare."

"To have the wedding and then a few days later the funeral—that's hard!"

I turned to Clem. "Your mother always insisted that we must pay our condolence calls on the day we arrive in the village, especially for a relative," I said. "And wasn't Benji a cousin of some sort?"

"He is, was, part of our clan," Clem said. "Or at least I think he was."

I expected Emma to confirm or deny the connection of the clan, or *umunna*. Then I realized we'd spoken English. His hearing was already failing, and he had not understood.

I turned to Emma, speaking in Igbo. "Benji's widow must still be in their home in Delta. But will you come with us to visit his mother?"

Benji had been with Shell Oil in the Delta region of Nigeria for at least fifteen years, for the last five as a senior engineer. He and his family lived near his work in Delta State, but his house in our village was an easy walk, just down the road from ours. Benji's mother, widowed years earlier, usually stayed there whenever she wasn't visiting Benji or one of her other children.

"No, no, you can't go," Emma said. "She isn't even there. She's away, and she does not know that her son has died."

"What?" I said. "He died weeks ago. Surely she must know, or at least suspect."

Nigeria's history with the oil industry has been turbulent. Oil was discovered in Delta in 1956, even before Nigeria's 1960 independence from Britain. For many years Shell and other major oil companies explored and drilled in the area, frequently leaving behind a damaged environment. Efforts to get restitution from the companies or from the Nigerian government have never been successful. Since the 1980s, much of the exploration and drilling moved offshore, but the area was—and is—still plagued by conflict.

During the early 1990s, Ken Saro-Wiwa became a strong environmental activist for his Ogoni people, the largest tribe in the area. He was a leader of the Movement for the Survival of the Ogoni People, or MOSOP. The organization had frequent run-ins with the Nigerian government.

He was arrested in 1992, and again a year later. Finally in 1995 he was executed by the military government of the time. Most people believed the murder charge for which he was executed was made-up. The government just could not abide his activism.

Strife continued in the region where Benji lived and worked. Shell, his company, was the most notorious for their damage to the environment. Because of the damage, economic opportunities are few. Theft of oil is rampant, both by locals and by people from other parts of the country, who steal crude oil from the pipelines. When they are successful, they sell the pilfered oil on the black market in Nigeria or truck it to neighboring Cameroon for sale. When they are unsuccessful, the oil may ignite. The attempt can and often does result in death for the perpetrators and bystanders. The oil company is responsible for repairs whenever the pipelines are damaged.

Benji did not die directly at the hands of activists or oil thieves, but his death was closely related. He died because he was a thoughtful manager. When he had to send workers to undertake the hazardous repairs to a pipeline that had been broken by the oil thieves, he went along. He believed he should be with his workers when they were carrying out dangerous tasks. There was an explosion during the repair operation, and he died alongside one of his workers.

"What will happen at the daughter's wedding in a few days?" I said. "Won't she have to be told then?"

"She won't be told until after the wedding," Emma said. "There is time enough before the funeral for her to be given the information."

In earlier times, the Igbos buried the body of anyone who died within twenty-four hours. Most family members lived in the village or nearby. Members of the clan would notify everyone, and they would gather for the burial. Then the family would mourn for several weeks. The stipulated mourning period for the widow was seven market weeks, each week having four days. Benji's widow would be in this mourning period now. However, living away from the village and with children in school, she was not following the usual custom. And her presence in the village as the mourning widow would of course have alerted Benji's mother.

I asked Emma and my husband to explain the need to hide Benji's death from his mother. Emma couldn't explain, nor did my husband know why. How could not knowing for a few weeks soften the blow for her? Or was that even the idea? I wouldn't learn the answer until the wedding was over.

While I was puzzling over the mystery that evening, a young person from Benji's household delivered the invitation to his funeral! I still find an invitation to a funeral quite strange. An announcement I can understand; that seems more normal to me. But invitations to funerals are now standard in Nigeria. Today they are nearly as elaborate as wedding invitations. This one had Benji's picture. He was wearing a red wide-brimmed hat and red native dress. Underneath his picture was *Engr. Benny Ezento, Aged: 56 years.* The title "engineer" is often used for people of the profession.

"The entire family of Ezento and Ezenekwe cordially invite the pleasure of . . . to the Burial Ceremony of our beloved Son, Brother, Nephew, Cousin, Father and Grandfather." The elaborate burial arrangements, spelled out in the invitation, included three events: a service of songs/crusade from four p.m. till dawn on Friday, January 9; the funeral service at ten a.m. on the tenth; and a thanksgiving service on Sunday, the eleventh. All would take place at his family's compound, called Gloryland Manor. I guessed the name was given to the compound for this event.

The invitation asked for an RSVP and listed four people with their cell phone numbers for the replies. On the back of the invitation was a map showing visitors how to get to Gloryland Manor. A nice touch, I thought, as some people would be coming from Shell in Delta State, on the other side of the Niger Bridge at Onitsha.

I was sorry that I would miss the funeral. I had to return to the US two days before, but Clem would stay on. As I read the funeral invitation I thought about the wedding in a few days. Usually a wedding is such a happy occasion, but I wasn't sure how joyful it could be with this shadow hanging over it.

The main topic of conversation all over the village for the next few days was Benji's death. Everyone knew and liked him. Whenever we ran into an old friend or acquaintance, we would say, "What a shame."

The other would reply, "Yes, how sad that this happened just before the daughter's wedding." No one besides me seemed surprised that Benji's mother was not at home and not aware.

I asked a cousin, "Where is Benji's mother?"

"She is staying with her family members outside the village. She will be back for her granddaughter's wedding," she said.

On December 30 I stepped out of the car in my gold sandals, cream silk blouse, and long blue satin skirt onto the red dirt of the path into Benji's home for his daughter's wedding reception. I wore my best jewelry, knowing I would still look bland and underdressed among the guests. Not only did I have white skin and blond hair, but my clothes and accessories were no match for the silks, satins, brocades, and gold the Nigerian women would be wearing. My husband is also not a fancy dresser. He wore a long maroon dashiki with maroon trousers and a green felt hat.

Huge white party tents covered the stone courtyards in the front and at the side of the house. Swags of white netting hung from the roof and the tent tops. The red carpet leading to the couple's seats of honor was lined with large pots of artificial flowers. There were chairs in both courtyard areas for the two hundred guests. A crowd was already assembled when we entered the compound. I spotted Benji's mother, the bride's grandmother, seated a couple of rows behind Clem's brother Geoffrey, and greeted her with a quick hug.

We were escorted to seats in the front row. Geoffrey was already seated with his wife, Ifeoma. I have become accustomed to these positions of honor at village events. Clem was the very first Nigerian to be chief engineer for the national electric power company. He has two degrees from British universities. He had replaced the British chief engineer a year after Nigeria's independence. Geoffrey is a leading professor of medicine in Nigeria. Their cousin Jonathan was bishop on the Niger and then archbishop of the Anglican diocese of the region. Only two or three other families in the village have such prominent and successful family members.

Geoffrey, in a white embossed robe, stood to fulfill his role as head, or chairman, of the event. Microphone in hand, he welcomed the guests already present and introduced the two masters of ceremonies, who took turns announcing the arrival of more guests. So much ceremony no longer surprises me, though I still find it almost overpowering.

"My own brother, Engineer C. C. Onyemelukwe, and his beautiful wife, Catherine, have entered. A round of applause for them," he said. The guests applauded dutifully.

Suddenly a white SUV drove right into the compound, stopping nearly in front of our seats. The bridal couple got out. Benji's daughter Ifeoma, the bride, looked gorgeous in her white lace wedding dress. I don't think I was imagining her distress; to me she appeared to be near tears. I wanted to weep too as I watched her alight from the car with the groom beside her.

On this day that should have been her happiest, her father was not there. She must have longed for him. But she couldn't speak about his death since her grandmother had not yet been told. Certainly everyone else in the village knew why Benji wasn't there for his own daughter's wedding and reception. I found it hard to believe that the grandmother didn't see that her granddaughter was carrying a great sorrow; it seemed so obvious to me. But the people around me

"Don't worry—she will be informed in a gentle way," she said. I remembered other times when a family member's death was kept hidden from close relatives. I knew that it was an attempt among the Igbos to respect the feelings of the bereaved and find the appropriate time to share the information. But this seemed extreme.

As the applause for the wedding couple died down, I was absorbed by the two MCs, who were trying to outdo each other with proverbs about marriage and comments about the guests who were still arriving. The vibrant reds, blues, and yellows of the *bubas,* or blouses, stiff satin head ties, and long embroidered or brocade wrappers of the women and equally colorful flowing robes of the men gave the occasion a festive air and helped disguise the unacknowledged sorrow.

I continue to be amazed by the pomp and pageantry, mixing traditional and modern customs, that accompany wedding receptions in Nigeria. And the amount of ceremony seems only to increase yearly.

The bride and groom walked gracefully to their decorated seats on an elevated platform at the corner between the two sides of the courtyard, where most people could see them. One MC gave the microphone back to Geoffrey for the afternoon's required formal opening.

No Igbo event can be considered complete without breaking kola. In fact, an event hasn't properly started until kola is broken. Geoffrey picked up a smooth pink kola nut from the tray in front of him. He raised it up, saying in Igbo, "Creator of the universe, we thank you for this kola. We honor our ancestors. He who brings kola brings life." The guests responded with the Igbo equivalent of amen.

He broke the nut into four pieces, took one himself, and placed the others back on the tray. He motioned to the servers to carry around the trays of kola that had been prepared ahead of time, distributing nuts to all the guests. I only pretended to put it in my mouth, instead dropping it into my bag.

After everyone was given kola, one of the MCs introduced the cake maker, an addition to the wedding reception that I had never seen before. "She will speak to us about the meaning of her cake," he said, handing her the microphone.

She pointed to the flowers adorning the cake. "The unique lily decorations stand for faithfulness and love," she said. How about truth, I thought.

Next it was time for cutting the cake. As the bride and groom came forward, the MC announced another new feature of the event that I had never seen before. He said that three guests would have the duty of observing and then reporting on the success of the cake cutting. Two well-known men were called. To my surprise I was the third person called forward.

I pondered what I would say when my turn came, and whether to speak in Igbo or English. Sonny, our friend and former lieutenant governor of our state, Anambra, was the first to speak. He announced that he would speak in English. "We have guests here from many parts of the country," he said, "and I don't want to exclude anyone."

The MC directed me to speak next. I enjoy demonstrating my command of the Igbo language, so I said in Igbo that I would follow his example and use English. Many people present already knew I spoke Igbo, but others were surprised. I am, after all, a white American. The audience laughed and applauded.

I turned to the couple. "Cutting the cake together was done well. You did it in partnership, and that's how the marriage should be," I said, to more applause. "You should always remember that you are equals." I knew most of the men present, and even a few of the women, would have challenged that statement if we were not in a public gathering. And I was certainly offending many of the elders, but then, the most traditional men at the event probably did not speak a lot of English. So my remark had little effect. By the time anyone could have commented, we had moved on.

There were more speeches and toasts to the bride and groom. Then the MC called the bride forward. Even though Ifeoma and her new husband had come from the church ceremony, entered together, and were seated next to each other on the chairs of honor, she had to perform the traditional ritual of sharing a glass of palm wine, as I had done at Papa's request forty-four years earlier.

While she walked forward to the MC, her husband slipped out of his chair and disappeared among the guests.

"You know that you have to show us who you have chosen as your husband," the MC said to her. "Take this cup of palm wine." He poured the fresh, milky-white wine, its aroma a mixture of sweet and acidic, from the jug on the table in front of me and handed the cup to her. "Find the man you agree to marry and kneel before him. Take a sip of the drink and give it to him."

Nowadays a similar ceremony may take place even if the wedding is not in the village. At receptions in Lagos, Abuja, and even the US, the bride must carry the cup of palm wine to give to her husband.

Ifeoma turned to give it to him. She had not noticed his quick exit from his seat. He was nowhere to be seen. She started walking toward her left, paused, and turned to the other side. People in the crowd began calling out, "No, not there," and "Go that way." At last she spotted him partially concealed behind a couple of his friends. She advanced slowly, holding the cup steady, knelt as custom required, sipped, and passed the cup to him, accompanied by loud applause from the audience of well-wishers.

With this, she was accepting her role as his wife and cementing the link between the two families, now joined by marriage.

Another new feature for me was the buffet lunch—I hadn't seen that at a Nigerian wedding reception. While I stood in line, I heard the woman behind me speak to her husband. "I'm sure Benji's mother must know," she said. It was the first time I heard anyone question the secrecy. "Mothers know such things," she said.

I had to agree. I wanted to ask them if they knew why the silence was being maintained, but they were deep in their own conversation and I had to move forward so I would not block the line. I placed a saran-wrapped ball of pounded yam on my plate, then a couple of spoonfuls of *egusi* soup, and headed back to our table. I continued to wonder, why the charade?

As I began eating, I remembered that I had first met Benji the year I lived in my husband's village. It was during the Biafran War, Nigeria's civil war in the late 1960s, and I was twenty-eight. Benji was a teenager. He was quiet, bright, and respectful. We saw him occasionally over the years and had followed his progress at Shell.

"Do you remember when we last saw Benji?" I said to Clem, who had chosen the jollof rice for his lunch.

"Yes, it was Sam's traditional wedding in 2006." That event had been in Asaba, near the Delta region. Benji came with his wife and children for the ceremony. We were grateful for his presence. The more people representing our son's family, the better we looked for our son's wedding. We had talked with him while we were waiting for the bride to emerge. Clem had been impressed with his seriousness, his command of the oil industry, and his position at Shell.

"I remember that I thought he might be helpful for my oil pipe project," he said. "That hope is gone."

We finished our food and drank the wine that had been placed on our table. Then the MC invited us to join the queue to present our gifts to the bride and groom. I stood in the heat, holding our elegantly wrapped gift of stainless-steel cooking pots, which Clem and I had purchased in the Lagos shopping mall a few days earlier.

I recalled again the surprise I had felt when Christian, Clem's cousin who is often in touch with us about local issues, called to tell us about Benji's sudden death. Now, a month later, we were at his daughter's wedding and awaiting his funeral. We returned home, still unable to feel anything but sad, despite the appearance of a happy wedding.

The next evening, we attended the New Year's Eve service at the church and held our yearly party back at our house for the close relatives. Clem opened bottles of champagne. We exchanged New Year's resolutions, but we were more subdued than the year before, with the wedding and the funeral coming in a few days.

The next day the masquerades appeared. I was always thrilled by their costumes, dancing, and flute playing, and I watched with amusement as women and children fled from them, while the men, including my husband, pretended that they were not afraid.

Suddenly I had a suspicion. What if Benji's mother did know, but couldn't admit it, because if everyone acknowledged the death, the wedding couldn't have happened?

That night I learned that my suspicion was right. "If the mother were told about her son's death, then the family would have to be in mourning," Geoffrey said.

His wife continued, "If they were in mourning, they could not have had the wedding for at least another six months. Think of all the wasted preparations."

"But when will they tell her? The funeral is in a few days," I said.

"I'm going with the brothers to tell her tomorrow morning," Geoffrey said. "I'll let you know what happens."

He came back from the visit the next day. "Two brothers and the daughter with her new husband were there," he said. "We had our script prepared."

"Mama, we have some very bad news for you," the older brother began.

"You can tell me," she said. "I'm ready now."

Geoffrey said, "We all looked at each other. Her son held her hand and said, 'You know?'"

"Of course I know, and I have already mourned for nearly two months. I had to do it privately," she said as she began to cry. "Now I can mourn with you. But tell me what happened." They related what they knew of how Benji had died, weeping and holding one another as they shared the sorrow they no longer had to hide.

Clem attended all three stages of Benji's funeral the next weekend. The service of songs and crusade on Friday afternoon and evening was led by the pastor of the church Benji and his family had attended in Delta State. The next day the body was brought back from the mortuary and buried, and on Sunday there was a more subdued church service. Many Shell employees came for part or all the funeral events.

Many family members from the new in-laws were present for all three events, as were other in-laws, already married to Benji's siblings. Benji's widow was surrounded by her family, who greeted the guests with her. His mother's family came in large numbers to support their relative. Each family brought money, usually a token sum, as a gift to the newly bereaved widow. Some also gave gifts to the mother.

The custom of having the widow shave her head and sit on the floor in rags, as I had seen my own mother-in-law and other widows do, was not practiced, Clem assured me. Maybe it has faded away.

When Clem came back to the US, I asked how Benji's mother had held up at the funeral. "Was she very distraught?"

"No, she was fine," he said. "She asked about you and the children and sent her regards."

I smiled at the thought. "How could she keep her sorrow to herself for so many days and pretend to be cheerful?"

"We Igbo men think we are so strong and can bear any trouble or tribulation," Clem said, "but really it's the women who are stronger." I had to agree.

I was relieved to know that I could talk to Benji's mother about her son on my next visit to the village. It would be a sad but satisfying conversation.

# 21

## IGBO SPIRITUAL LIFE:
## GODS, ANCESTORS, AND SLAVES

"I WAS WELCOMED VERY OPENLY when I went to your community as a naïve young American anthropologist in the 1950s," Professor Simon Ottenberg, age ninety-plus, said at an Igbo conference in Seattle in 2015. He told his audience, "My work would not have been possible without the help of some of your ancestors!"

The community Dr. Ottenberg referenced was a town called Afikpo. The US organization of Afikpo people was presenting him with an award for the work he had done in helping make African customs, especially their own, well known and respected. I knew Simon as our anthropology instructor during Peace Corps training in 1962. He was about thirty-nine at the time, and already established in the field of African anthropology. He was still publishing in 2014.

I love the way he wove in respect for ancestors in his speech accepting the award in Seattle. He and his wife, Phoebe, also a respected anthropologist, taught us that the Nigerian people honor their ancestors and call on them for help, advice, and blessings. They showed us pictures of shrines and described rituals invoking the ancestors' power. They spoke about the decline of these shrines and the weakening spiritual practices with the advent of the religion brought by the colonialists.

When I got to Nigeria in 1962, many of the traditional religious and spiritual habits had disappeared, just as the Ottenbergs had told us, replaced by Christianity. But a few remained. The central shrine in my husband's town of Nanka was still in place. It required a guardian. I was surprised to find out who the guardian was. On my very first visit to Nanka, I was with Clem's cousin Isaiah. Clem and I had been dating for only about six weeks. Clem had recruited him to show me around. I did not yet know I would become part of this family and this town!

We had just turned off the main road. There was a large church on our right. At the side of the road I spotted a disheveled man with matted hair and grayish-looking dry skin, carrying a long wooden staff. He was alone.

"Who is that?" I said.

"That's Akasinkpo. He's the guardian of the shrine," Isaiah said, pointing to our left as we rounded a curve on the narrow dirt road. "He comes from a family that is dedicated to protecting the religious sanctuaries in town."

I looked. There was a rectangular area about twenty feet deep, surrounded by a raffia wall with a narrow opening. I saw an overhang at the far end. I did not see anything inside that looked like a home.

"Where does he live?"

"He stays at the shrine. People bring offerings. During the day he wanders around the market." I accepted Isaiah's explanation and thought little more about the man. I was too engrossed in watching the passing huts, farms, and people as we drove down the road to Clem's village, one of Nanka's seven.

A year later I married Clem. My next trip to Nanka was for the naming ceremony for our son, in 1965. Clem was driving as we turned off the main road, and I saw Akasinkpo again.

"There's that man I saw when I came with Isaiah. Do you remember him? Has he been here your whole life?" I said to Clem. "Isaiah said he's a servant of the gods or something."

"Yes, he's osu, a slave. He stays at the shrine as its guardian," Clem said. "I was terrified of him when I was little. He must be old by now."

"What do you mean, he's a slave?"

"Akasinkpo is dedicated to the gods. His father or someone else in the family had the same role before him. They've always been slaves to the shrine."

"You mean he had no choice? This is really strange!" I said. "Who decides he's dedicated to the shrine?"

"It's our tradition. No one person decides. His family chooses the person who will follow the previous guardian."

"Isn't that Nanka family who live across from your parents in Onitsha also osu? They don't serve the shrine, do they?"

"No, they're different. I've never thought about it," Clem said. "But now that you ask, there are two types of osu, the people who were captured in war or taken in payment of a debt, and the ones dedicated to the shrine. They are all called osu."

"I thought slavery was outdated," I said. "Isn't it time to forget about slaves?"

"We don't really think about them," he said, "but we don't forget. You know they are not considered full citizens of the town. Other Igbo people cannot marry them."

As Clem spoke, I remembered the shock I had felt on hearing a story about osu from my Igbo friend Johnny during my first year in Nigeria, before I met Clem. Johnny said he had been in love with a woman whom he hoped to marry.

"You know we Igbo people marry another family, not just another person," he had told me. "When I knew I wanted to marry her, I asked my family to do the traditional checking into her family's background."

"What happened?" I said.

"They found that her people were osu. I had to abandon my wish to marry her. I still miss her," he said.

Throughout my year in the village, from September 1967 to September 1968 during the Biafran War, I continued to see Akasinkpo from time to time. He was frightening, sometimes speaking in words I didn't understand. His unkempt appearance was appalling. I forgot about him when I left the country halfway through the war. After the war was over in early 1970 and we returned to the village for the first time at Christmas that year, I saw him. But by 1974 or '75, he was gone. The shrine was still standing, though the area looked run-down. I occasionally paused near the entrance, but I never had the courage to look in carefully, and I certainly would never have ventured inside. A couple of years later the shrine too had disappeared.

Today I wonder how I so easily accepted, even adopted, the Igbo view of this man and the family that were osu. How could I have seen Akasinkpo as fearful? Was he anything other than a man consigned to an almost unendurable life, perhaps given the role because he was mentally disabled or driven mad by it? How could I have looked down on the family because of their status as osu?

The opinion of slavery that I brought to Nigeria with me was like that of many liberal white people at the time. Slavery in the United States had been despicable, but it was over. I knew there were civil rights demonstrations going on in the US. Some of my Mount Holyoke College classmates had participated in marches and protests during our last year, 1961–1962, though I had not joined them; indeed, I only became aware of their actions many years later. I did not know the extent of discrimination against African-Americans that continued, nor was I aware of the virulent racism that still exists. Dr. Martin Luther King was a distant figure.

Was I so eager to be accepted among the Igbo and my own new family that I overlooked the evil of condemning people and their descendants by their status of osu? Perhaps I accepted the practice as part of the package of Igbo culture, so much of which I admired, that I ignored the iniquity of this component.

Now that I know more about the history of slavery and its aftermath in the US, I feel compelled to be part of anti-racism work. I have led an anti-racism committee at my Unitarian Church. I am a member of the Westport town committee opposing racism and other forms of discrimination, and I facilitate discussions around the issue of race.

In Nigeria the stigma of osu is gradually disappearing, though few people whose families were osu are yet prepared to admit it. There is a law on the books that prohibits discrimination against osu. As far as I am aware, no one is today assigned to a life dedicated to a shrine, even though a few people still practice traditional religion. I am not proud of my original acceptance of osu. I am glad that it is fading. But for many older people, including my husband, the idea that a child or grandchild would marry someone who is osu is completely unacceptable.

With shrines mostly gone, and with them the practice of assigning slaves as guardians, is the regard for ancestors still critical?

I asked my husband, who has been a Christian his whole life, "What is the most important Igbo traditional practice related to spirituality?"

He did not hesitate. "Veneration for the ancestors. We believe the ancestors are still with us and can have an influence on our lives."

"Isn't this in conflict with your Anglican faith?" I said.

"No, I don't worship the ancestors. But I show them respect."

Ancestors are mentioned most frequently among the Igbo with the breaking of the kola nut. Before breaking the nut, the man performing the rite will call on the ancestors to bless the kola. The first words he utters will be something like, "We thank our ancestors for life, for family, and for bringing us this kola."

The ancestors are also invoked in a ceremony of marriage. In 2016 my husband and I went to Hemet, California, for the traditional wedding of our nephew Chidi. Chidi's father, Godwin, was two years younger than Clem. He died a decade ago, and my husband is the stand-in father. Our daughter, Beth, came with us as an additional witness to the union. With changing times and with the young people living in California, not Nigeria, there had been no investigation by one side of the other. The families were meeting each other for the first time.

The bride's two uncles welcomed us into the living room, a comfortable space with hardwood floors, a large sofa, a long occasional table behind the sofa, and a TV. They had arranged two dining room chairs to face the sofa. The brothers took seats there while they motioned us to the sofa. Beth sat between Clem and me. The bride was nowhere to be seen, and the groom, Chidi, was hovering in the background.

"I had never heard of Hemet," I said, "even though I lived in California in 1975 and '76 and visited again last year. It seems so remote. Are there other Igbo people living here?"

"We are many. My cousin had moved here. I came here for a teaching job, and never left. My brother joined me a couple of years later; he works for the town."

How like an Igbo family to resettle together, I thought.

The older uncle called his wife to bring him the bottle for the ceremony. "Our daughter doesn't drink alcohol, so we have to make do with this," he said, holding out the bottle of cider his wife had brought.

In a mix of Igbo and English he recounted how his niece had come to him a few months earlier to say she had met the man she wanted to marry. "She brought him to meet us, and we approved her choice," he said.

"So today we have the *iku aka na uzo* and *igba nkwu* together. You have come to 'knock on the door,' to ask for our daughter's hand in marriage. We will also expect a bride price from you," he said, smiling to show it would not be an onerous request. "We will let our daughter show her acceptance by carrying the drink to her husband."

He opened the bottle of cider and looked at me. "I have to honor the ancestors in Igbo," he said. "I apologize to those who may not understand."

"I understand Igbo, and our daughter can comprehend too," I said in Igbo. "But I can't speak for Chidi and your daughter; perhaps they do not speak the language of the ancestors."

The two men shouted. *"Chineke!* So you speak our language!" they said as one, using the Igbo word of surprise, and saying the rest in English. When they had calmed down from their excitement, the older man began. "We thank the ancestors for bringing us together to celebrate the marriage of your son and our daughter," he said as he poured a little of the cider on the floor.

"We ask the ancestors to bless this union and make it fruitful. Thank you to the ancestors for joining our families as one," he continued.

"What would he do if there were carpet on the floor?" Beth whispered in my ear.

"He'd ask for a bowl to be brought, so he could pour the cider into that," I said. "Or just pour it on the carpet!"

Once again, I observed the beloved custom of the bride sipping the "wine" and giving the cup to her husband-to-be. I'm sure the ancestors were pleased.

Another part of Igbo traditional practice that lives on is reverence for the major god and for lesser gods. The single god of Igbo spiritual practice, Chukwu, is omnipresent, responsible for life, the earth, the sky, animals, and people. Chukwu is honored more in the use of the name than as a source of inspiration or aid. Igbo people do not usually appeal to Chukwu on his own, in the way a Christian may pray to God.

*Chukwu gozie gi,* meaning "God bless you," is a phrase used in the market. One day when we were in the village during the Christmas holidays in 2017 I went to the market. After hearty bargaining for a minute or two, I agreed to pay 480 naira for a few tomatoes. I gave the seller a 500 naira note, about one dollar and thirty cents. "Chukwu gozie gi," she said to me when I refused the twenty naira note that was my change. "God bless you" seemed like large praise for such a tiny gift. Twenty naira at the time of that transaction was about six cents!

The phrase is used in more serious conversation too. Mama said, *"Chukwu gozie unu,* God bless you all," when I was departing Biafra with our two children, escaping the last year of the civil war and leaving my husband, her, and the rest of the family behind in the village. The word for "thank you," *dalu,* is often paired with "Chukwu gozie gi" when expressing gratitude for a favor, a task performed for someone, or a gift.

*Chi* is another word for god, usually used to mean a personal god or spirit that resides within each person. Both Chukwu and chi are part of many Igbo names, including those in our family. Chi, many Igbo people believe, is the most common element of Igbo names.

The chi or personal god in Igbo cosmology can influence someone's life deeply. An Igbo believer may say, "I could or could not do something because my chi did or did not allow it." The Igbo phrase is *Onye kwe, chi ya ekwe,* meaning "When one says yes, his god also affirms." I like the way it is seen to support one's decisions or prevent poor choices.

After the supreme being Chukwu and the personal god chi are lesser gods. I am familiar with only one, and only because of an encounter involving her. During the Biafran War, I was living in the village. There was a shortage of kerosene for our lanterns. I had gone to the outhouse next to the main building in the early morning without a light. I noticed something draped over the hole. I drew closer, thinking it was a piece of clothing someone had left.

It was a python, very long and very scary. Hearing my screams, several young male cousins came to prod and push it out of the small enclosure.

"It's getting away. Why don't you kill it?" I said.

"We can't kill it. Our tradition does not allow it."

"Why? Surely it's dangerous to leave it alive."

"The python is sacred," our younger cousin Chinedu said. "It lives close to Ani, the earth goddess. It walks on the earth. We've always regarded it as a god."

"You mean the snake is protected?" I said. "Won't it hurt someone?"

"Even if we wanted to kill it, the older people wouldn't let us," he said. "They would be very upset!"

After a couple of days of seeing the same snake curled up comfortably in a log at the front of our compound, I spoke to John, one of the older cousins, who seemed less committed to tradition than his siblings and other relatives.

"I'm so frightened I can barely sleep. I can't leave Beth on the veranda during the day without staying near her. What if the snake comes back?"

"You know it won't hurt Beth or the other children," John said. "It might take a chicken, but it won't harm anything else."

"How can you be so sure? I didn't grow up with snakes. And I don't see why this snake should be protected and I'm not! After all, the python is not sacred to my people!"

It was the only time I deliberately used my status as a foreigner and a white American. I didn't say, "Please kill the snake." But he knew what I wanted-ed. The next morning, I learned that the snake was dead. I was overjoyed. The umunna were angry. They held a meeting to decide what to do. No one confessed to being the culprit, so they couldn't punish any specific individual. But they did ask the Dibia what to do.

"You must bring five jugs of palm wine as an offering to appease the spirits for the offense of killing a python," the Dibia said. The umunna made the whole group of suspects responsible for getting the palm wine and carrying it to the Dibia.

Spirits and ancestors may take physical form among the Igbo as masquerades. Once, they were the feared enforcers of tradition. Today they are often entertainment.

# 22

## MASQUERADES, THE EMBODIMENT OF ANCESTORS AND SPIRITS

THE MASQUERADES, *MMANWU* OR *MMUO* in Igbo, are another powerful expression of spiritual life among the Igbo. A masquerade is the embodiment or the physical manifestation of a spirit. In some parts of Igboland, the masquerade is thought to be an ancestor, and in other places a lesser god. But he is always an intermediary between the spiritual and temporal worlds.

When I asked Clem about the masquerades, he said, "When I was little I knew they came from a hole in the earth. They were from the world beyond."

"But didn't you know they are men in secret societies who conceal their bodies and wear scary masks?" I said.

"I didn't know that. I did not like to think about them. If I misbehaved, my father told me the masquerades would take me away."

It took many years for him to admit that they were people. The revelation really crystallized for him one day thirty years ago during the Christmas holidays. Our son Sam, then sixteen, had gone out as soon as we finished lunch. Around four in the afternoon a masquerade entered our compound with his followers. I sat on the low wall around the veranda, the same place Beth had stood as a one-year-old when I worried about the snake. Clem stood behind me, not willing to be so close.

"Papa Chinaku," the masquerade called out in his reedy masquerade voice. Clem took one step forward, visibly frightened. In a normal young man's voice, the masquerade said, "Do you know who I am?"

"It's you, Okeke!" Clem said. "It's the son of our next-door neighbor Mg-bokwuocha!" He turned to me with a smile as he spoke and stepped back. Then one of the followers stepped forward, holding out his fan for our contribution. It was Sam!

The mmuo wear elaborate masks that may depict evil spirits, ancestors, animals, or warriors. There are even masks that depict women. In earlier times the men who were masquerades were charged with maintaining respect for traditions. They demanded obedience and could not be challenged. In the past they had the authority to enforce customs. If anyone stepped out of line, the masquerades could be called upon to enforce order.

Clem remembers a time when Papa hit a mmuo. He does not know how it happened, but Papa was nearly killed for this offense. Because the family was respected, he was spared.

Today the masquerades are a source of entertainment, widely appreciated by Igbo people at holidays such as the new yam festival or New Year's. They appear for funerals and other major celebrations. Yet the men who don the costumes to become masquerades are still sworn to secrecy and can still awaken fear in some onlookers.

Women were not supposed to look directly at a masquerade. That tradition remains for the most powerful mmuo, but can be modified, as I learned during the Christmas holidays in 2017. Clem and I had finished a late lunch on the day after New Year's.

"I'm going up to take a nap," Clem said as I went outside to wait for the masquerades to appear. "Call me when they come."

Sam, now forty-six, had taken his children out along the road to be closer to the action. "Did you see any masquerades?" I said to the children as they returned to our compound.

"I saw two," said Bruche, our six-year-old grandson. "I wasn't afraid," he said, though he was holding his dad's hand. "They didn't whip me."

"Mother, come," Sam said. "Our friend Obi has invited you to join him. He's reserved places at a bar overlooking the main road to watch."

I called Clem, and we followed Sam about a quarter mile up the busy road.

"Welcome, come sit—these places are for you," Obi said, indicating two chairs

Figure 15 Musicians performing in Nanka, January 2018

in the front row being vacated for us. We were just above the road where a group of musicians was playing.

One had an *udu,* a clay jug hit on the opening with the hand or a fan for percussion; two held ogenes, a double-sided hand bell made of forged iron, struck with a stick or iron rod. I saw one man shaking an *ichaka,* a gourd partially covered with cowrie shells to give it a distinctive rattle.

Soon a masquerade appeared, and the musicians stepped aside. The mmuo, wearing a yellow top with dark green stripes, one pant leg in the same fabric and the other in red, danced in front of us. His mask had large white-and-black horns, surrounded by a halo of blue hair. He had a white face with black outlining the eyes and mouth. The crowd on the road stayed a few feet away. A couple of men threw money at the masquerade. His followers collected the cash and moved on. Another came, then one more, this one in a bright magenta, purple, and blue outfit, with a flute player accompanying him. The musicians returned whenever there was a break.

An hour later the most frightening masquerade, called Agaba, raced down the road and halted in front of us, but only for a second. He turned as the crowd scattered, and he stalked back and forth to show his power. Sam's daughter moved behind her father, and Bruche, who'd been seated on Clem's lap, joined his sister.

Two men seated near me said I had to move to the back. "A woman cannot observe Agaba," they said.

Obi defended my presence. "Once a wom-an is over seventy, she can watch," he said. I stayed.

Agaba was taller than other masquerades and had shiny two-inch metal cones interspersed with multicolored feathers and fabric covering his body. His head was completely hidden by black raffia, with a headdress topped by four curved black horns and feathers. A single spike projected over his forehead.

Children who had run back when Agaba first came into view recovered their courage and approached, though were careful not to get too close. Adults did not shrink away as they might have done twenty years ago. A few men threw money, which his followers collected from the ground around him. After four or five minutes, he sprinted back up the road toward the market.

The musicians returned. Then came two mmuo impersonating women. They wore white masks with exaggerated black facial markings and high headdresses of green, yellow, and red ribbons. The tops they wore were covered with colorful geometric patterns. Most of their dancing was synchronized. Their movements were exaggerated feminine gestures.

We used to watch masquerades from our own compound. We would know they were approaching by the sound of the dried pods worn around their ankles and waists, which rattle and clatter when they run. Sometimes we would see a gang of children running on the road in front of our compound and know they were following or being chased by a masquerade.

Today fewer masquerades come to us. When they do, as the time our neighbor Okeke revealed himself to my husband, the masquerade calls out in his strange high-pitched mmuo voice. His followers stamp around, brandishing their whips. A flute player sometimes accompanies him; if so he will dance to the tune the flautist plays. He may call out someone's name. I have been called several times

Figure 16 One of the masquerades, January 2018

Figure 17 Agaba, the most feared masquerade, Nanka January 2018

in the eerie voice. I go forward with my head down, never looking directly at the masquerade, and say with deep respect, "Mmuo." One of the followers holds out a fan for me to place my gift. Then the mmuo jumps and turns with his followers and they race out of the compound.

I recognize the importance of deference. But I have felt fear only once! That was when the night masquerades came during the Biafran War. I had been in the village for seven months.

Figure 18 "Female" masquerades in Nanka, January 2018

Mama had given me warning before we all turned in. "Tonight, the *achikwu ocha,* the white masquerades, are coming," she said. "They will come when you are already asleep."

"What do you mean, white masquerades?"

"They are invisible. You will only hear them," she said, "but not see them. You must not show any light."

"What would happen?"

"They can do very bad things," she said.

When I was awakened by their screeching sounds, I peered carefully out the window, making sure my face was hidden. I could see nothing in the moonless night.

Several years later I understood the power of Mama's warning. Our neighbor and clansman Nnadi had been accused of placing a charm on his brother. When he refused to deny his act, he was exiled for seven years. The *achikwu* exacted further punishment and destroyed his house. I have heard nothing about them in recent years. Maybe they are no longer able to exert power.

Masquerades are an essential part of our visits to the village. They continue to be said to embody the spirits of the ancestors or the gods. Though few people are afraid of them today, their presence is key to holidays in Nanka. I hope they will still be there when our grandchildren take their children to the village!

# 23

## WHEN THERE IS NO SON

*"NNO, NWUNYEM!* WELCOME, MY WIFE!" Mgbokwuocha's booming voice and strong arms surrounded me as I climbed out of the car, stiff after nine hours on the road.

*"Kedu? Kedu maka ndi be gi?* How are you? How is your family?" I said.

Our family of five had come in two cars for the Christmas holidays in 1989—my husband and I with the driver and cook in one, the children with Chinaku, the oldest, driving the other. I was now living in the US, as were Beth and Sam, and Clem spent most of his time in London, but this was irrelevant to Mgbokwuocha. We had come to the village for the Christmas holidays. Where we came from was not of interest.

The late afternoon air was tinted with the reddish dust of the Harmattan. I caught the aroma of the bitterleaf soup cooking in Mgbokwuocha's compound to the left of ours. As I looked in that direction I was reminded of the snake that had curled up in the cement block wall separating our compounds twenty-one years earlier.

To the right of our compound the goats were bleating in their sheds near Obele's house. The wall that separated our home from Obele's and her sons' houses was about my height of five feet, seven inches, so too tall to see over. Clem's brother Geoffrey had planted ixora bushes along our side of the wall. I loved their small star-shaped reddish flowers and shiny green leaves. The orange tree that he'd planted near our generator house was now twenty-five feet tall, but I'd never tasted one orange. They were never ripe at Christmastime.

Papa's room over the gate had shreds of torn curtain hanging in the window. No one had taken over the room since his death a decade earlier, though John, a cousin, used it from time to time. Our second son, Sam, would not just sleep there, but take possession of this space for our two weeks in the village.

Two palms, one with coconuts and one with oil-bearing fruits, grew beyond the orange tree, nearer the gate. There were patches of grass on the red earth where the sweeping had been neglected. I relaxed easily into the serenity of the village, leaving the memory of the hectic drive behind me.

Mgbokwuocha was my husband's second cousin. I met her at our first son's naming ceremony in 1965. She had three sons then, the oldest in his teens and the youngest the same age as our son Chinaku.

By the time we fled the capital of the breakaway Republic of Biafra in September 1967 to take refuge in Clem's village, she had a daughter, Mgbokwu, three months old at the time, the same age as my daughter, Beth. I saw her frequently during my year in the village. Our daughters turned one. They often stood side by side at the railing in front of our house and laughed together.

Mgbokwuocha's appearance matched her voice. She was large, taller than me by at least an inch, and broad, her body almost square. Her dark, chestnut-brown skin was shiny with sweat. She had a large nose, wide-set eyes, and heavy eyebrows. Her clothes usually looked as if they needed washing, and occasionally her body too clearly sent the message that she needed a bath.

Over the years I heard bits and pieces about why she had children but never married. In 2015 I proposed a talk for the Igbo Women's Cultural Event at the School of Oriental and African Studies (SOAS) in London. I wanted to speak about inheritance, a woman's place, and land. I guessed that her story was a prime example.

I asked our cousin Chinedu to tell me about her. Through several email exchanges, I learned the facts, embellished here with my imagination, with what others have told me over the years, and with research in the related custom. Her story is based on the importance of land, critical to an Igbo man's preservation of his lineage. He may pass it on to his oldest son or, more commonly, divide it among his sons. But by tradition it can be passed only to sons, not to daughters.

Mgbokwuocha's father, Ezeofor, was the brother of our grandfather Ogbungwa. Ogbungwa had five sons, so inheritance was not an issue. But Ezeofor was less fortunate. He first married a woman who had a son, but she and the baby died. He then married another woman called Ebulonu. For years she did not conceive. Finally, she had to accept that she was not having any children. He had no one to inherit his land.

She turned to an Igbo custom called *nnochi,* to represent, or "to take the place of." It is used when someone must be brought into a marriage to fulfill a role that the wife herself cannot. Ebulonu decided to save her marriage and provide a son for her husband by introducing her younger sister Nwangbeke into the marriage. Her role was specifically to have a son. She did, but only after giving birth to three daughters.

Ezeofor's bad luck continued. The son was developmentally disabled and unable to inherit the land. Ezeofor was aging and did not feel ready to take another wife. If he had no one to whom he could pass on his land, it would revert to a brother or other male relative. His lineage would disappear. He was faced with a major problem.

Before he found a solution, he contracted leprosy. His illness made him lose interest in who would inherit. Instead, he became focused on finding the person who would give him a befitting burial and promised a portion of his land to this man. The question of inheritance was forgotten for the time being, and not resurrected until after his death and burial.

When he died, the two sisters, his widows, were left with three daughters and a disabled son. By Igbo custom the oldest of their late husband's brothers could marry them, or they could be forced to leave. The land would be lost to their children and they would have nothing. To secure their own place to live, and to fulfill the purpose of the nnochi, they had to act, and act quickly.

The older two of Nwangbeke's three daughters had already married. But the youngest, Mgbokwuocha, had just reached the age to marry. Nwangbeke had heard of a practice where a woman could be given the role of a man, thus ensuring her right to hold the land. Was this what she should do now with her remaining daughter?

She went to two senior men of the clan, men she trusted.

"You can have your daughter take on the role of a son," they told her. "You will have to conduct an 'inside marriage,' or *nnuikwa,* to give Mgbok-wuocha the role of 'female son.'"

"How does this happen?" she said. "What do I have to do?"

"You must bring two jugs of *nkwu-enu*—the 'up' palm wine from taller trees, two of *ngwo*—palm wine from shorter raffia palms, one live cock, and kola nuts. You and the other women will have to prepare food for the umunna who will be your witnesses. We will assemble them for this event." The elders smiled at the thought of the feast Nwangbeke, her co-widow, and other women married into the family would prepare for them to eat after the ceremony.

"Didn't the Christians object to this practice?" I asked Chinedu.

"At the time, although some people in Nanka were already Christians, her family was pagan, so there was no religious objection to this ceremony."

On the appointed day, the umunna assembled in the compound of the oldest male. There were ten men, all related to the deceased husband. The chief priest, or Dibia, had been summoned to perform the ceremony. The host held up a kola nut from the tray Nwangbeke had brought to him. "With this kola we honor you, our ancestors," he said. "Kola brings life." He broke the kola nut, took his own piece, placed several others on the tray, and instructed the youngest of the umunna to break them and pass them around. When each man had taken his own, the server held the tray out for Nwangbeke and the other women.

"*Ndi be anyi, kwenu!* Our people, shout!" the elder called out. The men responded with a loud "Yah!" Twice more he uttered the traditional greeting so loved by Igbo people. I've even seen it used when just women are present, though a woman would not dare say it if men were in the gathering!

Then the Dibia held up the rooster, addressing the ancestors. "We offer you this cock as a sign that we are bringing you our daughter and making her a son and your bride," he said. "The mother of this woman has also given us palm wine and kola to demonstrate her wish that we accept her daughter in the role of *nnochi.*"

He called Mgbokwuocha to come to him. "You are charged from this day forward to act in the place of a son of your father. You may live on the land and treat it as your own. You must have sons so you can pass the land on to them."

Her clansmen helped her repair her father's house, which had been neglected during the last days of his illness. She moved into the house, took over the yam and cassava fields that are usually the duty of a man, and entertained male visitors. Her mother moved in with her and helped with farming, gathering firewood, and cooking.

She now owned the land as a caretaker for the next generation. And because she did, she was able to barter small parcels of the land for cash or goods, sell a few profitable trees or their fruits, and grow her own crops for cash. She had a responsibility to produce heirs, and she did. The men of the village knew she needed them to father her children. "Responsible men came forward to help," Chinedu told me. "They were not threatening the birthright of their children, since Mgbokwuocha's children would inherit from her, not them."

The idea of a woman "becoming a man" to hold the land and the place in the line of succession was new and fascinating to me. In my research I found several accounts of this practice among the Igbo people, but no other individual stories. Mgbokwuocha's story shines a spotlight on the critical relationship between the land and the chain of ancestors. An Igbo man's land is such an important piece of his wealth and worth that he cannot bear the thought of losing it because he has no male heir. His place in the world is determined by having his own land. It is his claim to being part of the clan, the village, and the family.

During the twelve months that I stayed in the village and our daughters played together, Clem and I became aware that Mgbokwuocha was finding it difficult to grow and buy enough food for her family. We invited her to send her third son, Okeke, to eat with us every evening to ease her burden.

Her first son was away fighting in the civil war and died in the conflict. Her next son, Emmanuel, or Emma, grew into a serious young man. who got an education. The daughter never learned to speak fully, although she did interact with other children in the village. What I remember most about her is hearing her mother call her. "Mgbokwu!" she would yell, so loudly that her voice rang out through our compound and several others. We would eventually see Mgbokwu return to her mother.

When we rebuilt our house in 1990, we made an enclosed kitchen that protruded into her land. According to my husband, he bought that piece of land from Mgbokwuocha's son. But several years later she contested our ownership of that piece, about six by twelve feet. Finally, she exhausted my husband with her demands, and he had the kitchen knocked down. But after quarrelling over land, Mgbokwuocha didn't come to greet me anymore. I missed her.

Emma has married. He is working in eastern Nigeria but comes to their home during the holidays. Mgbokwuocha died in 2005. She was mourned by her sons and by our umunna. Emma's oldest son will inherit the land and maintain the lineage when his father dies.

For years after I learned her story I thought her life was constricted, that she was bound in a role she had not chosen. She was forced to become the head of the household. Yet in fulfilling the tradition of inheritance, she perpetuated her father's legacy. She preserved the land for her sons. For the umunna, having her take on this role was right and proper. And who am I to say that she did not enjoy the sexual freedom that was not open to other women? Not having a son to inherit is a worry for Igbo men. We have two sons, but Clem is concerned that our older son, who has the first rights to our compound and house, is not yet married. Clem wonders how our son will be able to preserve the land. There is no doubt a conflict between all these traditional Igbo practices and the recognition of women's rights. The tradition says the first son inherits; he may share with male siblings but not female. By tradition, widows do not have rights and can even be regarded as the property of their deceased husband's male relatives. Many people have articulated the idea that women's rights are human rights, maintaining that these practices are inhumane and counter to treaties to which Nigeria is a signatory, in addition to being contrary to the Nigerian constitution.

In 2015 the Nigerian Supreme Court affirmed the right of women to inherit from their fathers and husbands. They declared specifically that the Igbo practice of not allowing women to inherit was unconstitutional. I wondered if that ruling affected opinions in Nanka. "Has the custom of *nnuikwa* died out? What about a widow inheriting from her husband?" I said to Chinedu, my informant on oral tradition.

"I do not think the elders in the village are ready to allow a woman to inherit family land without some special reason, like Mgbokwuocha's case," he said. "They probably still do not think widows should inherit."

I am a champion of human rights and women's rights specifically. If I were asked, I would oppose forcing a woman to "become a man" to maintain ancestral rights to land. But the custom of *nnuikwa* was an integral piece of preserving the status of land ownership in the community. I have come to embrace many Igbo customs, and now understand how Mgbokwuocha filled a critical need in the family and umunna. I admire the capacity of the Igbo people to find this solution to an untenable situation.

# 24

## THE KOLA REACHES HOME: COMMUNITY AND CONNECTIONS

THE LURE OF BELONGING AND being part of a community has held me in its power since my early days in Nigeria. Even though I left the country to return to the US in 1986, it continues to guide me.

The stories of people from my husband's village and clan deepen my understanding of the many ways in which this sense of community is expressed. The first way is belonging to a place and a family. My father-in-law ran away from a ceremony he feared when he was seventeen. But he returned to his home to marry in 1929, knowing members of his clan would find a bride for him. My husband did not exactly deny but ignored the connection for years when he was in the United Kingdom. He finally succumbed to it under pressure from his mother's desire to see him and spurred on by his legal troubles.

Second is the connection formed between families through marriage. From the initial investigation by both sides of a union, to the ceremonies of knocking on the door and carrying the palm wine, to the final departure of the bride with her husband, the two families are becoming joined. They remain connected beyond the lives of the two who wed, into succeeding generations. These bonds link people from different towns or villages and strengthen a sense of shared lives.

Third is the importance of land. A West African man desperately wants to own land, no matter how small a plot it is. Papa's decision to abandon land he was given for fear of the mysterious mist was not made lightly. For years after, he struggled with his older brother to be given his own piece of property. Finally his uncle obliged him. Papa passed the land on to his son, my husband, together with a small area on the other side of the adjoining compound. Custom dictates that land is passed only to sons, and it is up to the father to direct whether it goes to only the first son or to all sons. Clem's father stipulated that Clem must give that small area to his brothers, Godwin and Geoffrey, which he did.

Mgbokwuocha's story illustrates the solution when there is no son to inherit. She had to remain on the land, treat it as her own, and produce a son to inherit. Thus the land was kept in the family. The practice of passing land to all sons, or even forcing younger sons to find other land in the village, means that the plots become smaller and smaller over time, leading to a high population density and less land for cultivation.

Fourth is respect for elders. When Samuel went to the ceremonies celebrating his marriage, he was always accompanied by elders from the clan. Likewise the hosts would assemble their elders to welcome the groom's family. At any breaking of kola nut, the oldest male present will be given the honor. When there is a dispute within a clan, the elders will convene to find a solution.

Fifth is the veneration of ancestors and the related devotion to those yet to be born. It is evident in the invocation when breaking the kola nut, asking the ancestors to bless the nut. The importance attached to having male children is to ensure that future generations will be present to preserve the family line.

Sixth are the spiritual beliefs of the Igbo people, like those of other Africans. The one supreme deity, Chukwu, is supported by lesser gods, who are found in the natural surroundings and in animate creatures, such as the python, who is close to the earth goddess. The role of the Dibia is related, as he is the intermediary between spirits or ancestors and humans. Masquerades, being the embodiment of ancestors and/or spirits, are part of this custom.

Seventh are the names given to children that signify important events, hopes for the future, reverence for God, or days of birth. Naming ceremonies involve burying the umbilical cord, or a bit of the baby's hair, in the compound to connote belonging.

Eighth is the way children are taught to share, again adding to the sense of belonging and being responsible for one another. A plate of yam and soup given to a group of children is divided among all, with the oldest taking his own first but assuring everyone that they will get a portion. Connected is the tradition that says every child belongs to everyone in the community. This is one of the starkest differences between African and Western culture. An adult in the West dare not correct someone else's children.

Lastly, palm wine and kola nuts are signifiers of connection and grease the wheels of community interaction. Palm wine is the most common gift to hosts at celebratory events, is often part of the bride price, and is carried by the bride to her new husband's family. It is the drink the bride will carry to her husband to signify her acceptance of him as her husband. Kola nuts are the prerequisite of every event; a visitor takes them home to show how well his hosts treated him.

Customs such as the treatment of widows and the killing of twins have changed over the years. Mary Slessor and other missionaries convinced the Igbo people more than a hundred years ago that twins were not evil and that the mother should not be blamed. Today multiple births are welcomed. Most widows are no longer required to have their heads shaved.

Funeral ceremonies have perhaps changed the most. They used to occur within twenty-four hours of the death; now they are held weeks, sometimes months, later. The more important a person, the longer it takes to prepare for the funeral, or so it seems.

Whereas decades ago most family members lived close by, today families are spread out around the country and around the world. To notify everyone can take several days, crossing time zones and schedules. Caring for the deceased before burial has become a big business in Nigeria. Mortuaries are thriving as more and more often bodies are stored for a serious length of time.

Divorces, multiple marriages, travel distances, and work commitments complicate funeral planning. Most Igbo people are Christian, with about half Anglican and half Roman Catholic. But many have embraced the modern evangelical churches, sometimes alongside their Anglican tradition. Relatives have to decide whether to have an Anglican or a modern evangelical funeral service.

Another consideration is whether to consult a Dibia, the traditional shaman, to determine the best time to hold the funeral. Then there is the question of where the burial will take place. In my husband's town, a woman is usually buried near her husband in the family compound. In some Igbo towns it is customary to return a woman's body to her place of birth. Clem's parents are buried in our compound and he expects to join them.

The family must gather the necessary funds to put on a good funeral. Many visitors come for days of wake-keeping, traditional ceremonies, and religious services. They must all be fed. Someone must design the invitation and get it printed. If the extended family will wear the same fabric in their clothing, someone must choose it, buy it, and distribute it to the family members, who will take it to their own tailors or seamstresses. Today I cannot imagine a Nigerian funeral without an elaborate program book to accompany the event.

In 1973 my husband's book *Men and Management in Contemporary Africa* was published. He wrote it based on research he and I carried out in several industrial plants in Nigeria in the 1960s and '70s. We found that certain habits of Nigerian workers were regarded negatively by their mostly European managers. For the managers, the practices were mystifying and frustrating. For the workers, the managers' complaints were unreasonable. They were miles apart in understanding one another's actions.

One such practice was that workers would send a good part of their wages or salaries "home" to their families. Sometimes they would ask for an advance, explaining that they had to support aging parents or an ill relative. The managers would bemoan the habit, stating that workers needed to take care of their immediate families, not far-off villagers. Yet West African workers have an obligation to help out those they have left behind in their villages, as well as those who have suffered illnesses or injuries. Not doing so would place both the worker and his parents in a shameful position.

When a worker's father, mother, or other close relative died, the worker would be absent for up to two weeks, sometimes even more. This was unheard of for a European manager, who would understand two days, maybe three, for the funeral of a close family member, but certainly not a week or more. Clem himself, who wrote the book, has never become accustomed to the Western response to a death in the family. Ed, our minister of music and choir director at the Unitarian Church in Westport, lost his mother. When I told Clem that Ed was present for choir rehearsal not even a week later, he was horrified. "It's not right," he said. "How could he come back so quickly?"

Another characteristic of Nigerian workers is their unwillingness to ask questions, even when instructions are not well understood. Nigerian teachers and parents demand obedience. They do not tolerate objections or questions to their authority. They do not even need to say, "Because I said so!" It is understood by both sides.

But the reluctance to ask questions can be damaging. Even if an employee does not understand what he has been asked to do, he will usually muddle through. In his mind, asking a question seems like insubordination, as if he is questioning authority, rather than a means to seek information. So tasks get done incorrectly, and then the worker is blamed. Of course, he had answered, "Yes, sir," or in Nigerian parlance by workers, "Yes, sah!" when given the directions and asked if he understood.

This happens in domestic situations as well as in factories and often leads to unhappiness on both sides. The female head of a household, whether foreign or Nigerian, is called "madam." The madam will tell her steward to cook a certain dish, provide directions, and ask if he understands. He will answer that he does. When the dish does not come out right, she is angry, and he is confused and unhappy. In restaurants, a waiter or waitress will say they understand a customer's order whether they do or not. Rather than question the customer, they will risk bringing the wrong dish.

Managers also felt that workers did not show initiative. They had to be told every step to take and would not seek solutions to problems on their own. They will wait for a manager to provide the answer.

The mismatch between managers' expectations and workers' responses is due to basic understandings among Africans about how to behave and foreign managers' complete unfamiliarity with African customs and norms. When Africans become managers, some adopt European practices and can exhibit the same impatience or dissatisfaction.

In the chapter "Environment for Business in Africa and Survey Strategy,"

Clem says, "The [African] family is conceived of as a large number of people, many dead, some living and countless numbers yet to be born. Every individual is taught to accept his place in this group and to behave in a way to bring honour [sic] to it. . . . Emphasis is placed on helping others in sickness or health, success or failure. A family member fulfils his obligation not by acquiring for himself but by giving to other members."[10]

Of course a worker will send money home or help a clansman in need. He must do this to fulfill his obligation. He would be ashamed of himself and unwilling to face his relatives at home if he did not.

In the next paragraph, Clem says, "Individualism is suppressed, and from his early days a person is taught to accept his place in the family-blood relations as determined by his age. . . . He is supposed to keep the company of his age group and take active, unquestioning part in its traditional roles. . . . His behavior and manners are closely scrutinized by his elders . . . the drive for individual autonomy and independent thinking in Africans is continually suppressed." Again, asking questions and seeking solutions on one's own have not been encouraged or even allowed for young African men.

My husband proposes solutions for these issues. He says in Chapter 11 that a new concept for business in Africa is needed. He calls it "the community concept . . . [which] sees the business organization as a community to which the individual belongs, not just as one with a fixed legal contract but as a member by choice." He envisions it "built on close interpersonal relationships and group interactions."[11]

In this community the African traditions regarding age and hierarchy will be honored. The European outlook is that a person should be rewarded with a promotion and given supervisory responsibility if his performance merits it. But for the African, hierarchy is based on age and time in the organization. Newer and younger workers should respect older and more experienced ones and cannot be promoted over those who were there before them or have a significant age advantage.

All these traits—individualism, taking initiative, being rewarded for merit over age, showing commitment to nuclear family over extended, and dealing with death "in a hurry"—are taken for granted in Western society. They are foreign to Africans. The sense of community, belonging, and being part of something larger is a source of satisfaction to people who grew up in an African setting. The connections forged in a family, clan, and village—by birth and through marriage, reinforced by respect for elders, attachment to land, and shared spiritual beliefs—are powerful. They provide African men and women with confidence in knowing they have a home where they belong and are needed. I believe that our American and European cultures today do not help us develop deep connections with others. We join with people who think like us or have similar experiences, but the bonds may not be lasting. Many of us are left unmoored with a vague sense of discontent.

Can we in Western societies consider adapting from African traditions that foster a sense of belonging? How would these enrich our lives? Would regard for African traditions help us deal with the divisions of racism in the US? These are weighty questions beyond the scope of this book. I do address them in several talks I gave in the last few years which you will find in the appendix. Here I will mention three possibilities.

First we can pay greater attention to links with extended family. I have found Facebook useful in connecting with cousins and getting to know a little about their lives. Many families have reunions, more could.

Second, caring for those in our extended family or in our town who face hardship would be a way of demonstrating we belong to one community. I remember not being willing or able to adjust my life to care for my father in our house when he could not live alone. Today there are efforts underway to keep elders at home while cared for and respected. We can encourage these.

Third, the US needs to address racism in all its individual and systemic manifestations. It is a serious blight in the United States. White Americans must understand the privilege we have and use it with courage, speaking up against racism when we see it. Black Americans can be rightly proud of their ancestors' traditions that foster community. Many African-Americans are already using values and traditions adopted from Africa. If these practices can become part of US culture, not just Black US culture, we would all be richer!

*Oji luo uno okwua ebe osi abia.*
*When the kola nut reaches home, it will tell where it came from.*

The kola nut has served its purpose. Just as a visitor takes home a kola nut to say how well he was treated by his hosts and to report on his visit, I brought back to the US the warmth, the sense of community, and the knowledge of lifelong connections from my years in Nigeria. When I went to the country as a Peace Corps volunteer in 1962, I had no idea I would marry, raise a family, have a business, and more importantly become part of a village. I returned to the US knowing that I have a home in Nanka whenever I want or need it. I was changed and enriched by my years in the country. I have given you a full report on what I experienced and shared with you how well I was treated, as the proverb says.

# Appendix A

"Breaking Kola," My Reflections for Summer Service, August 20, 2006, the Unitarian Church in Westport, Connecticut

I RECALL THE INSTRUCTION WE heard from our associate minister Margie in her sermon as a candidate last May. She said, "Draw the evidence of the past into the present to make sense of life's trajectory." She told her story well. I want to tell you the story of my path to finding my own tribe.

Early on, I felt like an outsider. There we were, living in a predominately Republican northern Kentucky town. With my German immigrant working-class father and my Vassar-educated liberal democratic mother, I was pretty sure we didn't fit.

I left home for Mount Holyoke College. Though I liked my years there, I still thought others knew secrets to belonging that I didn't quite get. During junior year, William Sloane Coffin came to campus to speak about Crossroads Africa. A few months later the Peace Corps formation was announced. I felt compelled to apply and was accepted. I prepared to head to Africa, to the amazement and puzzlement of friends. Why would I want to do that? Africa?

But I identified with the underdeveloped people of the world—weren't they excluded from the world's bounty as I had been excluded from the inner social circles? I thought I could help bring them from outsider to insider status,

I believe, and although I didn't think it at the time, give myself an insider role too.

My Peace Corps assignment was far from typical. I did not live in a village in rural Nigeria. Instead, I had a two-bedroom apartment in the main residential area of Lagos, the capital. I was assigned to a postsecondary science school, where I taught German to very bright sixth-form students.

I was also assigned to a school nearby, a new one-room school. There was no reliable transport, so Peace Corps, contrary to their usual policy, supplied me with a tiny car, a Fiat 500, which led to meeting Clem. But I didn't know it at the time!

What I knew was that after eighteen months in Nigeria, I felt very much at home. I was surrounded by many expatriate and African friends. I knew the customs and had learned some Yoruba—the language of the village where I taught part-time—when one day I received a letter, a memo, from the chief engineer of the Electricity Corporation of Nigeria. The company was surveying consumers about electricity usage. The survey takers had called at my apartment several times, but I was never home. Would I kindly report to the chief engineer in his office?

Why the chief engineer should concern himself with this survey puzzled me a little, but off I went, where I was ushered into a huge office. Seated behind the very large desk was a very proper Nigerian in his suit, tie, pocket handkerchief, and all. I was a little indignant—I made clear that I was a Peace Corps volunteer and used very little electricity. Clem was all apologies, so sorry for the inconvenience, and on learning that I was Peace Corps asked about my work and how I liked Nigeria. I left somewhat mollified.

A week later, he showed up at my door with a woman I knew from school. I didn't recognize him, but he reminded me that he was the chief engineer, Clement. The custom then as now in Nigeria is that people drop in—no invitation needed. The woman explained that Clem had been visiting her and her husband; she had mentioned she wanted to see me, and Clem had kindly offered to drive her over. I served them native palm wine, which I usually had on hand. We had a lovely conversation. Clem invited us both to his home a week later. That was the start of our relationship, as I knew it then.

Not more than a month later, I was going to eastern Nigeria, Ibo[12] country, for the Christmas vacation to help in a day camp. Clem arranged for his cousin who lived there to meet me, take me to meet his family, and show me around—a cultural experience. Isaiah took me right to the village, Nanka, where Clem is from. Their home was down a long dirt road—at least two miles off the main road. We passed few other cars on the way down, but lots of mud-walled thatched huts. To enter the compound, we had to park and walk around a long six-foot-high brown mud wall and then duck through the gate. Straight in front was the hut of Clem's uncle Ejike, the patriarch of the family. Ejike was tall and slender, a commanding presence. I was introduced to everyone, but since I didn't speak any Ibo at the time, I have no idea what was said. A couple of months later, back in Lagos, when pressed, Clem confessed that he had asked Isaiah to take me to his family because he wanted them to meet me—he wanted to marry me! I was furious at having to force him to say it, but it didn't take long for me to agree that I wanted the same. Neither race nor height differences were issues in Nigeria or in my mind.

Certainly the chemistry was right. And I was ready to belong to the Nigerian society I had come to love. We were married a year later, on Boxing Day, December 26. Our wedding turned out to be news around the world—including a centerfold photo in *Life Magazine!*

I learned that marrying an Ibo means marrying the whole extended family, clan, and even village. I was shocked during an early visit to the village to have strangers address me as "my wife." Of course, being the only white woman for miles around, I was pretty easy to spot.

Our first son, Chinaku, was born the next year. Soon after, the Nigerian government was overthrown in a coup, and before long, whispers of Biafran secession started. The Ibos are the dominant tribe in eastern Nigeria, and there was resentment that the Nigerian government at independence, in 1960, was controlled by Hausa northerners.

By the time our second child was due, secession and war were imminent, and we succumbed to the wishes of Clem's parents that we leave Lagos for the East. The war started a few days before Beth was born, and within months we found ourselves living back in Nanka, Clem's village. Over a year of my early parenting time was spent living with Clem's parents. This close proximity only highlighted the variations in in our expectations of child rearing.

Major differences emerged around taking risks and being independent—Clem and his parents believing that children should be obedient and respectful, and never question authority. Nigerian or at least Ibo society supports the man imposing his will on his children and even his wife, who should not be too independent! But we cleared that up early! Ibo men do not take part in domestic chores. Clem eventually learned that washing dishes wouldn't harm him or mean that he was giving up his freedom, but it took a long time. When something is a family matter for Clem, that means he should decide what the family should do. I on the other hand believe it means the family should decide.

The war ended and we returned to Lagos and picked up our lives. We returned to the Anglican Church where we had been married. I helped start the Sunday school, when our children were the age for it. I helped found Nigerwives, a society to support foreign wives of Nigerians and teach other women how to adapt. I was president of the American Women's Club, where I saw part of my role as helping the expatriate women understand the culture where they found themselves for a few years.

Five or ten years later, when Clem was running his own business, he was busily drafting a memo to be sent to clients. "We regret to inform you that the import duty on steel has been raised by the order of the federal government. Therefore, as our contract provides, the price of steel to be used in the project will be raised accordingly."

I said, "Why are you sending this as a memo as if it is going to many people? You only have one client using steel, don't you?"

He said it looked better that way. He did not want the company to think they were being targeted. "It will be easier for them to accept it; they won't argue," he said.

Suddenly I remembered that memo about the electricity survey that had brought me to his office so many years earlier.

"How many people received the memo about the survey?"

He denied everything, but eventually the truth came out—he had seen me in my little Fiat at the Mobil station and had followed me home. The memo was his creation to get to meet me.

As our children each went away to boarding school at age eleven, we drifted away from the Anglican Church where we had been married and I had run the Sunday school. I was relieved, no longer able to comfortably recite the Apostles' Creed or the Lord's Prayer. By the time I came back to the US in

1986, I could barely imagine going to church.

At that point, although I felt at home in Nigeria, I recognized that our children were more likely to live in the US or Europe and I wanted to be near them as I grew old. So I was torn between staying in Nigeria and making our home back here. In that frame of mind, I had a significant "outsider" experience. Ejike, the first person I met in the village, died in 1990. He was buried in his own compound, right beside his house. I returned to Nigeria for the funeral. By then I had lived back in the US for four years, and was working at getting Clem to consider coming this way more permanently.

At the funeral, I had the most powerful feeling of being an outsider that I can remember. We were standing around the gravesite in a large circle—the clan, who had fully accepted me. I suddenly felt that no one there had any idea of who I really was. I found myself wondering what I was doing there. The feeling only lasted a few minutes, and then I was back among my adopted family. But it reminded me of living in two worlds and being a bridge.

Soon after, Clem agreed to spend more time in the US. We moved to Westport. I found this church. I recall telling my sister-in-law that I was pleased to have found people like me—in the town, and in this church. She said I had found my tribe.

Today, I find myself in a setting where I really feel at home. I am an insider here, but feel my role is to be a bridge between those on the outside and those inside—to create understanding, empathy, and to expand horizons. I believe that we all have to reach out, stretch, and open ourselves to understanding each other's stories and our own.

# Appendix B

## "Georgina and Our Sixth Principle," Sermon for UN Sunday, October 23, 2011, the Unitarian Universalist Congregation of the South Fork, Bridgehampton, New York

THANK YOU FOR INVITING ME to be here with you for UN Sunday. And thanks to Mark and the others who helped create this service. I will tell you a story about a relative. First I will give you a little lesson in Ibo.[13] Then I'll remind you of our sixth principle, and I'll tell you about my husband's cousin Georgina and why her story inspires my belief in the UN and my participation in the UU-UN Office.

My husband, Clem, is Ibo. This is his tribe and his language. It's one of the three major languages in Nigeria, though there are over two hundred other languages. The language is tonal, so to say the name correctly you have to use the tones. O-nye-me-lu-kwe—it goes mid tone, high, low, low, mid. Let me hear you say it.

And what does it mean? Onye means a person, or someone. This person did a great deed and then boasted about it. Clem says it probably came from victory in a fight, either in war or in wrestling, very popular among Ibos a long time ago.

I just came back from Nigeria, where I attended the funeral of Clem's cousin Jonathan. I was reminded, as I am each time I visit, of the richness of the culture, traditions, and language. But I'm going to tell you about another cousin.

Do you know our UU sixth principle? It says, "We covenant to affirm and promote the goal of world community with peace, liberty, and justice for all."

I love this principle. Before I knew there was such a thing as a UU sixth principle, it was a guide to my life. But I don't see how, in good conscience, we can believe that we promote the goal of world community while poverty is so prevalent in large parts of Africa. The civil wars, the coups d'état, the rebellions—all have their roots in poverty and disenfranchisement.

I admit that African countries have not done themselves any great service in the years since independence. But there were great kingdoms in Africa long before missionaries arrived. The years of missionary activity, the slave trade, colonialism, disruption of tribal loyalties and languages all took their toll. With the carving up of Africa after European wars, tribes were split across country boundaries. With independence in the 1950s and '60s, the governing structures that were foreign remained foreign, never integrated with African customs or mores. So while I don't blame all the ills of Africa today on these forces, I do think the Western world bears some responsibility. I believe that promoting the goal of world community means we have work to do, right here in our homes and in our congregations.

Georgina's story is about being on the outside, missing out on basic human rights that we take for granted, not being part of the world community that enjoys peace and justice. Her story is one of lack of opportunity and lack of women's rights.

Georgina was a lovely preteen when I first met her in 1964. I had gone to Nigeria as a Peace Corps volunteer. Partway through my second year as a Peace Corps teacher, Clem and I met, dated, and fell in love. We were married a year later in Nigeria.

My parents came to our wedding in Lagos, Nigeria. So did the Nigeria Peace Corps director and many friends from the Nigerian and expatriate community. Our wedding photo made Life Magazine—with a caption something like "Peace Corps volunteer marries native." Apart from the cake nearly capsizing in the heat at our outdoor reception, the event was fabulous. My mom and dad had a great time, except for one upsetting experience. In the evening after the wedding, my father went to the fridge to get some ice cubes. He opened the freezer to find the head of a goat staring at him! No one thought to warn him! He was in a state of shock for an hour afterward.

My parents returned home to northern Kentucky to a barrage of hate calls. After all, there were still laws against interracial marriage in Kentucky.

When we'd been married just two years, Nigeria was wracked by civil unrest and then a civil war, the Biafran War, from 1967 to 1970. It was fought between the Ibos, from the eastern part of the country, who were determined to secede, and Nigeria, which was unwilling to let them go. We lived in the Nigerian capital, Lagos, but right before the war started we went to the East at the urging of my husband's parents and our own awareness of what was to come. Ibos had been slaughtered in their homes in northern Nigeria. Ibo families who had lived, sometimes for generations, in the North and other parts of the country were also returning home to the East. We went to Enugu, which was declared the capital of the new country, Biafra, soon after we arrived. After the war started, we left the Biafran capital and went to Clem's village.

I had met Georgina and all the other relatives before, but during my year in the village I got to know them well. Georgina was the daughter of Clem's youngest uncle. She was always cheerful, pleasant to have around, and hardworking. She had a couple of younger brothers and she helped care for them. She also helped me care for our daughter, Beth, who was just three months old when we went to the village.

Georgina had started school later than her brothers, and the school was a couple of miles away. There was no electricity, so children had little time for reading after their long walk, fetching water, and cooking. And then school was suspended during the war.

I remember seeing her and other women and children fetching water from the spring a couple of miles away, climbing down a ravine with their empty clay pots balanced on their heads, and back up again with their full pots, again carefully balanced.

She finished elementary school a couple of years after the war was over. Today there is a girls' secondary school in the village, but there was none then. To attend secondary school she went to live with another cousin, my brother-in-law, in northern Nigeria. There she was expected to help around the house in return for her room and board.

When she finished secondary school, there were only a few universities in Nigeria. She was not a stellar student, and she wasn't able to pass the entrance exam. Nor did anyone have the money at that time for her to attend university, so she stayed with various relatives as a housemaid or nanny. There were no job opportunities for young women or anyone to suggest that she do something other than pursue a degree. During the late '70s, more universities were established, and finally in the '80s, she was able to pass the entrance exam and, with help from relatives, attend university. She graduated with a degree in journalism and some hope for a life outside the village.

But her training was meager. Even if she'd been an excellent student, there were no jobs available without good connections, and she didn't have any. We and other relatives tried unsuccessfully to find her a position. She went back to the village and stayed with her now elderly parents, working on the farm. She was by then too old to attract the village men who wanted younger wives, and not interesting to more educated men who wanted a woman with career prospects.

Every time we visited the village, we saw her. As the years went by, she was no longer so cheerful. There was no longer hope of a brighter future. Then her mother died and she stayed on to care for her father, who had lost his sight. She was one of so many subsistence farmers, growing their own food and selling any surplus to buy what they couldn't grow.

When her father died two years later, she no longer had a real home. Though her brothers might have let her stay on in the village home, it didn't belong to her, but to them. Daughters did not, and do not, have rights to their parents' property.

She went to live with her oldest brother in Lagos, the capital. He was married and raising his own family. She was always the odd one out, the maiden aunt, with little to do except help with the children and the housekeeping.

Lagos, like most of the large cities in Africa, is full of people with little hope of finding jobs, who get by with petty trading, living with relatives. Electricity is scarce, the water supply suspect, and the politicians seem to get richer and fatter on oil revenue while most people live on pennies a day. Medical care is sparse and expensive and not a priority for unmarried women who have no income. In 1998 we heard that she was ill, and a few months later, still not fifty years old, she died. I immediately suspected AIDS, but we later learned that she most likely died of cervical cancer, one of the leading killers of women in Africa.

What a waste of a life. She would have been a wonderful wife and mother, or a teacher of young children. She ended up a disappointed woman, and met an early death. Last week in Nigeria I told her brother that I would talk about her. He was very pleased to learn that her story would serve a purpose.

In the 1980s I came back to the US to pursue a graduate degree in management. In 1994 I became a Unitarian. Or maybe I should say, as I'm sure many of you do, I became aware that I was a UU. I learned about the seven principles. I believe in them—all of them. But the sixth principle holds special meaning for me.

"We covenant to affirm and promote the goal of world community with peace, liberty, and justice for all." When I learned that UUs have a presence at the UN, I saw the connection with my life and my beliefs. I joined the UU-UNO.

I had seen the UN agencies at work in Nigeria. Friends who were Peace Corps volunteers in my group came back a few years later with UNICEF. I believed then and still believe today that the UN, despite its flaws, is our best hope for a world community with peace, liberty, and justice for all.

The director of communications for the UN mission in Iraq said of the UN, "The UN is precious." He wrote those words in August 2004, a year after the bombing of that very UN mission that took the lives of twenty-two of his colleagues.

"The UN is precious," he said, "not because of its name, but because it struggles, however imperfectly, to reach global consensus on the world's critical issues."

The world's critical issues, for me, are the issues that affect the lives of people like Georgina. They are sustainable peace; sustainable development; a sustainable environment; human rights; education; empowerment of women; the elimination of poverty, discrimination, and disease. These critical issues are addressed by the United Nations. I want my voice and my values there in the debates and conversations.

Though there is now piped water in parts of the village, the women and children still have to walk long distances to collect water. People die needlessly for lack of medical care, even basic medicines. Girls have less chance at an education, and all children face lack of teachers and equipment. Though primary education is free in theory, children must buy uniforms and in many places have to supply their own desks. Though there are highly skilled faculty members at the universities, they are often on strike for lack of pay, or the universities are closed because of unrest. There are insufficient jobs for the graduates.

Unmarried and widowed women are dependent on male relatives for support. The environment is under stress. Our village is threatened with destruction because there is huge uncontrolled erosion in the area. Homosexual behavior is against the law in Nigeria.

There is a new organization at the UN, UN Women, with a focus on women's rights and social justice, promoting equal and good education for girls and young women, job opportunities, health care, and freedom from domestic and sexual violence. It's easy to think that we're out of the woods on these issues. Liberia has a woman president who just shared the Nobel Prize with two other African women. A woman in Kenya received the Nobel several years ago for her work on the environment. But the truth is that without continued advocacy, basic rights for women in many parts of the world are not secure. Women like Georgina have little opportunity for advancement when they cannot get good education and are dependent on their male relatives, who may not wish to, or be able to, pay for their health care.

So I support the UU-UNO, working with others at the UN and with the new UN Women to advocate for policies that address these critical issues. I count on the UU-UNO to advocate with my values, and I count on the UU-UNO to keep me and other UUs informed about the work of the UN.

I joined the board of the UU-UNO in 2007 and became president in 2010, following Marilyn Mehr. This June, our board voted to return the UU-UNO to its original home at the UUA [Unitarian Universalist Association], though keeping the office in New York across the street from the UN.

But it still needs us as members.

As you know, when you advocate you need the strength of numbers. That's why we need you to become members of the UU-UNO.

And the people who are so far from peace and justice in their own communities need you now more than ever! I hope you will join as a member and consider joining our UN Committee so your voice can be added to urge action on these critical issues.

For Georgina and for our sixth principle, keep our UU voice at the UN powerful. Let's work together for the goal of world community with peace, liberty, and justice for all.

The next generation of Georginas thank you. And I thank you.

# Appendix C

WHEN I WAS YOUNG I belonged to a Presbyterian Church in Fort Thomas, Kentucky, with my family. My brother and I sang in the choir and belonged to the youth group together.

Within the youth group I felt fortunate to have a role as an officer. Then I attended statewide retreats and conferences and became an officer at the state level, going to Louisville, Kentucky, for board meetings. I loved the leadership opportunity it gave me.

I spoke from the pulpit on Youth Sunday. I shared joys and sorrows with other youth group members. I recall that we shared the sad secret when our adult leader had cancer, a word we didn't even utter at the time.

I was among the youth group members who participated in voter registration drives with the NAACP in Black neighborhoods. Because I valued the community I had, I was happy to give my time and talent to support it. I even made a few gifts of my "treasure" from babysitting earnings.

After college, I joined the Peace Corps and I traveled far away—to Nigeria—to find a new home. I grew and changed, learned new customs and a new language. I used skills I didn't even know I had.

When I met my husband, Clem, in Nigeria, I began attending the Anglican Church in Lagos, St. Saviours, with him. We married there and had our first child christened there.

When the Biafran War was looming, we left Lagos and went to the eastern part of the country, the part that seceded to become Biafra. Our second child was born then, and we attended the Anglican Church in his town.

After the war was over, we returned to Lagos and St. Saviours. We had our third child. When the children were little I started the Sunday school in that church.

But it was never really my community—it was Clem's. I found it less and less of a spiritual community for me—I was saying, and then finally stopped saying, words I didn't believe anymore.

I made friends and a career in my home in Nigeria. I made music as a teacher, and took part in musicals and a singing group. I joined other American women in the Women's Club, and even had the good fortune to become president of the American Women's Club.

With friends, I started an organization of foreign wives of Nigerians. I felt fortunate again to have a leadership role when I became the first national president of the organization, which I'm proud to say continues more strongly than ever today, with branches in the US as well as in many cities in Nigeria. So I really had two communities—the expatriate and the Nigerian.

But I didn't have a religious or spiritual home.

Then I came back to the US and I had to find a new place to belong. First I found one with fellow students at Yale's School of Management. Then I found community in places where I worked, and in groups of former Peace Corps volunteers, but I was still looking for a place to call a spiritual home.

Finally I found this congregation. Here I felt I had come home to a community where I belong. Here I found people who have broad interests, and among them I could find people who are similar to me, who like and understand me. I have grown to love this community because it shelters me and makes me whole. It gives me much more.

Not too surprisingly, what I love here is similar to what I loved in my Fort Thomas Presbyterian Church.

I have a role here; I am needed. I can be a leader in the wider spiritual community. I work for racial justice. And I sing; I share joys and sorrows; I contribute my time, talent, and treasure.

How do I know I am needed? When I first joined the church, I was asked to become part of the Endowment Committee. Sally Dimon handed the leadership to me in my very first meeting. She sealed my sense of being needed in this community.

Through Denny's intervention I became a board member of the Unitarian Universalist Women's Federation, the UUWF. I joined the UU–United Nations organization and became its president. In that role I led the return of this organization to its original home at the UUA.

In this community I strive for racial justice, as I did in the youth group in Fort Thomas. Here I find people who share my vision of a more just life. I find people who will go with me for voter registration, or walk with me, as Linda Hudson did in the NAACP protest of "stop and frisk" in New York last year. I have friends like Ruth, Kathy, Lorna, Jean, and others who share discussions on books that educate us about racial issues and inspire us.

I make music here, as I did in Fort Thomas and in every community I join. Only here I have not just one choir, but the richness of three. Each one provides community for me, and I'm part of the community for others.

I remember one morning in spring a few years ago thinking as I rehearsed with the women's choir at eight fifteen in the morning, there's no place I'd want to be right now but here, doing this. I've had the feeling other times. Maybe that's grace. It feels like I'm in the right place for me, because I have a community where I can sing.

Not only at candle lighting, but at choir practice, after services, and in meetings when I'm with church friends, I share joys and sorrows. My own newest joy—our fifth grandchild—has had his picture viewed by many friends here, and I feel their joy when they ask me about him. In the same way, I share their happiness when they talk about their own grandchildren or children, and I share their sorrow when a loved one is ill or dies.

And I share my time, talent, and treasure. Even my professional skills are useful here. I have joined the Year Round Stewardship Committee to share what I know about raising money. Because this is what I know how to do, I want to use that skill here. After all, if I weren't willing to use what I know to support this institution, would it be fair to expect others to do so?

**I share, because that's what you do in a community.**

I started with a community in Kentucky with my family, in the Presbyterian Church and its youth group. Then I found a community—a home—in Nigeria, with Clem and his family, his clan and his village, and then with others in Nigeria.

Since coming back to the US, in the last nineteen years I have found a community, a home, here, where I share my gifts, become whole, and receive sanctuary. Here I am part of the community and I have a spiritual home.

And incidentally, I have found here a great source of discussion with Clem, who sticks to his Anglican faith no matter what. "You people," he says, "some of you don't believe in anything." But he's wrong. I do—I believe in the community I have found here. It gives me a community I call a spiritual home.

The words Denny read in the opening are meaningful for me, and I hope they are for you too. A few phrases speak most clearly to me:

This church is ready for you to make community,

to create beauty, to bend it toward justice.

This church is ready for you to be here.

This church is your church.

Here we are home.

Here we are whole. From Rev. David S. Blanchard.

**Candle Lighting**

An email from our colleague Matt Peterson inspired Denny and me to talk about community.

Matt said, "I feel so lucky to have this community. The support I have received has strengthened my connection, not only because of what it has done for our family, but because I know that every day, someone else is going through a hardship, and that s/he feels that same level of support. This validates for me the true meaning of fellowship, love, and community beyond words."

If you would like to light a candle and make a statement about the meaning of this community, I invite you to follow Matt's example with one or two sentences about its importance for you.

**Closing Words**

One special joy I have found here which I haven't shared with you so far is my love of astronomy. The summer after sophomore year in college, I worked in the Maria Mitchell Observatory in Nantucket, photographing and studying variable stars. It was an amazing experience. I knew that Maria Mitchell had been a professor of astronomy at Vassar in the 1860s. But I didn't know she was a Unitarian.

I was thrilled when I found a reading by her in our hymnal, called "Our Whole System."

It added to my sense of being at home in my community. I want to share it as our closing words. If you would like to follow along, you can find it in the hymnal *Responsive Readings*, #537.

# Appendix D

"Born to a Village and a Network of
Mutuality," Summer Service, August 9, 2015,
the Unitarian Church in Westport, Connecticut

"THROUGH OUR SCIENTIFIC AND TECHNOLOGICAL genius, we have
made of this world a neighborhood and yet we have not had the ethical commitment to make of it a brotherhood. But somehow, and in some way, we have
got to do this. We must all learn to live together as brothers or we will all perish
together as fools. We are tied together in the single garment of destiny, caught
in an inescapable network of mutuality. And whatever affects one directly affects all indirectly."

Dr. King's words make me think of my husband's village in eastern Nigeria. It is called Enugwu-Nanka, and it is one of seven villages that make up the
town of Nanka. For in this village the commitment, the sense of belonging,
is so strong that it is inescapable. People from the town—as is true of most
towns in sub-Saharan Africa—are tied together in a network of mutuality.
They know that what affects one, affects all.

My husband, Clem, is Igbo, one of the three largest tribes in Nigeria.
Like others of his tribe, and others in much of sub-Saharan Africa, he has
always known he was part of a place and group of people. He knew from
childhood that whatever affects one directly, affects all indirectly. He felt the
network of mutuality.

"How do you learn this sense of belonging?" I said.

He said, "I was born with it. It's part of me." In fact, Clem wasn't even born in the village. His parents lived in midwestern Nigeria, where his father was working in the logging industry.

So I challenged him. "I don't think you were born with this sense. But I do think it is taught so strongly that it feels inborn."

As I look at the strength of the ties, I have come to believe there are many factors that make an Igbo know that he is not only part of but responsible for his family, clan, and village. They form ties that bind him for life and after. They cannot be broken and cannot be ignored.

The first is language. I don't mean just that the people share a common language, though that is certainly part of belonging. No, I mean the words people use for relationships.

I was surprised and a little disturbed the first time I visited my husband's village after we were married. Men and women both called me *nwunyem* or *nwunye anyi,* "my wife" or "our wife."

A man I had never seen before, or at least didn't remember seeing, came up to me in the market at *Afor Udo. "Nwunyem, kedu?* My wife, how are you?"

Who is this? I thought. Why is he addressing me like this? I was still new to the Igbo language, though I understood the words he was using.

*"O di mma.* I'm fine," I said. But I'm not his wife. What does he think, addressing me so familiarly?

"What do they mean?" I asked my husband.

"They are telling you that you are part of the village and part of our family now," he said. I relaxed and came to enjoy being greeted so familiarly.

In Igbo custom, we say *nna anyi,* "our father," to speak to an older male in the village, whether directly related or not. And we speak to children with a similar phrase, saying "our child" or "my child," again whether or not the child is a direct relative. We all belong to each other in the village.

We even address mothers with the name of their first child. I am still called "Mama Chinaku" by many people in Clem's village and town. Most wouldn't know my name if asked.

Clem's father taught me the customs of language every day I was with him. He consistently called me Mama Chinaku. I never heard him or Clem's mother utter my name. As I tell his story and then hers, I keep hearing his voice and hers in my head. I knew they loved me and valued me as part of the family. I could hear it in how they addressed me!

Second is the way children are given their food in a traditional setting. In the village and in times past, children ate together out of one bowl. The rules were strict—the oldest child takes first but cannot take more than his or her share. In Clem's childhood, there was often only one piece of meat for each person. The children would finish the other food first, then take the pieces of meat one by one, with the oldest taking the largest.

Clem's mother taught me this custom. For the year we were together in the village during the civil war, she consistently cooked enough for everyone, shared the food beginning with us—her oldest son and his family—then her husband, then the others. Eight months into the war, as the currency was losing value, imported goods had disappeared from the markets, and meat was becoming more and more scarce, as northerners couldn't travel into the Igbo-held territory with their cattle, she announced that eating should be twice a day instead of three times. I realized this was not the first time such an idea surfaced. It was typical during a famine or even toward the end of a year, right before the harvest, when the supply of yams was nearly exhausted.

I protested, and she assured me that we would not be included in this reduced food allocation. But she instituted the program for the others.

I was often the one who went to the market, sometimes with her and sometimes on my own. I did sometimes cook separately, but always knowing she was in charge. I learned from her how to preserve coconut over the open fire, how to reheat food so it wouldn't spoil when we didn't have a fridge, and how to soak cassava for eight days to drain away the poison.

The ceremonial breaking of kola nut is a common experience; it's the third method of teaching people that they belong, and not just to their current relatives but to the ancestors and those to come. Several men, but never women, demonstrate this custom  and the sayings that go along with it in many chapters of *Breaking Kola.*

Children will observe it from a very young age. Presenting kola is a requirement to welcome visitors, whether at a wedding party for hundreds or when your neighbor shows up at your door for an evening chat. The guest or guests are invited to take home a nut, or one lobe of a nut. The people who are visited and the visitors are united by this sharing.

The fourth, sharing belongings, is also taught from early childhood. When a child is given something special, a treat, a toy, a book, a grown-up will often ask for it back. The message—we share our belongings—is reinforced.

I remember feeling bad for my own children before I knew this custom. They thought they had been given something for themselves, and then they were immediately asked to give it to another grown-up. But I soon learned, as they did, that the adult always says in the end, "No, you keep it."

From Clem's cousin Mgbokwuocha I learned about assisting other family members. We asked her to send her son Okeke to us for his main meal every day during the Biafran War to give her a little assistance. I helped her when she tried to deliver her baby during the war. I cut the umbilical cord for her and drove her to the maternity hospital, though the baby did not survive. Through her relationship with us I learned about the fifth, the commitment to help out relatives, other clan members, even fellow villagers.

I was introduced to this necessity in many other ways as well. Every time we went to the village for Christmas, as we did annually for as long as we lived in the country, we would be besieged by people seeking help. Money was the most frequent request.

Since we belong together and are all part of the family or community, we are obligated to help when we can. People ask for many forms of help beyond money. Often they ask for help in finding a job. Sometimes an African hires a relative. What we in the West term nepotism is often fulfilling a responsibility. Relatives or clansmen may ask for help to get a visa or go on a call to a prospective bride.

Sixth is for events. When there is an occasion like a wedding, an anniversary celebration, or a funeral, all the family members wear clothes from the same fabric. For our fiftieth wedding anniversary in Nanka, there were about forty people, all related, who were dressed in the same cloth.

The system of belonging to an age grade is the seventh. Every child belongs to his or her age group or age grade in an Igbo village. The groups are children born within four or five years of each other. During their teens, they may give themselves a name. There are certain village duties assigned to each age grade as they reach a certain level, so the older teenage boys are tasked with roadwork.

When our daughter performed her traditional wedding in our village, the girls in her age grade surrounded her as she came before the assembled guests, a jug of palm wine on her head. The men of the age grade served as surrogate age grade members for her husband, an American who had no group of his own.

The last is what ties a child to his place forever. It is customary to bury a lock of a new baby's hair, the placenta, or the umbilical cord in the family compound. An older male relative undertakes this task. He prays to the ancestors and declares the connection to the earth, the clan, the immediate family, and the place. In my memoir I described the naming ceremony for our oldest child, our son Chinaku.

I said, "The stub of Chinaku's umbilical cord had fallen off when he was two weeks old. Clem had told me to save it and bring it along for the naming ceremony. Now Papa asked me to bring it to him.

"'I bury this cord which binds Chinakueze to Nanka, to our compound, and to our people forever,' he said. 'Whenever he returns he will know that he belongs here. When he is away, he will always know that part of him is here.' He placed the cord in the small hole that had been dug earlier."

What can the lessons from an Igbo village teach us about living comfortably within the "inescapable network"? How can we make the "single garment" fit us all? Can we use these lessons of belonging to address racism, anti-Semitism, and the other divisions that that permeate our society today?

# SUGGESTED DISCUSSION
# QUESTIONS FOR BOOK CLUBS

1. Do you think Mama and Papa loved each other? Why?
2. The umunna are both a powerful and a supportive group. How did they show support to Samuel (Papa)? How did they exercise power in the case of the man without a son? Would they have been able to force Ejike to give land to his younger brother?
3. The author describes the ceremony of carrying palm wine by a bride to her husband. Are there similar ceremonies you've performed or seen performed?
4. Do you think the family was wrong to keep the news of Benji's death from his mother so the wedding of his daughter could proceed? What would have happened if they had told her?
5. How did you feel about the requirement for Mgbokwuocha not to marry yet have sons to preserve the lineage? Would you have abided by tradition and obeyed?
6. How did the author demonstrate the sense of community she felt in Nigeria? How different was her experience at Yale?
7. What is your favorite Igbo name and its meaning?

# FOOTNOTES

1 Rosemary Keen, "General Introduction and Guide to the Archive," Church Missionary Society Archive, http://www.am pltd.co.uk/digital_guides/church_missionary_society_archive_general/editorial%20introduction%20by%20rosemary%2 keen.aspx.

2 Adam Paddock, "A World of Good to Our Boys": Boy Scouts in Southern Nigeria, 1934–1951, in *Children and Childhood in Colonial Nigerian Histories*, ed. Saheed Aderinto (New York: Palgrave Macmillan, 2015), 124.

3 Paddock, "World of Good," 124.

4 *Annual Report on the Social and Economic Progress of the People of Nigeria, 1938* (London: His Majesty's Stationery Office, 1939), 24, http://libsysdigi.library.illinois.edu/ilharvest/Africana/Books2011-05/3064634/3064634_1938/3064634_1938_opt.pdf.

5 Leprosy and Yaws: Points of Contact * by T. F. DAVEY, O.B.E., M.D., M.Sc., Senior Specialist, Nigeria Leprosy Service Research Unit, Uzuakoli, Eastern Region, Nigeria in JOHN MANTON London School of Hygiene & Tropical Medicine, Keppel Street, London Accepted for publication 27 May 2011 Lepr Rev (2011) p. 13

6 Patrick E. Nmah, "Spiritual Dimension of Land Identity Crisis in Igboland of Nigeria: An Ethical Reflection," *UJAH: Unizik Journal of Arts and Humanities* 12, no. 2 (2011), 138, http://dx.doi.org/10.4314/ujah.v12i2.6.

7 Wikipedia, "Igboland," last modified June 1, 2018, 7:57, https://en.wikipedia.org/wiki/Igboland.7

8 Luft, J.; Ingham, H. (1955). *"The Johari window, a graphic model of interpersonal awareness"*. Proceedings of the western training laboratory in group development. Los Angeles: University of California, Los Angeles, from Wikipedia.

9 Simon Ottenberg, "Comments by Simon Ottenberg After Accepting Dike of AOI Award," YouTube, accessed July 22, 2018, https://youtu.be/8SOKBeVHWMY.

10 C. C. Onyemelukwe, *Men and Management in Contemporary Africa* (London: Longman Group Limited, 1973), 25.

11 Onyemelukwe, *Men and Management,* 123.

12 This sermon was given before the change from Ibo to Igbo in the spelling of the language became widespread.

13 This sermon was given before the change from Ibo to Igbo in the spelling of the language became widespread.

14 Rev. Dr. Martin Luther King Jr., quoted in John A. Powell, *Racing to Justice: Transforming Our Conceptions of Self and Other to Build an Inclusive Society* (Bloomington, IN: Indiana University Press, 2012), 27.

Made in the USA
Middletown, DE
17 February 2019